Peter A. Jackson
Gerard Sullivan
Editors

Lady Boys, Tom Boys, Rent Boys: Male and Female Homosexualities in Contemporary Thailand

Lady Boys, Tom Boys, Rent Boys: Male and Female Homosexualities in Contemporary Thailand has been co-published simultaneously as *Journal of Gay & Lesbian Social Services*, Volume 9, Numbers 2/3 1999.

Pre-publication
REVIEWS,
COMMENTARIES,
EVALUATIONS . . .

"**D**emonstrates how negative stereotypes have pervaded the dominant scholarship on sexual minorities in Thailand and caused barriers to needed health education, counseling, and health services . . . This book illustrates how the cultural notions of family and community may be positive resources in providing effective services."

Eldon L. Wegner, PhD
Professor of Sociology
University of Hawaii at Manoa, Honolulu

Lady Boys, Tom Boys, Rent Boys: Male and Female Homosexualities in Contemporary Thailand

Lady Boys, Tom Boys, Rent Boys: Male and Female Homosexualities in Contemporary Thailand has been co-published simultaneously as *Journal of Gay & Lesbian Social Services*, Volume 9, Numbers 2/3 1999.

Lady Boys, Tom Boys, Rent Boys: Male and Female Homosexualities in Contemporary Thailand

Peter A. Jackson
Gerard Sullivan
Editors

Lady Boys, Tom Boys, Rent Boys: Male and Female Homosexualities in Contemporary Thailand, edited by Peter A. Jackson and Gerard Sullivan, was simultaneously issued by The Haworth Press, Inc., under the same title, as a special issue of *Journal of Gay & Lesbian Social Services*, Volume 9, Numbers 2/3 1999, James J. Kelly, Editor.

Harrington Park Press
An Imprint of
The Haworth Press, Inc.
New York • London • Oxford

1-56023-119-X

Published by

Harrington Park Press, 10 Alice Street, Binghamton, NY 13904-1580 USA

Harrington Park Press is an imprint of The Haworth Press, Inc., 10 Alice Street, Binghamton, NY 13904-1580 USA.

Lady Boys, Tom Boys, Rent Boys: Male and Female Homosexualities in Contemporary Thailand has been co-published simultaneously as *Journal of Gay & Lesbian Social Services* ™, Volume 9, Numbers 2/3 1999.

Cover design by Ray Howard. Photograph by Peter A. Jackson.

Library of Congress Cataloging-in-Publication Data

Lady boys, tom boys, rent boys : male and female homosexualities in contemporary Thailand / Peter A. Jackson, Gerard Sullivan, editors.
     p. cm.
    Includes bibliographical references.
    ISBN 0-7890-0656-1 (alk. paper). -- ISBN 1-56023-119-X (alk. paper)
    1. Homosexuality–Thailand. 2. Transsexualism–Thailand. 3. Gay men–Thailand. 4. Lesbians–Thailand. 5. Male prostitution–Thailand. 6. Transvestism–Thailand. I. Jackson, Peter A. II. Sullivan, Gerard. III. Journal of gay & lesbian social services, v. 9, no. 2/3.

HQ76.3.T5L33 1999
306.76′6′09593–dc21
                                                 98-55912
                                                    CIP

INDEXING & ABSTRACTING

Contributions to this publication are selectively indexed or abstracted in print, electronic, online, or CD-ROM version(s) of the reference tools and information services listed below. This list is current as of the copyright date of this publication. See the end of this section for additional notes.

- *AIDS Newsletter c/o CAB International/CAB ACCESS*

- *BUBL Information Service, an Internet-based Information Service for the UK higher education community*

- *Cambridge Scientific Abstracts*

- *caredata CD: the social and community care database*

- *CNPIEC Reference Guide: Chinese National Directory of Foreign Periodicals*

- *Contemporary Women's Issues*

- *Criminal Justice Abstracts*

- *Digest of Neurology and Psychiatry*

- *ERIC Clearinghouse on Urban Education (ERIC/CUE)*

- *Family Studies Database (online and CD/ROM)*

- *HOMODOK/"Relevant" Bibliographic Database*

- *IBZ International Bibliography of Periodical Literature*

- *Index to Periodical Articles Related to Law*

- *Mental Health Abstracts (online through DIALOG)*

- *Referativnyi Zhurnal (Abstracts Journal of the All-Russian Institute of Scientific and Technical Information)*

(continued)

- *Social Work Abstracts*

- *Sociological Abstracts (SA)*

- *Studies on Women Abstracts*

- *Violence and Abuse Abstracts: A Review of Current Literature on Interpersonal Violence (VAA)*

Special Bibliographic Notes related to special journal issues (separates) and indexing/abstracting

- indexing/abstracting services in this list will also cover material in any "separate" that is co-published simultaneously with Haworth's special thematic journal issue or DocuSerial. Indexing/abstracting usually covers material at the article/chapter level.
- monographic co-editions are intended for either non-subscribers or libraries which intend to purchase a second copy for their circulating collections.
- monographic co-editions are reported to all jobbers/wholesalers/approval plans. The source journal is listed as the "series" to assist the prevention of duplicate purchasing in the same manner utilized for books-in-series.
- to facilitate user/access services all indexing/abstracting services are encouraged to utilize the co-indexing entry note indicated at the bottom of the first page of each article/chapter/contribution.
- this is intended to assist a library user of any reference tool (whether print, electronic, online, or CD-ROM) to locate the monographic version if the library has purchased this version but not a subscription to the source journal.
- individual articles/chapters in any Haworth publication are also available through the Haworth Document Delivery Service (HDDS).

CONTENTS

ABOUT THE EDITORS

Peter A. Jackson, PhD, is a Research Fellow in Thai History in the Research School of Pacific and Asian Studies at Australian National University in Canberra. Fluent in spoken and written Thai, Dr. Jackson has conducted extensive research on gay and lesbian communities in Bangkok and nearby provinces. Dr. Jackson was a founding member of the Australian Gay and Lesbian Immigration Task Force and helped develop a Thai language curriculum in Australian high schools. His book, *Dear Uncle Go: Male Homosexuality in Thailand* (1995), was the first major study of male homoeroticism in Thailand. His other books include *Buddhism, Legitimation, and Conflict: The Political Functions of Urban Thai Buddhism* (1989), *The Intrinsic Quality of Skin* (1994), and *Multicultural Queer: Australian Narratives* (The Haworth Press, Inc., 1999).

Gerard Sullivan, PhD, is Senior Lecturer in the Department of Behavioural Sciences at the University of Sydney in Australia. His research interest in gay and lesbian studies includes civil rights, health issues, and the social construction of homosexuality in different cultural contexts. A board member of the Australian Centre for Lesbian and Gay Research, Dr. Sullivan is also co-editor of *Gays and Lesbians in Asia and the Pacific: Social and Human Services* (The Haworth Press, Inc., 1995) and *Multicultural Queer: Australian Narratives* (The Haworth Press, Inc., 1999).

Acknowledgments

A former Director of the Australian Centre for Lesbian and Gay Research at the University of Sydney, Robert Aldrich, persuaded us to collaborate and organize a conference in 1995 on homosexuality in Asia, which led to the idea for this book. The project was supported in part by the Department of Behavioural Sciences and the Faculty of Health Sciences at the University of Sydney, the Sydney Gay and Lesbian Mardi Gras, the Australian Agency for International Development, the AIDS branches of the Commonwealth Department of Human Services and Health, and the New South Wales Department of Health. Tony Hassett, Stephanie Cooke and Inthira Padmindra provided administrative support for the project.

Peter A. Jackson and Gerard Sullivan

FOREWORD

Some tourists and casual visitors to Thailand mistake the "Land of Smiles" as being a paradise for sexual minorities. A *kathoey* or drag queen in full female regalia is a common sight on the streets of Bangkok and provincial towns alike. On both the small screen and the silver screen, effeminate men commonly play minor roles in television soap operas and in Thai movies. Many popular male entertainers whose trademark is their showy cross-dressing are frequent guests on TV talk shows and game shows. Moreover, many television comedy programs feature "straight" actors taking the roles of female characters.

Visitors to Thailand may also think that male and female homosexuals lead happy, normal lives in the kingdom as well. Female homosexual lovers walking hand-in-hand, often caressing each other, can be spotted anywhere from streetside noodle stalls to the lobbies of five star hotels, and are especially visible amongst the crowds of window shoppers who throng the shopping malls that have mushroomed across Thailand in recent years. Gay male holiday makers from both western and Asian countries might feel that when they are here in Thailand they are free to be openly gay without being subject to the heavy criticism that is common in their home countries. This image of apparent freedom is reinforced by the open existence of dozens of gay venues–bars, saunas, restaurants, karaoke parlours and

[Haworth co-indexing entry note]: "Foreword." Rattachumpoth, Rakkit. Co-published simultaneously in *Journal of Gay & Lesbian Social Services* (The Haworth Press, Inc.) Vol. 9, No. 2/3, 1999, pp. xvii-xxiv; and: *Lady Boys, Tom Boys, Rent Boys: Male and Female Homosexualities in Contemporary Thailand* (ed: Peter A. Jackson, and Gerard Sullivan) The Haworth Press, Inc., 1999, pp. xiii-xx; and: *Lady Boys, Tom Boys, Rent Boys: Male and Female Homosexualities in Contemporary Thailand* (ed: Peter A. Jackson, and Gerard Sullivan) Harrington Park Press, an imprint of The Haworth Press, Inc., 1999, pp. xi-xviii. Single or multiple copies of this article are available for a fee from The Haworth Document Delivery Service [1-800-342-9678, 9:00 a.m. - 5:00 p.m. (EST). E-mail address: getinfo@haworthpressinc.com].

xi

discos–across Bangkok and in other cities such as Pattaya, Chiang Mai and Phuket.

However, the assumption of many casual visitors that sexual minorities in Thailand are free from prejudice, criticism, ostracism and discrimination is in need of radical revision. Although anti-gay, anti-lesbian and anti-*kathoey* sentiments never provoke any violent homophobic attacks, no Thai homosexual or transgender person feels that they are living in a gay or homosexual paradise. On the contrary, many feel that their lives are miserable, if not a living hell, where they are threatened by public denunciation, job discrimination, malicious gossip and indirect interference in both private and working spaces.

Although there are no legal sanctions against homosexual or transgender behaviours or lifestyles in Thailand, sexual minorities nevertheless exist in a legal limbo. The new civilian-drafted constitution, which began to be implemented on 26 December 1997, has been widely praised as enhancing the Thai people's civil and political rights, matters which had been overlooked in previous constitutions drafted by the military. But sexual minorities are not mentioned in the new pro-democratic constitution, let alone their rights. Under current Thai law, same-sex marriage is not recognized, and same-sex couples are denied access to the spousal benefits accorded heterosexual couples, such as tax benefits, social welfare and insurance benefits. Furthermore, sex change is not officially recognized, which means that post-operative transsexuals face a lot of difficulties in leading a new life after having a sex reassignment operation. For example, they are not able to change their sex on their I.D. cards, drivers licences, passports, and so on. Despite the rising number of people, men and women, who undergo sex change operations in this country every year, no amendments have been made to either the civil or criminal legal codes in order to take account of the special needs of individuals who have undergone sex change operations. For example, there have been several reports of male-to-female transsexuals arrested on criminal charges being incarcerated in men's prisons and being subjected to rape and persistent sexual harassment.

In addition to being invisible in the eyes of the law, sexual minorities also have to survive in a cultural climate dominated by biased stereotypes. Homosexuals and *kathoeys* are widely perceived as being irrational, violence-prone, jealous, oversexed, a threat to young people, social misfits, psychologically aberrant, or just plain sick.

These misperceptions are nurtured by media presentations. While more and more gay and *kathoey* characters are being included in TV soap operas (often based on best-selling novels or short stories by heterosexually identifying authors), almost none of these characters are portrayed as being ordinary people. Their characterization is primarily based on some or all of the above biased stereotypes. The effeminate men who often appear as guests or co-hosts on TV game shows or talk shows rarely project any positive image of the characters they portray. They appear in these programs just to make the audience laugh, and reinforce the common image of homosexuals and *kathoeys* as being sources of humour and objects of ridicule.

Thai language gay magazines, of which there are about 15 monthly titles, often feature one or two short stories as well as serialized novels by Thai gay writers. But the theme of this gay fiction for the local readership often revolves around a romance which ends in tragedy. That is, even Thai gay fiction perpetuates negative stereotypes of gay people's lives. All these negative stereotypes–perpetuated by both the heterosexual and gay press and media–contribute to the prevalent anti-homosexual attitudes in Thai society and encourage the widely practiced social sanctions, ostracism and discrimination mentioned above.

Thai people tend to turn a blind eye to homosexual lifestyles and gay/lesbian issues. They may express tolerance if they happen to meet homosexuals in public, be they gay, lesbian or obviously *kathoey*. But problems often arise if people find out that a close acquaintance or a member of their own family is attracted to the same sex. Commonly a first reaction is to deny or reject their friend's or relative's sexual preference, and in many cases this rejection leads to people being ostracized from family ties. Putting gay and lesbian people and *kathoeys* under this kind of pressure is tantamount to a mental crime, and automatically prevents most people from coming out of the closet.

Anti-homosexual discrimination had long been practised in Thailand but was not formalized until the recent Rajabhat Institutes case. This involved a ban against homosexual students enrolling in courses leading to degrees in kindergarten and primary school teaching. This ban had apparently been in force, albeit on a limited basis, since 1993. But the Rajabhat Institutes, the governing body of the 36 teachers colleges nationwide, opened a veritable Pandora's box in January 1997 when it announced that the ban would be formalized and extended to all campuses from the beginning of the 1997 academic year. Widespread public criticism of the ban ensued, especially after the then Education Minister, Sukhavich Rangsitphol, attempted to justify the Rajabhat Institute's ban by equating people with a "wrong sexual orientation" to drug addicts and denied that the anti-homosexual ban was a human rights issue. Minister Sukhavich was also quoted saying that "sexually aberrant people" needed rehabilitation and should be kept in a camp for the efficient administration of "treatment."

However, the controversy ended later in 1997 without anyone losing face, by a traditional Thai method of dealing with problems that are likely to tarnish the reputations of the parties involved. The ban was simply quietly removed from the Rajabhat Institutes' ordinances when a new Education Minister was appointed after a cabinet reshuffle.

Perhaps a more typical example of the prevailing character of anti-homosexual and anti-*kathoey* sanctions occurred in the sporting arena in 1996. At the Thailand National Games in June that year, the male volleyball team from Zone 10 (Bangkok), which included several prominent national team players, was beaten by a dark horse team from Zone 5 (the northern province of Lampang). This sporting upset received an unusual degree of media coverage because six of the 12 athletes from the Zone 5 team did not even try to hide their transgender lifestyles and their attraction to men. The team, calling themselves Satri Lek ("Iron Ladies"), became the center of attention whenever they appeared on the volleyball court because of their pony-tail hairdos, heavy makeup, and effeminate screams and gestures. Their appearance and personalities attracted hundreds of sport admirers, who unanimously agreed that matches with the Zone 5 team were as enjoyable as they were spectacular. The athletic skills of the "Iron Ladies" exceeded those of the national level male players in the favoured-to-win Zone 10 team, and their charisma captivated audiences, both in the gymnasium and on live TV broadcasts of their matches. The "Iron Ladies" team immediately raised the profile of the sport of volleyball in Thailand, which until then had usually been overshadowed by other sports such as basketball or football.

However, the underdog Zone 5 team members who took home the national volleyball trophy failed to convince the Volleyball Association of Thailand (VAT) of their capacity to represent their home country in international sporting competitions. The effeminate male volley-ball players were quoted by the Thai language press as saying that some influential figures in the VAT suggested to them that it would be better if they did not compete for a place on the national volleyball team. Their obvious transgender lifestyles and homosexual preference were obstacles for them to be considered qualified candidates for the national team. It was suggested that if they were selected to represent Thailand in international competitions, the country's reputation would be tarnished. The VAT made it clear that only "straight looking" male athletes could bring sporting honour to the country, whereas a cross-dressing sportsperson could bring nothing but national humiliation.

The cross-dressing athletes, all college students or graduates, seemed to have a good understanding of Thai social expectations and rather than challenging this discrimination opted to remain quiet and not try out for a place on the national team. The successful cross-dressing athletes then kept a low profile and have since quietly quit the sporting field.

Many openly gay or effeminate men and lesbians choose to work in the private sector because, as is widely known in Thailand, the government sector in this country does not operate by the merit system. Job promotion in the public service or in government universities or colleges is often based on personal favoritism. In job selection the actual qualifications of a particular candidate are only a secondary criterion. A homosexual orientation is widely considered a weak point or disadvantage, and bars many openly gay men, lesbians and *kathoey* government workers from winning promotions.

When Dr. Seri Wongmontha, one of the few outspoken openly gay men in Thailand, competed for the presidency of the prestigious state-run Thammasat University in Bangkok ten years ago, some competitors for the senior position attacked him because of his openness about his homosexual preference. Seri, who had previously excelled in his performance as Dean of Thammasat's Faculty of Mass Communications and Journalism, was in the end defeated. He is the first and still the only openly gay man who has ever held the position of a university faculty dean. Because of persistent opposition, Dr. Seri quit his teaching career in the late 1980s and has since started his own public relations company. This type of discrimination is evidence of the subtle but persistent cultural violence which haunts members of sexual minorities in Thailand.

Despite the existence of widespread anti-homosexual discrimination, Thailand does not have any gay political organizations, nor any formal gay social groups. There is no gay residential ghetto in Bangkok as in many western cities, although five years ago a group of gay businessmen attempted to establish a real estate project named Meuang Dork-mai or "Flower Town" in Nakhonratchasima Province about 180 kilometers northeast of Bangkok. The project was billed to be the first exclusively gay housing estate and residential complex in the world, but received heavy social criticism and in the end did not proceed. However, the failure of the project may also have stemmed from a downturn in the real estate market in the kingdom. Also absent in Thailand is a distinctive queer cultural presence outside the commercial gay and *kathoey* venues. The only activist group in the country which promotes the rights of sexual minorities is the Anjaree lesbian group. This group organized a public seminar on lesbian issues in Bangkok in December 1997. The group also organizes social activities for lesbians and circulates a regular newsletter to its 500 members in Bangkok and around the country. Feminist-inspired lesbians have been politically active in Bangkok, and they played an impressive role during the Rajabhat controversy in publicly countering the discriminatory ban against homosexual students and appearing before a parliamentary committee which inquired into the ban.

Compulsory heterosexuality is at the core of Thai social norms, and people who are labelled "sexually deviant" are often criticized as being threats to social order. Because of the dominance of heterosexual and patriarchal attitudes the problems of sexual minorities are overlooked. Not one baht of the Thai government's funding of social services and social welfare activities is directed towards the specific needs of homosexual or transgender people. Even in the area of HIV/AIDS education and prevention, homosexually active men are ignored, with unprotected heterosexual sex and intravenous drug use often being represented as the only risk activities. Ignoring a problem is often considered to be a traditional method of "solving" social issues in Thai society. At first glance, this neglect of sexual minorities might be seen as some sort of tolerant compromise, but in fact it is a form of suppression and denial that causes mental torture for many gays, lesbians and *kathoeys*. Sexual minorities who are marginalized from the rest of society are in fact being denied the expression of their rights. By being criticized, or more commonly simply "ignored," they are forced to hide their actual needs and conform to compulsory heterosexual lifestyles. (In the 1990s one of the most common "gay problems" discussed in the Thai press has been the issue of "gay husbands," men who marry to avoid social criticism but then cause problems for both their wives and children by continuing to seek out male partners.) Despite increasing discussion of gay, lesbian and *kathoey* issues in the Thai press and media, few people even think that members of sexual minorities might have special needs requiring specific social services, let alone consider how to provide or how to best deliver such services.

While social services of any form, whether publicly or privately provided, are extremely limited in Thailand, some services are available for homosexual men and women. A volunteer-staffed telephone counselling hotline operates in Bangkok to provide advice for the general public, and gay men and lesbians not infrequently call this line for information and support. However, while the telephone counselling staff are generally sympathic to homosexual callers, they are not necessarily gay or lesbian themselves and Thailand has no dedicated gay/lesbian/transgender counselling service. Some HIV/AIDS health and support services, in some cases supported with overseas funding as part of non-government organization (NGO) projects, have explicitly included men who have sex with men in their brief. In the late 1980s and early 1990s the Fraternity for AIDS Cessation in Thailand (FACT) provided safe sex advice and counselling to men who have sex with men in major cities, and in the mid-1990s the Chai Chuay Chai ("men helping men") project also provided HIV support services to homosexually active men in Chiang Mai. As Prue Borthwick mentions in her paper in this book, there are also a small number of village-based HIV projects which openly involve local homosexual men. However, some of these gay men's health projects are no longer operating and it is true to say that Thailand's sexual minorities are very poorly served in terms of counselling, health support and other areas. The data and information in the articles in this book are therefore extremely important in beginning to provide a detailed understanding of these groups' special needs. This is a vital first step towards designing and implementing effective social services.

The Thai academic arena also tends to overlook the concerns of homosexual and transgender people. Sexual minorities/related topics are marginalized within academia for the fallacious reasons that information about different sexual orientations is already available and the issues are already well-understood and so do not need to be touched. As a result, knowledge about sexual minorities in this country is still an "infant science."

This book, *Lady Boys, Tom Boys, Rent Boys: Male and Female Homosexualities in Contemporary Thailand*, is therefore an important contribution to the academic study of the diversity of male and female homosexual lifestyles, identities and subcultures in contemporary Thailand. As several of the following articles point out, there is only a limited amount of solid research on male homosexuality and transgender issues in Thailand, and much less on female homosexuality. Furthermore, as Peter Jackson and Gerard Sullivan point out in their introductory article, a significant proportion of the Thai language research that has been undertaken has been unsympathetic towards homosexual people and based upon stereotypes and prejudices. This book presents foreign (Thai: *farang*) perspectives on these issues rather than local or Thai perspectives. However, the efforts of all authors in this volume to present balanced analyses that move beyond stereotyping marks a very important step, one that I hope all future academic studies in Thailand will follow. I hope that Thai academics and other interested people in this country will read the insightful articles in this book. I also hope that an informed and open Thai-*farang* dialogue can be established to exchange research findings, views and opinions in order to contribute to improving social understanding and social services for sexual and gender minorities in this country.

It is important that academic understanding of sexual minorities convey the message that society will not collapse if sexual variations are accepted openly. It is necessary to emphasize that the more flexible a society becomes, the better it will be for all members of that society. Misperceptions and biased stereotypes can only be removed by thorough studies of the lives of Thailand's *kathoeys* and homosexual men and women, and for this reason this book has an important cultural and political role in promoting the welfare and well-being of sexual minorities in this country.

Rakkit Rattachumpoth

A Panoply of Roles:
Sexual and Gender Diversity
in Contemporary Thailand

Peter A. Jackson
Gerard Sullivan

INTRODUCTION

This book presents a series of case studies of contemporary forms of male and female homosexuality and transgenderism in Thailand. The studies concentrate on the three most visible, and within Thailand, most stigmatized homosexual behaviors and identities, namely, *kathoey*[1] (transgender and transsexual males), *tom boys* ("masculine" or "butch" lesbians) and male sex workers who service male clients. The title of this book derives from the focus of the following papers on these three groups. In Thailand, transgender *kathoey* are also commonly called "lady boys," butch lesbians are called "tom boys" or simply "toms," and male sex workers are also called "boys" or *dek*. In English the use of the term "boy" in such expressions would often be considered derogatory or demeaning. However, English terms borrowed into Thai often take on distinctive local

---

Address correspondence to: Peter A. Jackson, Division of Pacific and Asian History, Research School of Pacific and Asian Studies, Australian National University, Canberra ACT 0200, Australia.

[Haworth co-indexing entry note]: "A Panoply of Roles: Sexual and Gender Diversity in Contemporary Thailand." Jackson, Peter A., and Gerard Sullivan. Co-published simultaneously in *Journal of Gay & Lesbian Social Services* (The Haworth Press, Inc.) Vol. 9, No. 2/3, 1999, pp. 1-27; and: *Lady Boys, Tom Boys, Rent Boys: Male and Female Homosexualities in Contemporary Thailand* (ed: Peter A. Jackson, and Gerard Sullivan) The Haworth Press, Inc., 1999, pp. 1-27; and: *Lady Boys, Tom Boys, Rent Boys: Male and Female Homosexualities in Contemporary Thailand* (ed: Peter A. Jackson, and Gerard Sullivan) Harrington Park Press, an imprint of The Haworth Press, Inc., 1999, pp. 1-27. Single or multiple copies of this article are available for a fee from The Haworth Document Delivery Service [1-800-342-9678, 9:00 a.m. - 5:00 p.m. (EST). E-mail address: getinfo@haworthpressinc.com].

1

nuances, losing some of their original meanings. "Lady boy" and "tom boy" (or *tom*) are self-chosen terms that are widely used with pride by transgender males and butch lesbians, respectively. Use of the term "boy" for male sex workers is arguably more problematic and suggestive of social inferiority, but reflects current Thai usage where adolescent and adult males who work in any service capacity (sexual or otherwise) are widely called *dek*. Male sex workers also not uncommonly refer to other workers as *dek*, when it can be imbued with a sense of solidarity. The papers in this collection do not deal with pedophilia.

Thailand is located in mainland Southeast Asia and has an area roughly the same as France. The country has a population of around 60 million, of whom somewhat more than twenty percent live in major urban areas. The capital and largest city is Bangkok, with a population in excess of 9 million people. The country is divided into four geographical regions, each of which has a distinctive local Thai dialect and cultural traditions. Ranked from the largest to the smallest in terms of population, these four regions are: the northeast (called Isan by the Thai) which borders Cambodia and Laos, the central region focussed on Bangkok, the north bordering Laos and Myanmar and centered on the city of Chiang Mai, and the south, bordering Malaysia. About ninety five percent of the population identifies as Theravada Buddhist, with a significant Muslim minority (especially in the southern region) and small numbers of Christians, Sikhs and Hindus. Thailand has undergone rapid socio-economic change in recent decades, being transformed from an agrarian economy based on rice exports to an emerging industrial society. Between 1985 and 1995 GDP more than doubled to over $US 2,000 per capita (Phongpaichit & Baker, 1996). However, rapid economic change has produced widespread social dislocation, environmental degradation and growing popular disenchantment with corrupt bureaucratic and political practices. The dramatic collapse of the Thai economy in the latter part of 1997 has highlighted these stresses in the country's social and political fabric. At the time of writing (October 1997) a new anti-corruption, pro-democratic constitution had been signed into law by Thailand's constitutional monarch, King Bhumibol.

THE SOCIAL CONTEXT OF HOMOSEXUALITY IN THAILAND

Thailand provides a productive site for testing Western-derived understandings of sexuality. The only Southeast Asian nation to retain its independence throughout the colonial period into the modern era, Thailand has experienced a unique continuity of institutions and cultural forms uninterrupted by direct imperialist rule. At the same time, however, the country has been open to a complex array of influences over the centuries, first from ancient India and imperial China, then from the West, and most recently from Japan and other economically and politically emergent East Asian societies. While incorporating cultural, intellectual and linguistic elements from all these sources, Thailand nevertheless remains a distinctive cultural domain within one of the most culturally and linguistically diverse regions of the world.

In this ancient, complex and rapidly developing society, are found some of the largest, most visible and most diverse sexual subcultures outside the West. Thailand has a rich indigenous history of complex patterns of sexuality and gender, with an intermediate category, the *kathoey*, historically being available to both males and females and existing alongside normative masculine and feminine identities. Gay identity among masculine homosexual men in Bangkok dates to at least November 1965, when the Thai language press in Bangkok reported that there were several hundred Thai homosexual men in the city who collectively called themselves "the gay association" (*chom-rom gay*).

In parallel with Thailand's rapid economic development, the Thai gay subculture has also bloomed in the past decade and a half. In 1980 John Stamford's *Spartacus International Gay Guide* listed 10 gay venues in Thailand, all in Bangkok. Eleven years later Eric Allyn (1991) listed over 100 gay bars, saunas, restaurants and discos around the country. Until 1983 there were no Thai language magazines published by and for Thai gay men. In 1997 almost 20 monthly Thai language gay magazines competed on newsstands across the country, and also in 1997 the first edition of an English language magazine for lesbians and gay men was published in Bangkok.

While tolerated in certain contexts, male and female homosexuality remain unacceptable behaviours in Thailand. Jackson (1989a, 1995a) has described the psychological, interpersonal and social difficulties faced by Thai homosexual and transgendered men and has developed an account of anti-homosexual sanctions in Thailand. These are not based on legal or religious[2] interdictions as in the West, but rather on cultural norms of appropriate and inappropriate masculine or feminine behaviour. Thai sanctions concerning both male and female homosexuality are generally non-interventionist, involving the withholding of approval rather than active attempts to force a person to desist from what is considered to be inappropriate behaviour. But even these sanctions, mild by Western standards, usually only come into play when inappropriate sexual behaviour becomes publicly visible or explicitly referred to in discourse. So long as a Thai homosexual "man" or "woman" maintains a public face of conforming to normative patterns of masculinity or femininity, respectively, he or she will largely escape sanctions.

The size and openness of Thailand's multiple queer scenes–male, female and transgender–leads many visitors, especially those who do not speak Thai, to mistakenly conclude that homosexuality and transgenderism are accepted and considered normal in Thailand. While the sanctions against alternative sexual expression (i.e., outside the confines of marriage) are different from those in the West (as outlined above), they are still pervasive, deeply felt and discriminatory. Male sex workers of course have clients; *kathoey* often have gender normative partners and *toms* have feminine female partners. However, homosexual men and women who do not breach gender norms often remain invisible, trying to avoid social sanctions by "passing" as normatively masculine men and feminine women, respectively.

One of the most stunning features of Thai discourses of gender and sexuality in recent decades has been the proliferation of male and female identities. Historically, three forms of sexed or gendered being, called *phet* (pronounced like "pairt") in Thai, were recognized within local discourses, namely, normatively masculine men (*phu-chai*) and feminine women (*phu-ying*) and an intermediate category called *kathoey*. *Kathoey* variously denoted a person, male or female, who expressed hermaphroditic features or exhibited behavior considered inappropriate for their sex, and were commonly called a "third sex" (*phet thi-sam*) within both popular and academic discourses.[3] *Kathoey* is now almost exclusively used to refer to biological males. Since the 1960s, a complex range of new male, female and transgender identities have emerged in local discourses. These include masculine women (*tom*, from "tom boy"), who are increasingly visible in public, and their feminine partners (*dee*, from "lady"); bisexual men (*seua bai* or "bi-tigers"); *queen*, *king* and *quing* varieties of gay men (i.e., those who play the receptive or insertive role in sexual encounters or both, respectively); and transsexuals (*kathoey plaeng phet*). All of these identities have been much remarked and much debated phenomena in the Thai press and electronic media. De Lind van Wijngaarden's paper in this volume elaborates on some these categories.

Rosalind Morris (1994) has also noted the proliferation of Thai identities, interpreting this phenomenon in terms of the emergence of new, Western-modelled discourses of sexuality. Following Kosofsky Sedgwick (1990), Morris (1994, p. 34) suggests the co-existence of the older *kathoey* category with newer homosexual and bisexual identities indicates that contemporary Thai sex/gender discourses represent a complex of "two irreconcilable but coexistent sex/gender systems," one indigenous and based on gender, the other borrowed and structured around the Western notion of sexuality. Morris adopts a Foucauldian model, proposing that the older "man–*kathoey*–woman" system of three identities was constructed within a system of gendered discourses, while the recent gay, lesbian and bisexual identities have emerged as products of the eruption of a new discursive domain of sexuality.

Jackson (1997a) has challenged the proposition that the proliferation of Thai identities reflects the emergence of a new discourse of sexuality, tracing the historical development of Thai psychological and biomedical accounts of same-sex and cross-gender behaviours from the 1950s to the present. A summary of this research is included below. Jackson reports that while Western discourses of sexuality have had an increasing impact on both popular and academic accounts of eroticism in Thailand, indigenous discourses have resisted the formation of a domain of sexuality distinct from gender. All Thai discourses continue to be framed in terms of the indigenous category of *phet*, a notion that incorporates sexual difference (male vs. female), gender difference (masculine vs. feminine) and sexuality (heterosexual vs. homosexual) within a single discursive regime.

Within Thai discourses, gay and *kathoey* are not distinguished as a sexuality and a gender, respectively. Rather, gay, *kathoey*, together with "man" (*phu-chai*), "woman" (*phu-ying*), and the lesbian identities *tom* and *dee*, are collectively labelled as different varieties of *phet*.

In Thailand, the new identities have not been interpreted in terms of the emergence of a new domain of sexuality, but rather as a multiplication within the pre-existing domain of *phet*. This is indicated by the fact that Thai discourses have not borrowed the Western "gay"/"straight" binary. The term "gay" has been borrowed but it has been re-inscribed within a gender discourse beside "man," *kathoey* and "woman," rather than constructed in opposition to a category of heterosexuality (see Jackson, 1997b). This suggests that *phet* remains an integral discursive domain, where, for example, the English distinction between gender identity and sexual identity has little relevance. Indeed, within Thai academic discourses a single expression, *ekkalak thang-phet*, is used to translate both "gender identity" and "sexual identity." To date, the discourse of *phet* has remained so powerful that all western discourses of gender and sexuality have been appropriated and re-inscribed within its frame.

In Thailand, there is a general lack of the notion of "gay community" as understood in the West. It is more accurate to think in terms of many local networks linked loosely by a common argot and ethos rather than of community (Sullivan & Leong, 1995). These networks are defined geographically and by class, educational and occupational differences. Jackson's paper in this volume indicates that even in a moderately sized country town in Thailand, at least three distinct and relatively non-interacting networks of homosexually-active men exist, namely, transgender *kathoey*s, younger gay-identified middle class men, and poorer rural and urban working class men. In some respects, it may be that this feature of the social construction of homosexuality in Thailand is not very different from the situation in many western societies.

While there is no gay, lesbian or transgender rights movement in Thailand, some gay and lesbian organizations have been formed in the past decade. In the late 1980s Natee Teerarojjanapongs established the Fraternity for AIDS Cessation in Thailand, or FACT, which conducted HIV/AIDS education activities among gay men, published a regular newsletter called *Kunla-gay* and for a period in the early 1990s operated Bangkok's first gay drop-in center, called FACT House. Also in the early 1990s, Anjana Suvarnananda and a small group of other Thai lesbians established the Anjaree group to give a public voice to issues concerning Thai lesbians and to organize social activities for isolated "women-loving women" (*ying rak ying*). Anjaree publishes a regular newsletter called *Anjaree-san* and now has several hundred members throughout Thailand.

WHEN FARANGS (CAUCASIANS) WRITE ABOUT THAIS: REPRESENTATIONS IN SEXUALITY RESEARCH

Readers may be interested in issues of motivation, representation, participation and positionality in the production of this volume and the papers it contains. All of the authors and the editors are Westerners: from Australia (Borthwick, Jackson, McCamish, Sullivan), New Zealand (Storer), the United States of America (Murray, Sinnott) and the Netherlands (Brummelhuis, Wijngaarden). All contributors except Sinnott and Borthwick are men, and with the exception of Sinnott's paper on lesbianism and aspects of other papers which deal with transgender issues, the contributions deal primarily with expressions of male sexuality.

This volume grew out of a conference held by the Australian Centre for Lesbian and Gay Research at the University of Sydney in 1995 called "Emerging Lesbian and Gay Identities and Communities in Asia," which attracted participants from around the Southeast Asian region. In order to cater to the interests of many who were unable to attend, the convenors of the conference, who are the editors of this volume, invited those who had presented papers as well as others to submit papers for a book on the same subject. The response to the call for papers was overwhelming and we gathered enough material for three volumes.[4]

The call for papers elicited a disproportionate number of articles about Thailand written by Westerners rather than Thais. This presented the editors with a dilemma. A major purpose of the conference had been to provide an opportunity for people outside the cultural mainstream of the international lesbian and gay movement[5] to discuss their experience. Ironically, but perhaps not surprisingly given that it is published in English, this volume duplicates the observed dominant patterns in writing about homosexuality. All the papers in this volume have been written by members of the white middle-class, and, with two exceptions, are by men. Although they have been written from different perspectives from those which the conference strove to emphasise, we felt that these papers were valuable in interpreting aspects of homoerotic behavior in Thailand for a western audience.

A number of the contributors speak Thai and have spent considerable periods of time in the country. However, all of the authors included in this volume are outsiders to Thai society. The editors have
not wished to produce a text which would instruct Thais about their
culture and society, and we make no claim that the papers represent a
comprehensive view of Thai (homo)sexuality. Two papers (Jackson
and Murray) interpret Thai writings on homosexuality through Western eyes. Three contributions (McCamish, Storer and Wijngaarden)
examine aspects of the male sex industry. One paper (Sinnott) examines the dynamics of some lesbian relationships; one (Brummelhuis) examines the world of the expatriate Thai *kathoey* (the male-to-
female transgendered community) in Europe; and one (Borthwick)
describes HIV/AIDS education programs by and for gay men in northern Thailand.

Most of the papers include reports of fieldwork in Thailand. The
authors of these papers lived in Thailand and collected information
about the issues that their papers address. The editors encouraged authors to explain to readers how they arrived at their conclusions. Rather
than representing their reports as objective reality, as so much Western
(social) science has done until recently, the editors believed that many
readers would want to gain an understanding of who the authors are and
how they arrived at the understandings reported in their papers. Information about how many people the authors spoke to or observed, what
the characteristics of these people were, and how they were selected,
undoubtedly helps readers form an opinion of the representativeness of
observations. However, such an approach focuses on "the other," that
is, the Thai subjects of the research, and can obscure the western ob-
server and his/her involvement in the research process. Knowing something about the authors and their involvement with those about whom
they have written, and the extent to which those written about were
participants in the research, would assist in assessing the adequacy of
observations. Generally, the authors of the papers have presented little
about themselves or the research process. In this regard this text can be
understood as a product of the authors' and editors' training as researchers, training which is almost exclusively western and for the most
part not significantly influenced by feminist, post-structuralist or participatory action research frameworks.

It should be added, however, that the contributions to this collection
are representative of much current Thai and English language research on

Thailand, which to date has been little influenced by post-structuralist, post-colonialist and related trends in western academic analysis. In some ways this marks the discursive distinctiveness of Thai studies research. Thailand's lack of a colonial history gives it a unique position in Southeast Asia and has produced a different relationship between western and indigenous discourses from that which exists in some formerly colonised Southeast Asian countries. Unlike the case in some neighbouring countries, Thailand's intellectual elites never lost control of the production of indigenous discourses, and western knowledges have been selectively appropriated by these elites rather than being imposed by western imperial powers. Post-structuralist analyses are one aspect of contemporary western discourses that Thailand's intellectual elites have so far felt no need to appropriate in producing knowledge about their own society, and post-colonialist theory has a problematic status in the study of an Asian society which was never a European or American colony.

Readers may also be interested in the editors' involvement with this project. Peter Jackson has conducted research in Thailand since the early 1980s, and has published several books and articles on Thai cultural history. His work focuses on the history of Thai Buddhism (Jackson, 1988, 1989b), on the one hand, and the history of sexuality and gender, on the other hand. He has also published a novel (Jackson, 1994) about a western gay man whose relationships with Thai homosexual men force him to confront the culturally specific nature of his understandings of masculinity and sexual identity. In the mid 1980s Peter was a foundation member of the Canberra chapter of the *Gay and Lesbian Immigration Task Force*, which successfully lobbied the Australian Government to grant immigration rights to the overseas partners of Australian gay men and lesbians.

Gerard Sullivan has only visited Thailand twice. While he was born and raised in Australia, travel, friendships and research experience at the East-West Center in Hawaii and the Institute of Southeast Asian Studies in Singapore have together prompted an enduring professional and personal interest in Asia. Since returning to Australia in 1990, Gerard has conducted research on ethnicity and health care in Australia and lectured on multicultural issues. In the early 1990s, together with his partner, he was a member of the *Asians and Friends* group in Sydney, a social, support, and HIV education group for gay Asian men and their friends. Both Gerard and Peter are members of the Australian

Centre for Lesbian and Gay Research at the University of Sydney, and because of their interests in Asia were invited to co-convene the Emerging Lesbian and Gay Identities and Communities in Asia conference, from which this collection has emerged.

RESEARCH ON HOMOSEXUALITY IN THAILAND

This volume takes its place among a considerable body of Thai language research on homosexuality and transgenderism. Much Thai academic writing on the subject has been reviewed by Jackson (1997a), who conducted a content analysis of 207 Thai language books, chapters, articles and postgraduate dissertations published between 1956 and 1994. He found that over three-quarters (76 percent) dealt with male homosexuality, almost one-fifth (19 percent) with *kathoey* and only six percent dealt exclusively with female homosexuality. Almost one-third (31 percent) were written from the perspective of psychology or psychiatry, 21 percent in the fields of sociology and anthropology, 14 percent in the biomedical sciences, and 11 percent were related to education. Almost all of these books and articles were written by authors who identified themselves as gender normative heterosexuals. Much of this research (64 percent of publications dealing with male homosexuality) was written from the perspective of trying to determine the aetiology of homosexuality and the formulation of interventions to prevent people from becoming homosexual. In addition to the supposed causes of homosexuality which western readers will be familiar with–such as poor sex role modelling by parents, distant fathers or dominant mothers–rapid socio-economic and cultural change was considered by a number of Thai authors to be responsible for a perceived increase in homosexual orientation among Thai adolescents. A series of studies was undertaken to determine the extent of homosexual experience among Thai youth in the late 1980s and early 1990s. (Jackson's paper in this collection reviews aspects of this research in more detail.) Many of these articles assumed homosexuality to be a pathology and perversion, and many were concerned about an apparently growing number of male sex workers who serviced other men.

Few of the recommendations of the Thai studies dealing with interventions to prevent homosexuality were implemented. This is partly because much of the Thai population remains poor and beyond the limited resources of social and child welfare workers, whose services rarely reach beyond the urban middle class. It has been argued that the Thai middle and upper classes, especially those of Chinese ancestry, are less tolerant of homosexuality and transgenderism than others in Thai society. Thai academics are mostly drawn from the more privileged classes and to a considerable extent this may explain the homophobic nature of much of their writing, as well as the fact that their concern has not been taken up as an important social issue in Thai society generally. Academic knowledge of homosexuality is not necessarily representative of popular attitudes, which vary according to social class, urban or rural residence, ethnicity, age and other factors (Jackson, 1995a, esp. pp. 64-77; 1997b).

As noted above, much of the opposition to homosexuality in Thailand operates at the level of discourse rather than institutional practices affecting everyday life. Exposing a person's non-normative sexuality by naming it is often a traumatizing action which damages the labelled person's public image. Jackson (1997b, p. 176) has observed that, apart from shaming aberrant individuals by naming their deviance, Thai sanctions against both homosexuality and transgenderism are markedly non-interventionist. Thai law does not criminalize homosexuality[6] and neither the state nor Buddhism, which is extensively practiced, attempts to enforce compliance to heterosexual norms. So long as a Thai homosexual man or woman maintains a public face of conforming to normative patterns of masculinity or femininity, respectively, he or she will largely escape sanctions.

Only four percent of Thai studies reviewed by Jackson (1997a) saw gender-normative male homosexuality (what would probably be called "gay men" in the West) as unproblematic. However, most research conducted by Westerners tends to be consistent with this category of research. This volume extends research in this tradition, which seeks to avoid problematising homoeroticism and transgenderism, and the authors in this volume have in common the aim of presenting an unbiased view of the topics and people they investigate.

It is a sign of the openness of Thai society that the authors of the following papers were permitted to conduct their research. Another sign of this openness is the participation of foreigners in relationships with Thais and in the local sex industry. Similarly, western aid and social service organizations have been allowed to operate in Thailand for many decades. All of the articles in this volume deal with one or more of these intersections. Because many Westerners are involved with Thai people, Thai organizations or Thai culture more generally (for example, as health, social service or community development workers; life partners; or sex tourists), there is a need for a volume like this one which extends knowledge, especially for outsiders, about the intersections between Thai and western sexual cultures and discourses of gender and sexuality. This volume does not pretend to present a comprehensive survey of sexual behavior in Thailand, nor even of homosexual behavior. Rather, it looks at a number of specialized situations involving one or more forms of homoeroticism which are relevant to providers of specific social services.

In some ways it is much easier for the non-Thai authors of the papers in this volume to reflect on the sensitive topic of Thai homosexuality than it is for Thai scholars. The observations and analyses of non-Thai researchers are limited by their position as "outsiders." However, this external position as discursively privileged native English speakers and as culturally privileged *farang* (Caucasian foreigners) paradoxically also enables us to say more about these topics than most Thai researchers, and also to be listened to (if not always agreed with). Thai scholars are often hindered by an academic environment that generally devalues this topic of research as unimportant and which, when it is undertaken, subjects it to moralistic critique.

It is a regrettable but unavoidable reality of the global dominance of English language academic discourse, and of the dominance of United States discourses within the English speaking world, that books and articles emerging from the United States' presses have an unwarranted impact and value within Thai academia. The "foreign expert" (more often pseudo-expert) is often listened to more readily in Thailand than Thai academics, although if the "foreign expert's" message is unsavory he or she may be politely listened to and reported, but then just as politely ignored. Western observers can easily misunderstand and misrepresent phenomena in different societies, but in Thailand they do have the capacity to create a discursive space within which Thais can contribute. A number of the authors in this volume have received private encouragement from Thai gay and lesbian colleagues, friends and informants to conduct and publish research on these topics because they find it difficult to breach the strong discursive sanctions against representing homosexuality in an unproblematic way.

The homophobic discursive environment within Thai universities and colleges was clearly demonstrated in late December 1996, when the Rajabhat Institutes Council, the governing body for all of Thailand's 36 teacher training colleges, decreed that "sexually deviant" and "wrong-gendered" students would be barred from enrolling in teacher training courses.[7] The ban was justified in terms of such students supposedly being "short tempered" and presenting inappropriate role models to impressionable youth. In early 1997 the ban became a focus of intense public debate, with critics claiming it violated the right of academically qualified students to receive an education. The anti-homosexual student ordinance was not part of any wider trend to institute legal or other restrictions on queer people in other areas of Thai social life. It emerged from the decades-long history of anti-homosexual research within Thai academia and was not instituted in response to any antipathetic movement within the wider society. The highly contested nature of the ban, which apparently was never enforced, also demonstrated the contradictions between academic homophobia and more liberal sectors of contemporary Thai society–notably elements of the press, opposition political parties, human rights groups and some social commentators, all of whom vehemently attacked the ordinance. In September 1997, after a cabinet reshuffle saw the appointment of a new Minister for Education, the Rajabhat Institutes[8] lifted the ban, apparently in response to both international and local pressure.[9] Given the difficulties faced by many Thai gay and lesbian academics in researching and writing about the lives and cultures of homosexual men and women in their own country, we hope that this volume will help expand the space for Thai queer voices to be heard, listened to and taken seriously.

THE FOCUS OF THIS COLLECTION

Male sex workers, *kathoey*s and *tom*s are the most visible faces of homosexuality and transgenderism within Thai discourses and in everyday life. These three categories are the most stereotyped and stigmatized in Thailand, and perhaps not coincidentally, also the most accessible to study and research. Male sex workers can easily be located in gay bars; *kathoey*s and *tom*s are visible by their cross-dressing.[10] Almost all the papers in this volume focus on these three groups. This volume is an attempt to "normalize" research on homosexuality in Thailand and free it of unnecessary moralism. In this regard, it is the figures of the male sex worker, the *kathoey* and the *tom* who are most in need of demystification, of being seen as people rather than as comical or fearful figures.

The negative stereotyping widely attached to *kathoeys*, *toms* and male sex workers is one of the reasons gender normative homosexual men and women in Thailand are often so fearful of coming out. In effect, all homosexually active and transgender men and women in Thailand suffer under the burden of the stereotypes that attach to these figures, and research on all aspects of same-sex eroticism is also affected. Large numbers, perhaps the majority, of homosexual men and women in Thailand seek to distance themselves from the stereotypes which are attached to these three figures, and they resist coming out publicly, partially for fear of being tarred with the same brush. When male sex workers, *kathoeys* and *toms* are seen and treated as human beings, their partners will also be freed of the imputed stigma and will be able to become more visible figures, both in discourse and in everyday life. Very little material that is not judgmental or moralistic exists on any of these categories of people. The papers in this volume attempt to look beyond the stereotypes and to lift the veil of prejudice under which homosexuals and transgendered people live in Thailand.

The first article in this volume is by Peter Jackson, who helps establish a context for the other articles by reviewing what is known about the rates of homosexual behavior in Thailand. Much of this research was undertaken by people who disapproved of such behavior, but more recently it has been conducted as a basis for developing HIV/AIDS education programs. That there is disapproval of homosexual behavior may come as a surprise to some Westerners who know of the vibrant male sex industry and have heard about tolerance toward, if not acceptance of, this behavior in Thai society. Jackson's paper helps shatter simple stereotypes like this and shows some of the diversity and complexity of modern Thailand. It is worth emphasizing that most of the research which Jackson reviews has been conducted in the past ten years. Accordingly, while his article gives readers an indication of contemporary attitudes and behavior throughout Thailand, it does not consider the history of Thai homoeroticism. Readers are directed to Jackson's other writing for further information on that topic (e.g., Jackson, 1995a, 1997b).

AIDS is also an important determinant of Prue Borthwick's paper.

Borthwick went to school in Thailand in the 1960s and returned there in 1992 to work on a Thai-Australian HIV/AIDS education and prevention program in the Chiang Mai region. Borthwick had previously worked on a series of educational cartoon magazines for street children and other disadvantaged groups in Sydney, and has published a book on lesbian parenting (1993). Her paper examines models of community organizing and service delivery among men who have sex with men in northern Thailand. In this contribution Borthwick provides insight into some of the ways that patterns of male homosexuality in Thailand differ from gay life in the West. Here we see a mixture of modern and traditional gay life, and she touches on how transgenderism, which is common throughout Southeast Asia, is integrated with homoerotic identity and behavior, particularly for those from rural or working-class backgrounds.

Stephen Murray's article analyzes letters to a gay advice columnist, known as Uncle Go, and translations of Thai gay erotic writing. Murray conducted a content analysis of the letters and stories in order to discern patterns of homoerotic concerns and behavior in Thailand. While there is no way to determine how representative the letter writers and other materials are of men who have sex with men in Thailand, the article provides valuable insight into changing patterns of male homoeroticism. Murray addresses the issue of "nativism" (Garcia, 1996) and places Thai homosexuality within a conceptual framework which he uses to compare and contrast it with homosexual behavior in other societies. Murray is well regarded internationally for his work on comparative expressions of homosexuality and he has published numerous books on the subject (e.g., Murray, 1992, 1995; Murray & Roscoe, 1997, 1998).

Megan Sinnott's paper is the only one in this volume which deals with lesbian relationships in Thailand and she documents the pervasive nature of butch-femme or *tom-dee* relationships, as they are called in Thailand. Sinnott recognizes the existence of lesbian relationships which fall outside this model, but she explains that *tom-dee* couples are widespread, and she considers the dynamics of these relationships. While butch-femme relationships were unfashionable among many American lesbians in the 1970s and 1980s (Faderman, 1993; Miller, 1995), they have re-emerged and western readers will no doubt be interested in contrasting western lesbian relationships with the Thai form. Sinnott's article raises the issue of gender rigidity and suggests that lesbian expression is both regulated by and transcends traditional male and female roles. To the extent that *toms* see themselves as men in women's bodies and *kathoey* see themselves as women in men's bodies, they may not have lesbian or gay identities.

In some respects, *toms* are the analog of *kathoeys*, who are discussed by Han ten Brummelhuis in his article. Unlike the other papers in this volume, Brummelhuis writes about Thai homosexuals outside Thailand. His informants were *kathoeys* in Amsterdam. One might wonder how much this changed locale would affect the identity and behavior of Thai homosexuals. This issue will be an important one for many readers of this volume because they will be relating to people from Thai backgrounds who are now living abroad. However, it is not a question that is easily answered. There are many ways that migration can affect people's identity and behavior and readers would be well advised to avoid stereotyping Thais who have sex with people of the same sex–especially those who may reside in other countries–on the basis of what they read in this volume. This is not to say that these articles do not provide valuable insights into Thai sexual expression. Rather, readers should avoid assuming that any individual conforms to the patterns identified by authors in this volume. Having said that, interestingly, Brummelhuis' observations differ very little from Jackson's research (1995a, 1996) on *kathoey* in Bangkok. However, no information is provided by Brummelhuis about how long his informants had been living in Amsterdam, whether or not they spoke Dutch or languages other than Thai, if they were educated in the Netherlands, or if they regularly mixed with friends of other cultural backgrounds. These are some of the factors which may effect cultural change.

The final three articles in this volume explore the world of Thai male sex workers whose clients are other men. The Western media are often wont to sensationalize and moralize about Thailand's sex industry (see Jackson, 1998b), yet it must be recognized that male sex work is prevalent in all Western countries. Gay publications in Australia, North America, Great Britain and most West European countries contain pages of advertisements for male sex workers, often with photos and mobile telephone numbers. There is a strong orientalist tendency in much Western reporting of Thailand, which tends to portray a "shocking Thailand" and overlooks and ignores the prevalence of precisely the same phenomena in the West. Fortunately this is less apparent in academic writing. While there is a literature on this topic based on research conducted in other countries (e.g., Boyer, 1989; Mathews, 1987; Reiss, 1961), relatively little is available in English on the situation of male sex work in Thailand.

The authors of the three articles on male sex workers conducted their research in different cities–the capital Bangkok (Storer), the tourist resort of Pattaya (McCamish) and the old northern capital of Chiang Mai (De Lind van Wijngaarden). Their findings reveal both similarities and differences in the culture of male sex work in these cities. For example, De Lind van Wijngaarden reports a close rapport among sex workers in Chiang Mai, while McCamish says that relations among workers in Pattaya are often characterized by mistrust. These findings suggest the possibility of regional differences in male sexual cultures, but the limited number of studies to date do not permit us to explain such differences with any certainty.

Nevertheless, we can say that each of the three locations is very different, with Pattaya, Bangkok and Chiang Mai each having distinctive histories and urban lifestyles. Pattaya is a very new city, built as a beachside resort town and is populated almost entirely by migrants from other parts of the country, most of whom are separated from peer and family networks. Pattaya also has a street culture of homeless youth. Bangkok is a huge metropolis where many people feel anonymity and alienation, as in any city of over 9 million inhabitants. Like Pattaya, many of Bangkok's residents have migrated from rural areas over the past few decades, resulting in significant social dislocation. Until only a couple of decades ago Chiang Mai was a large country town, but recent rapid growth has seen it become a middle-sized city of half a million people. It has a long history dating back to the thirteenth century and a well-established and proud culture built on a distinctive local dialect and religious customs. Many of the young male sex workers in this city continue to live and work within the supportive networks of family and friends in the city or province in which they grew up, and this may explain the greater degree of group solidarity and support between Chiang Mai male sex workers that De Lind van Wijngaarden reports.

The clients and organization of sex work also differ from place to place in Thailand. There is a higher proportion of foreign tourists (and presumably, clients of sex workers) in Pattaya than in either Bangkok or Chiang Mai. In his paper, Jackson summarises a study of networks of homosexually active men in a country town in northeast Thailand which attracts very few tourists but where significant numbers of male sex workers service local Thai men. To the extent that this is typical of other locations in Thailand, it suggests that large segments of the male sex work industry cater to local demand rather than to gay sex tourists from overseas.

Borthwick's paper points out the existence of two distinct types of commercial sex venues in Chiang Mai. The most visible type of venue, and the type most studied by both Thai and foreign researchers, are the gay bars. These are formally established commercial enterprises clearly marked with their name on a sign out front, and which often advertise their services in the local press or gay magazines. The gay bars in Chiang Mai, like those in Pattaya and Bangkok, have full time regular workers. The less visible commercial sex venues in Chiang Mai are simply called *ban* or "houses" in Thai. These are not formally registered businesses, have no trading name, advertise only by word of mouth and often only have casual workers. The *ban* cater almost exclusively to local Thai men, and anecdotal reports by a resident in Chiang Mai indicate that such *ban* exist in all provincial towns in the north of Thailand, being linked by word of mouth networks.

The three papers in this volume which take male sex work as their primary interest focus on workers rather than on bar managers or clients. As Graeme Storer notes in his paper, this research focus is a response to the widespread concern about male sex work in Thailand. Storer observes that this "concern" often centres on a misplaced anxiety that these men will become gay (i.e., lose their masculinity) by engaging in sex with gay men, and Thai research on the topic has often betrayed a distinct unease with both sex work and homosexuality. Storer considers some recent Thai research on male sex workers in Bangkok which was based on the belief that homosexuality is "contagious," noting the moralistic character of this work and its greater interest in "saving" male sex workers from becoming gay than in these men's health or other welfare concerns. The papers by Storer, McCamish and De Lind van Wijngaarden all attempt to get beyond these homophobic anxieties to portray the lives of male sex workers in non-sensational, everyday terms, which is essential if their actual needs and requirements are to be met.

IDENTITY

Much Thai research on same-sex eroticism has failed to distinguish homosexual behavior from homosexual identity, and has also failed to grasp the diversity of behaviors and features that are linguistically distinguished within most populations of homosexually active men and women in Thailand. De Lind van Wijngaarden distinguishes more than half-a-dozen types of distinctively labelled homosexually active men in Chiang Mai. The tendency of previous studies to label all homosexually active men as *kathoey*, "gay" or "homosexual" (*rak-ruam-phet* or *homosekchuan*) fails to grasp this diversity. De Lind van Wijngaarden's paper examines the sexual identity of male sex workers in Chiang Mai and finds that to a considerable degree this is not determined by sexual practices. The confusion over identity and behavior also helps explain some of the inconsistent findings of the studies reviewed by Jackson. Homosexuality can be defined in terms of sexual behavior, sexual desire, or sexual identity. There is a consistent research result both in the West and in Asian contexts that many people who have sex with others of the same biological sex do not necessarily see themselves as homosexual. Indeed, the issue of what constitutes "having sex" varies from person to person and according to time and place, or context and situation. The concept of a homosexual is a relatively new cultural development (e.g., Vance, 1995) in the West and it should not be assumed that it has wide currency in other cultural circumstances. In the general population in Thailand, *kathoey* is a much more readily understood concept than is gay (as used in its Western sense). It is important that the articles in this volume be understood in this light.

SOCIAL SERVICES

This volume will be first published as a special issue of the *Journal of Gay & Lesbian Social Services*, which is oriented towards social workers and policy makers and analysts. While most of the authors are primarily researchers rather than practitioners, they have been asked to explicitly address the implications of their work for social service providers, and there is much that the latter can learn from these articles. It is well known that Thailand has one of the highest incidences of HIV infection and AIDS illness in Southeast Asia. It is to the credit of Thai policy makers that this issue has been confronted and preventive education and programs to help people affected by the virus have been implemented. Jackson discusses some of the research related to these issues in his paper. Several authors have discussed the need to provide HIV/AIDS education, especially for men who have sex with men in Thailand, and the articles in this volume suggest ways that these programs could be designed so that they are culturally sensitive and likely to be effective.

One of the most important issues for HIV/AIDS educators to keep in mind is that there are many men who engage in sexual behaviors which put them at risk of HIV infection but who do not see themselves as gay and who may not even consider that they have sex with other men. These men conceptualize "gay" and "sex" in very different terms from those used by most Westerners. Among other ideas for social services mooted by the authors in this volume, are the need for helping sex workers maintain good relations with family members and other people in their communities of origin; the development and enforcement of non-exploitative labor relations and employment practices in sex work establishments; and the need for a gay community center in Thailand to assist the increasing number of "gender-normative" homosexual men who see themselves as gay (more or less in the Western sense of the word) as well as to help *kathoeys*, *toms* and others deal with the discrimination and other problems that they confront in their lives.

FUTURE RESEARCH

The focused studies in this book reflect the need to resist sweeping generalizations about Thailand. Even among informed people it is not uncommon to hear sweeping statements such as "Thai people are . . . ," "Thailand is . . . ," and so on. Western students and even established academics, coming from a society which in recent decades has produced volumes of historical, sociological, linguistic and other studies of homoeroticism in the West, often betray ethnocentrism by expecting one book or even one article on Thailand to survey and summarize the totality of Thai sexual culture. In both academic and popular English language discourses the West is often portrayed as complex and diverse, while the cultural "other" of Asia is often seen as uniform and capable of being addressed in simplistic generalizations.

There is much scope to elaborate the articles in this volume and to explore other aspects of homosexuality and its social context in Thailand. Among topics still to be explored are the lives and networks of gender normative homosexual men and women who are generally invisible and often overlooked. Research to date has been less concerned to describe the clients of male sex workers, the gender normative male partners of *kathoey*s and feminine female partners of *tom* boys.[11] In the case of male sex work we need to ask who are the customers of sex workers? What are the backgrounds, indeed the self-identities, of people who buy sex from other men or from *kathoey*s? In order to develop a complete picture of male sex work in Thailand we need to know as much about the clients, and about the bar owners and managers, as we do about the workers. A starting point would be to ask how clients perceive workers, and vice versa. One of the challenges of future research on this aspect of homoeroticism is to develop a comprehensive socio-cultural and economic understanding of all aspects of sex work, including the demand from clients, the supply of sex workers and "marketing" by bar owners and managers. Our current knowledge is limited and one-sided.

The authors of the articles on male sex workers have not focused on issues of child labour; recruitment related to poverty, family disintegration or dislocation; or exploitative relationships between managers, clients and sex workers. There is some mention of these concerns, as well as problems that sex workers face due to widespread social disapproval of their occupation. These are vitally important issues where the provision of relevant social services could help alleviate suffering. However, it is a mistake to think that all sex workers operate under such abject circumstances and we hope that the articles in this volume will help readers obtain a balanced understanding of this occupation. Nevertheless, there is a need for further research which explores the best policies for social service providers to assist those who are hurt in the sex industry.

To humanize the male sex worker, the *kathoey* and the *tom* is a vital first step in challenging the dominant stereotypes that affect perceptions and self-perceptions of all homosexually active men and women. Admittedly this volume offers only a small contribution to this much larger project. We need detailed ethnographies of networks and communities of homosexually active men and women, life histories and studies of intra-group and external group dynamics. We also need careful histories that trace changing patterns and attitudes reflected in popular culture, film, literature, television soap operas, music, and so on. Perhaps most importantly, we need Thai scholars to feel that they can reflect on these topics as issues of genuine academic and social concern, free from moralism and free from the fear that working on these topics will damage their career or stigmatize them within academia.

NOTES ON THE THAI LANGUAGE

Thai is a tonal language with a number of vowel and consonant sounds not found in English. While Thai has its own phonetic script (derived from ancient Indian scripts via medieval Khmer), there is no generally agreed system for transcribing Thai words using the Roman alphabet. In this book a modified version of the Thai Royal Institute system is adopted. While not strictly phonetic, this system is the one most commonly adopted by the English language press in Thailand, in romanised street signs and other official usages within the country. Some key features of the Royal Institute system are as follows:

- Tones are not marked and long and short vowel lengths are not distinguished.
- *k-kh*, *p-ph*, and *t-th* represent pairs of unaspirated and aspirated guttutal, labial and dental consonants, respectively. The Thai *k*, *p*, and *t* sounds do not occur at the start of syllables in English and are closest to the short, unaspirated sounds that occur as the second elements in the English consonant clusters "s*k*," "s*p*," and "s*t*." *Kh* is similar to the English "k" or hard "c" sounds as in "cake"; *ph* is the usual English "p" as in "pop" and is never pronounced as "f"; while *th* is the aspirated "t" sound as in "*Th*ai," and is never pronounced as in the English words "the" or "bath."

Note that the word which is spelled *kathoey* in the Royal Institute system, and which variously denotes a transgendered person or an effeminate homosexual man, is notoriously difficult for English speakers to pronounce accurately. To assist readers to pronounce this word, Allyn (1992) uses *gatuhy*. This is also Stephen Murray's preferred orthography, but for the sake of consistency in this volume all renderings have been altered to *kathoey.*

The system used here differs from the Royal Institute system in some minor respects. The letter *j* is used with its common English value as in "joy" instead of the "c" which is used for this sound in the Institute's system. In order to avoid possible confusion, in some cases *ee* is used to transcribe the long vowel sound written simply as *i* in the Royal Institute system. For example, the colloquial feminine prefix or title is here written *ee*, not *i* (e.g., *ee aep:* "a closeted homosexual man"), and the term for a feminine lesbian is written *dee* not *di* (abbreviated from the English "la*dy*"). Lastly, where English words such as "gay," "gay queen," "gay king," and so on have been borrowed into Thai and become naturalized parts of the language, the original English spelling is preserved even though this may not always reflect precisely how the term is pronounced by Thai speakers.

Orthography of Thai Names

Many Thai people transcribe their names using roman script in idiosyncratic ways that do not accord with the principles of the semi-phonetic Royal Institute system. For example, it is common for the roman script spelling of Thai names, including place names, to include silent letters that are written in Thai but not pronounced. It is also common for names derived from Sanskrit and Pali to be spelled as in these ancient Indian languages, despite often having radically different pronunciations in modern Thai. It is customary and respectful practice to spell Thai people's names in roman script in the way in which they prefer.

Note also that it is customary for lists of Thai names to be arranged alphabetically by first name, not surname. For example, Thai telephone books (both Thai and English language versions) arrange all subscribers' names alphabetically by first name. This reflects the fact that the universal use of surnames was only introduced at the beginning of this century, and all Thai titles continue to be prefixed to given names rather than surnames (e.g., in Thai one says Dr. Mary, not Dr. Jones). Bibliographies in Thai libraries and Thai language publications also list Thai authors alphabetically by first name. However, to complicate matters, most English language publications, including those written or co-authored by a Thai person, follow the English system of alphabetizing authors by family name. In this book, citations of Thai language publications by Thai authors will refer to authors by given name, while citations of English language publications will refer to authors (both Thai and non-Thai) by family name. Lastly, Thai language publications are dated using the Buddhist Era (B.E.) calendar, which began in 543 B.C., and which remains the most common calendrical system used in everyday life in Thailand. In this volume, for Thai language publications Buddhist Era publication dates are included within parentheses after the equivalent Christian Era year, e.g., (1997, B.E. 2540).

Terminology and Semantics

The various papers in this volume often reflect differing understandings of the array of new sex/gender terms that have emerged in popular and academic discourses in Thailand in recent decades. Slightly different emphases and nuances for terms such as "gay" and *kathoey* indicate the lack of uniformity in the meanings attached to these terms in different regions of the country and even between different socio-economic strata in the same locality. For example, at least three distinct meanings attach to the term "gay" in the papers here. In places it is used in its western sense to refer to gay men or gay cultures in western societies. In other places the term "gay" reflects the common understanding of this word in the general Thai heterosexual population to mean all homosexually active men, both *kathoey* and masculine-identified. "Gay" is also used to reflect the sense of the term as it is used within local subcultures, where masculine "gay" is differentiated from feminine "*kathoey*," and where "gay" itself is differentiated into *gay queen* and *gay king* varieties. Increasingly in Thailand, gay-identified men use the simple term "gay" to mean a man who rejects the *queen/king* dichotomy and is simply a masculine-identified homosexual man. Note also that in Thai "gay" can be a noun as well as an adjective. Thais talk of "a gay" or of "gays" as a group. The expressions "gay man" or "gay men" do not occur in Thai, because "gay" is classified as a different type of sex/gender being (i.e., a different *phet*) from "man" (*phu-chai*).

NOTES

1. See discussion later in this section on the romanization of Thai words.

2. We here refer only to the sexuality of laypeople in Thailand. All forms of sexuality, including heterosexual, homosexual and autosexual, are explicitly prohibited for Buddhist monks. For an analysis of Thai Buddhist attitudes towards homosexuality, see Jackson 1995b and 1998a.

3. The long-standing reference to *kathoey* as a third *phet* (sex or gender) appears to be of local origin, and is unrelated to the very similar late nineteenth century western notion that homosexuals constitute a "third sex."

4. Two other volumes related to the conference themes are currently in production. One deals with the intersection of ethnicity and homosexuality and is titled *Multicultural Queer: Australian Narratives* (The Haworth Press, Inc., 1999). The other book deals with male and female homoerotic experience in a diverse range of Asian societies, and is provisionally titled *Gay and Lesbian Asia: Identities and Communities* (The Haworth Press, Inc., 2000).

5. Certainly in the case of gay and lesbian cultures in Australia, the published discourses on issues about homosexuality are dominated by white, middle class men and women.

6. This was not always so. When Thailand introduced a revised criminal code in the first decade of the twentieth century based on western codes, crimes "against human nature," including homosexuality and bestiality, were identified. No prosecutions were made under this statute, which was abolished in the 1950s during a subsequent revision of the criminal code.

7. *Bangkok Post*, 26 December 1996, p. 2.

8. *Bangkok Post* (Internet Edition) 11 September 1997, "Education college lifts its ban on gay entrants–Regulations relaxed after NGO pressure," by Sirikul Bunnag.

9. However, at the same time as withdrawing the ban on "sexually deviant" students, the Institutes proposed a new rule to keep out what Sawat Udompot, Deputy Secretary-General of the Rajabhat Council, described as "sexually abnormal" people, including those who copulate with inanimate objects, expose themselves in public, derive pleasure from sado-masochistic acts, and harass others orally. One member of the Institutes Council, Dr. Wanlop Piyamanotham, told the press that the old ban had been imposed out of a misunderstanding of the nature of sexual deviance. "The institutes misunderstood and used the wrong word . . . Sexual deviants [i.e., homosexuals] are not always sexually abnormal. Sexual abnormality is worse. They can't be good teachers–they're emotionally abnormal." At the time of writing, the proposed revised ban was being forwarded to the Rajabhat Council for consideration and if approved will take effect in the 1998 academic year.

10. The clients of male sex workers, the gender normative male partners of *kathoey*s, and the feminine female partners of *tom*s are less easily identified and apparently are less threatening to the Thai social order.

11. One of the few exceptions is Jan Jordan's (1997) research on male clients of female sex workers.

REFERENCES

Allyn, E. (1991). *Trees in the same forest: Thailand's culture and gay subculture.* Bangkok: Bua Luang.

Allyn, E. (Ed.). (1992). *The dove coos: Gay experiences by the men of Thailand.* Bangkok: Bua Luang.

Borthwick, P. (1993). *Mothers and others: An exploration of lesbian parenting in Australia.* Sydney: Jam Jar Publications.

Boyer, D. (1989). Male prostitution and homosexual identity. *Journal of Homosexuality, 17* (1-2), 151-184.

Dynes, W.R., & Donaldson, S. (1992). (Eds.). *Asian homosexuality.* New York: Garland.

Faderman, L. (1993). The return of butch and femme: A phenomenon in lesbian sexuality of the 1980s and 1990s. In J. C. Fout & M. Shaw Tantillo (Eds.), *American sexual politics.* Chicago: University of Chicago Press. (Originally published in *Journal of the History of Sexuality, 2* (4), 1992.)

Garcia, J.N.C. (1996). *Philippine gay culture: The last 30 years.* Quezon City: University of the Philippines Press.

Jackson, P.A. (1988). *Buddhadasa–A Buddhist thinker for the modern world.* Bangkok: The Siam Society.

Jackson, P.A. (1989a). *Male homosexuality in Thailand: An interpretation of contemporary Thai sources.* New York: Global Academic Publishers.

Jackson, P.A. (1989b). *Buddhism, legitimation and conflict–The political functions of urban Thai Buddhism.* Singapore: Institute of Southeast Asian Studies.

Jackson, P.A. (1994). *The intrinsic quality of skin.* Bangkok: Floating Lotus Publishing.

Jackson, P.A. (1995a). *Dear Uncle Go: Male homosexuality in Thailand.* Bangkok: Bua Luang Books.

Jackson, P.A. (1995b). Thai Buddhist accounts of homosexuality and AIDS. *Australian Journal of Anthropology (TAJA), 6* (3), 140-153.

Jackson, P.A. (1996). The persistence of gender: From ancient Indian *pandakas* to modern Thai gay *quings. Meanjin* (University of Melbourne), *55*(1), 110-120.

Jackson, P.A. (1997a). Thai research on male homosexuality and transgenderism: The cultural limits of Foucauldian analysis. *Journal of the History of Sexuality, 8*(1) [forthcoming].

Jackson, P.A. (1997b). *Kathoey* <> gay <> man: The historical emergence of gay male identity in Thailand. In Lenore Manderson & Margaret Jolley (Eds.), *Sites of desire/economies of pleasure: Sexualities in Asia and the Pacific* (pp. 166-190). Chicago: University of Chicago Press.

Jackson, P.A. (1998a). From *kamma* to unnatural vice: Male homosexuality and transgenderism in the Thai Buddhist tradition. In Winston Leyland (Ed.), *Queer dharma: Voices of Gay Buddhists* (pp. 55-89). San Francisco: Gay Sunshine Press.

Jackson, P.A. (1998b Forthcoming). Tolerant but unaccepting: Correcting misperceptions of a Thai "gay paradise." In Peter Jackson and Nerida Cook (Eds.), *Transforming Sex/Gender Orders in Twentieth Century Thailand.* Chiang Mai: Silkworm Books.

Jordan, J. (1997, March). User pays: Why men pay prostitutes. *Australian and New Zealand Journal of Criminology, 30*(1), 55-7.

Kosofsky Sedgwick, E. (1990). *The epistemology of the closet*. Berkeley, CA: University of California Press.

Mathews, P.W. (1987). Some preliminary observations of male prostitution in Manila. *Philippine Sociological Review, 35*(3-4), 55-74.

Miller, N. (1992). *Out in the world: Gay and lesbian life from Buenos Aires to Bangkok*. London: Penguin Books.

Morris, R.C. (1994). Three sexes and four sexualities: Redressing the discourses on gender and sexuality in contemporary Thailand. *Positions, 2*(1), 15-43.

Murray, S.O. (1992). *Oceanic homosexualities*. New York: Garland.

Murray, S.O. (1995). *Latin American male homosexualities*. Albuquerque: University of New Mexico Press.

Murray, S.O., & Roscoe, W. (1997). *Islamic homosexualities*. New York: New York University Press.

Murray, S.O., & Roscoe, W. (1998). *African homosexualities*. New York: St. Martin's Press.

Pongphaichit, Pasuk, & Baker, C. (1996). *Thailand's boom*. Sydney: Allen & Unwin.

Reiss, A.J., Jr. (1961). The social integration of queers and peers. *Social Problems, 9*(2), 102-120.

Stamford, J. (Ed.). (1980). *Spartacus 1980 international gay guide for gay men*. Amsterdam: Spartacus.

Sullivan, G., & Leong, Laurence Wai-Teng (Eds.). (1995). *Gays and lesbians in Asia and the Pacific: Social and human services*. New York: Harrington Park Press.

Sullivan, G., & Leong, Lawernce Wai-Teng (1995). Introduction. In Gerard Sullivan & Laurence Wai-Teng Leong (Eds.), *Gays and lesbians in Asia and the Pacific: Social and human services* (pp. 1-10). New York: The Haworth Press, Inc.

Vance, C.S. (1995). Social construction theory and sexuality. In Maurice Berger, Brian Wallis & Simon Watson (Eds.), *Constructing masculinity*. New York: Routledge.

Same-Sex Sexual Experience
in Thailand

Peter A. Jackson

SUMMARY. In this paper I consider a number of studies of rates of
same-sex sexual experience among young men and women in Thailand
which have been conducted since the late 1980s. Interest in conducting
these quantitative studies was prompted, first, by concerns among Thai
educators and social commentators about a perceived increase in homosexual behavior among both male and female adolescents and, second,
by the need to determine the prevalence of different sexual behaviors
considered to be associated with the risk of transmitting the human im-
munodeficiency virus (HIV). Studies of rates of same-sex experience
have a more recent history in Thailand than in the United States or other
western countries, beginning in the second half of the 1980s. The first
studies were undertaken by researchers working within a psychological
framework which problematized homosexuality and which was motivated by a concern to reduce the incidence of homosexuality. This anti-
homosexual research program is detailed in Jackson and Sullivan's
introductory essay in this volume. The second, HIV/AIDS-influenced
set of studies, have been undertaken by epidemiologists and demogra-

This chapter has been prepared as part of the research project "Thai Sexualities:
The Emergence of Sexual Subcultures," funded by the Australian Research Council.

Address correspondence to: Peter A. Jackson, Division of Pacific and Asian
History, Research School of Pacific and Asian Studies, Australian National University, Canberra ACT 0200, Australia.

The author wishes to thank Dr. Stephen O. Murray and Dr. Gerard Sullivan for
their valuable comments on earlier drafts of this paper.

[Haworth co-indexing entry note]: "Same-Sex Sexual Experience in Thailand." Jackson, Peter A.
Co-published simultaneously in *Journal of Gay & Lesbian Social Services* (The Haworth Press, Inc.) Vol. 9,
No. 2/3, 1999, pp. 29-60; and: *Lady Boys, Tom Boys, Rent Boys: Male and Female Homosexualities in
Contemporary Thailand* (ed: Peter A. Jackson, and Gerard Sullivan) The Haworth Press, Inc., 1999, pp.
29-60; and: *Lady Boys, Tom Boys, Rent Boys: Male and Female Homosexualities in Contemporary Thailand*
(ed: Peter A. Jackson, and Gerard Sullivan) Harrington Park Press, an imprint of The Haworth Press, Inc.,
1999, pp. 29-60. Single or multiple copies of this article are available for a fee from The Haworth Document
Delivery Service [1-800-342-9678, 9:00 a.m. - 5:00 p.m. (EST). E-mail address: getinfo@haworthpress
inc.com].

29

phers operating within a framework that has not problematized homoeroticism. In reviewing the Thai research, I critically assess the methodologies of the various studies and point to possible biasing factors in data gathering techniques. I conclude by considering the implications of these studies for the provision of social services to homosexually active men and women in Thailand. *[Article copies available for a fee from The Haworth Document Delivery Service: 1-800-342-9678. E-mail address: getinfo@haworthpressinc.com]*

INTRODUCTION

The notions of "homosexuality" as a condition and "the homosexual" as a type of person characterized by same-sex erotic preference entered academic and popular discourses in western societies in the late nineteenth and early twentieth centuries as categories of illness and moral perversion (see for example Foucault, 1980; Weeks, 1991).[1] While these categories entered Thai academic discourses much later, in the 1950s and 1960s, I have shown elsewhere (Jackson, 1997) that the vast majority of Thai research on homoeroticism has also problematized same-sex interest as illness or perversion. Thus, when Thai investigators have asked "How many people have had a homosexual experience?" or "How many homosexuals are there?," these questions have not been posed as parts of a disinterested inquiry into human sexual diversity. Rather, efforts to measure rates of same-sex experience in Thailand have emerged from contexts in which same-sex eroticism has been prefigured as a social problem to be solved or prevented, or as being associated with potential risks to health. In considering the results of the quantitative studies reviewed below, we need to keep in mind the research problematics which have made same-sex eroticism a matter of academic concern. These studies were not undertaken merely to satisfy some innocent curiosity, but as parts of academic power/knowledge complexes. Indeed, the results of the studies were often intended to be used as ammunition in public debates about appropriate and inappropriate sexual behavior and in devising behaviour-modifying interventions. In some cases, Thai quantitative research has been fundamentally homophobic and antagonistic to same-sex activity. However, this does not appear to have been the case in HIV-related research, where measuring the prevalence of same-sex activity has been used to argue for interventions aimed at reducing the spread of HIV infection and thus protecting the well-being of homosexually active men.

While there are many limitations and problems of interpretation associated with the data reported below, there are a number of important reasons why the results of these Thai quantitative studies should be more widely known.

- Almost all current data on rates of same-sex experience come from studies in western societies, some of which are summarized below. Despite their limitations, the Thai studies provide some of the first quantitative results from outside the western cultural sphere and as such are of intrinsic interest to researchers working in the field of cross-cultural studies of sexuality. There is an unfortunate tendency in many countries, including Thailand, to use the results of research on homoeroticism in western countries (especially the United States) as benchmarks, despite the fact that historical and ethnographic research strongly suggests that patterns of human sexuality are often culturally specific rather than cross-cultural universals. There is a need to challenge the current Amero-centrism of sex research by making data from diverse societies much more widely known.
- While the precise results of the Thai studies may be questioned, the figures nevertheless suggest trends and the impact of cultural values on local sexual behaviors. The purpose of this paper is not to compare rates of homosexual experience between cultures. Methodological differences and disparate understandings and constructions of sexuality between Thailand and the West make direct comparisons problematic. However, considered reflection on the Thai data augments our understanding of the culturally specific character of local constructions of sexuality, and a careful reading of these studies can assist in framing questions and topics of inquiry for qualitative ethnographic, sociological and historical research on homoeroticism and transgenderism in Thailand. While the various Thai studies, like those in the West, have produced widely disparate findings, their results suggest important cultural parameters that impact on the construction of patterns of homoeroticism. In particular, the Thai data point to class-based differences and urban-rural differences in rates of male homoerotic experience, and the possibility that rates of fe-

male homoerotic experience are considerably higher in Thailand than in western societies.

• The sequence of Thai studies considered below show that as methodological problems in data gathering have been identified and corrected in subsequent research, progressively increasing rates of same-sex experience are reported, at least among young men (who have been the major focus of Thai research). That is, the most recent and methodologically more sophisticated studies have reported the highest rates of same-sex experience among Thai men, providing increasingly reliable evidence that a significant minority of around 20 percent of 21 year-old Thai men have had at least one same-sex experience to orgasm.

While homosexually active men were initially demonized as the purported "source" of HIV/AIDS in Thailand in the mid-1980s, since the late 1980s this section of the population has increasingly been neglected in government-sponsored HIV/AIDS education and care programs. In many cases men who have sex with men have disappeared completely as a target group for Thai HIV/AIDS interventions, which have increasingly focussed on female sex workers and their clients and intravenous drug users. The data on rates of same-sex experience among Thai men indicate that the omission of these men from HIV/AIDS programs is a serious oversight, and that significant numbers of Thai men are failing to receive adequate (or any) education about avoiding risk of HIV infection in their sexual encounters with other men. Above all, the Thai studies indicate the pressing need for nationwide HIV/AIDS interventions targeting homosexually active men.

PROBLEMS IN MEASURING RATES
OF SAME-SEX SEXUAL EXPERIENCE

The measurement of rates of "homosexuality" is beset by both theoretical and practical difficulties. As already noted, "homosexuality" and "the homosexual" are historically and culturally variable categories that do not exist as objective phenomena like height or weight. That is, measurements of rates of homosexuality or of the number of homosexuals in a population may tell us less about the cross-cultural commonalities of human eroticism than they do about patterns of sexual behavior within specific cultural and historical contexts. This makes cross-cultural comparisons of rates of various forms of sexual experience a problematic undertaking. The problems associated with interpreting data from another culture are demonstrated by the culturally relative character of even such a fundamental notion as what constitutes "having sex." In reporting the results of a nationwide survey of sexual attitudes and behaviors, Wiresit et al. (1991, p. 109) observed that in Thailand different erotic acts are differentially perceived as constituting "having sex" (*ruam phet*). The relevant results of the study are reproduced in Table 1.

To summarize, most respondents thought that only heterosexual penis-vagina contact constituted "having sex." Fewer than 50 percent of both male and female respondents regarded oral or anal sex between men as "having sex." The survey did not enquire about views on mutual masturbation to orgasm between men, but significantly fewer than 10 percent of both men and women regarded a man kissing and caressing another man, or a woman kissing and caressing another woman, as constituting sex. However, roughly double this number or about 20 percent of respondents regarded heterosexual kissing and caressing as "having sex." Similarly, fewer respondents regarded male-male orogenital contact as "having sex" than those who thought male-female orogenital contact was real sex. This survey indicates that it is not a particular form of erotic contact per se which defines that act

TABLE 1. Definitions of "Having Sex" (*ruam phet*) by Sex

	N = 2902 (More than one response possible)	
	Male	Female
	%	%
Man caressing/kissing a woman	19.4	24.9
Man caressing/kissing a man	6.8	7.4
Woman caressing/kissing a woman	7.4	7.0
Placing penis in vagina	98.3	98.3
Male placing penis in male anus	48.7	44.2
Male/female orogenital contact	33.6	33.8
Male/male orogenital contact	25.0	22.5

as "sexual" within Thai culture; the gender of the partners is also important. Various forms of homoerotic contact are less likely to be viewed as "having sex" than similar forms of heterosexual contact. This finding has important implications for surveys of rates of "homosexuality," for it suggests that many informants may under-report the incidence of same-sex contact if asked a question such as "Have you ever had sex with another man?" Questionnaires thus need to be carefully constructed and specify the precise form of a sexual act–such as "Have you ever been fellated by another man?"–in order to avoid this problem.

Even within a given culture, lack of conceptual clarity in framing survey instruments can render data all but meaningless. In particular, one must be clear whether same-sex sexual experience or homosexual or gay/lesbian identity is to be measured. A person can consider him or herself to be "a homosexual," "gay" or "lesbian" and yet be celibate or even a virgin, while another person can engage in frequent same-sex erotic activity and still consider himself to be a "heterosexual." That is, measuring rates of homoerotic experience does not tell us how many "homosexuals" there are, and certainly is not an indicator of numbers of gay-identified men or lesbian-identified women. A number of the studies summarized below do not make these conceptual distinctions and conflate the indigenous Thai transgender category *kathoey* with the newer analytic category of homosexuality (*rak-ruam-phet, homosekchuan*) as well as with gay identity. That is, some of the Thai academic studies have not distinguished between transgenderism and homoeroticism, or between homoerotic behavior and homosexual identity. This reflects a sexual culture within which the categories of gender and sexuality are less clearly differentiated than in the contemporary West and in which gender role remains an important factor in most expressions of homoeroticism. In contemporary Thailand it is often possible for a male to avoid being labelled "gay" or "homosexual" provided he plays a masculine sexual role, and especially if his partner is an effeminate or feminized male who is labelled or self-identifies as a *kathoey* (see De Lind van Wijngaarden in this volume). However, this gender-focussed construction of homoeroticism is beginning to be challenged, especially in urban centres such as Bangkok, where it is increasingly common for a male to be labelled simply as "gay" if he engages in any form of homoerotic activity (see Murray in this volume).

Another difficulty besetting quantitative research is that in Thailand, as in western societies, homosexuality is widely regarded to be aberrant, deviant or wrong and participants in surveys may not be prepared to reveal their sexual history to an interviewer whom they feel they cannot trust or do not know well. Given the stigma attached to homosexual behavior, anonymity and comprehensiveness are crucial to the accuracy of any survey. Face-to-face interviews may lead to under-reporting of rates of homosexual experience as some informants may avoid the embarrassment or shame of admitting to having had a same-sex experience. Secondly, if survey responses are voluntary, then some respondents may not answer questions about homosexual experience, even when anonymity is guaranteed, because of the sensitivity of the topic. This may also lead to under-reporting. As will be seen below, anonymity and comprehensiveness are important methodological factors in interpreting variations in the Thai data.

Given the importance many Thai researchers have attached to the findings of the Kinsey team's studies of human sexuality, it is perhaps useful to summarise these studies before considering the Thai data in detail. The work of Kinsey et al. (1948) in the United States was the first large scale quantitative study of sexual experience conducted in any country and, in brief, the team found that:

- 37 percent of men and 13 percent of women had at least one homosexual experience to the point of orgasm some time between adolescence and old age;
- 18 percent of men had at least as much homosexual as heterosexual experience for at least three years of their lives;
- 8 percent of men and 4 percent of women had been exclusively homosexual for at least three years of their lives; and
- 4 percent of men had been exclusively homosexual throughout their lives.

These results have often been taken as benchmark figures for rates of homosexual experience, and in the 1970s were widely cited by gay liberation activists to support the claim that one-in-ten people in western societies were gay. However, no subsequent Western study has found similar levels of homosexual experience, and surveys conducted in the light of the HIV/AIDS pandemic have reported significantly lower levels of homosexual activity. In 1988 the US National

Academy of Sciences (see Goddard, 1994, p. 6) funded a study which, based on interviews of 1,719 men, reported that:

- 2 percent had experienced sex to orgasm with another man in the past year; and
- 20 percent had sex to orgasm with another man at least once in their lives.

A 1993 study conducted by the Batelle Human Affairs Research Centre in Seattle, USA (see Goddard, 1994, p. 6), reported that 1.1 percent of men had been "exclusively gay" over the previous decade and only 2.3 percent had any homosexual experience in the past ten years. A 1994 British survey (partly funded by the British Government and subsequently by the Wellcome Trust when then Prime Minister Margaret Thatcher withdrew Government support) found that 6.1 percent of men and 3.4 percent of women had "some kind of homosexual experience–maybe only kissing and cuddling–at any time in their lives" (Goddard, 1994, p. 6). For 0.6 percent of women and 1.7 percent of men this experience involved genital contact. The study also found that only 1.4 percent of men and 0.6 percent of women had a partner of the same sex in the past five years.

Note: All statistical data cited in this paper accurately reproduce information given in the Thai sources referred to. Where minor discrepancies exist, such as percentages not rounding to precisely 100, these reflect errors in the original text.

QUANTITATIVE STUDIES BY PSYCHOLOGISTS– ANXIETIES ABOUT AN "EPIDEMIC" OF HOMOSEXUALITY AMONG THAI YOUTH

Studies of rates of homosexual experience among Thai youth were first undertaken in the 1980s in response to a widespread anxiety among educators and psychologists that an "epidemic of homosexuality" (*rak-ruam-phet rabat*) appeared to have hit Thailand (Apha, 1985; Prachan, 1988; Wanlop, 1988). This widely discussed concern appears to have emerged from anxieties about the effects of rapid socio-economic and cultural changes on Thai youth. In recent decades morals campaigners in western countries, such as the American Anita Bryant, have campaigned against gay rights by arguing that impressionable youth may be influenced to "become gay" if exposed to images and information about homosexuality or by coming in contact with gay people. The Thai anxiety was somewhat different, being a concern that large numbers of youth had already become homosexual rather than a fear that they might be influenced to become homosexual.

Mahidol University Studies of Senior Secondary School and Vocational College Students

In the late 1980s and early 1990s several Masters level students in clinical psychology at Bangkok's Mahidol University undertook a series of studies of rates of homosexual experience among senior secondary and vocational college students around the country. All these studies were conducted under the supervision of Prof. Udomsin Srisaengnam M.D., who has written extensively on the clinical aspects of homosexuality over several decades (see Udomsin, 1978), and appear to be part of a research program initiated by Prof. Udomsin. The main aim of the studies supervized by Udomsin was to provide data to substantiate the anecdotal claims of Wanlop (1988) and others that rates of homosexual behavior among youth were high as part of a campaign to alert what was seen as a largely indifferent public to the "dangers" of homosexuality. Each graduate student focussed on one of the 12 geographical regions into which the Thai Ministry of Education groups schools and colleges, interviewing several hundred male and female 17 to 19 year olds from a variety of institutions in their selected region.[2] The findings of the various studies are listed in Table 2 (completed from Chalorsak, 1991 and Sujitra, 1991).

All studies had the same four objectives, namely, to (1) undertake a statistical study of the origins of homosexuality among teenage students; (2) study the tendency towards homosexual behavior of teenage students; (3) study factors associated with the homosexual behavior of students; and (4) study the attitudes of teenage students towards homosexuality (from Nujari, 1989, p. 4). Nanthirat Khunakorn's (1989) study of students from the region immediately adjacent to Bangkok indicates the tenor of these studies, which pathologized homosexuality:

> . . . it was found that the number of those who had homosexual behavior and those who had a high risk of being homosexual was very high. Therefore, their parents, guardians, instructors, mass

TABLE 2. Summary of Mahidol University Studies

Educational Region	Students Who Reported Homosexual Experience					Assessed At Risk of Homosexual Behavior	Total Number in Sample
	Females	Males	Female/Male Ratio (approx)	Total No.	%		
1	37 (3.8%)	8 (0.8%)	5:1	45	4.7	24.4% f, 8.5%m	965 (495f, 470m)
2	15	5	3:1	20	2.4	15.6%	832 (451f, 381m)
4	4.7%	1.9%				15.2%	891 (467f, 424m)
5	26	2	13:1	28	2.8		877
6	20	11	2:1	31	3.3		953
7	19	6	3:1	25	3.1		812
9	17	5	3:1	22	2.5		902
10	26	7	4:1	33	3.3	9.2%f, 7.4%m	922 (485f, 437m)
11	19	5	4:1	24	2.4		936
12	34	3	11:1	37	3.5		1052

Note: The results of the various studies were not reported in a consistent format in all dissertations. Only a small number provided breakdowns by male and female respondents, here marked "m" and "f," respectively. Sujitra provided only percentages, not actual numbers of positive responses.

media, and those who are involved in the Ministry of Education should realize this important problem and hurry to find the prevention [sic]. That is, they should be careful not to let the adolescent students–the adults-to-be who are going to be the national resources in the future–have homosexual behavior so that Thailand will lack both real men and women for the future. (Nanthirat, 1989, Dissertation Abstract, no page number)

Sujitra (1991) reported that she found the following factors to be "significantly related to homosexual behavior in female students":

These students' fathers were disrespectful and gave less time [to their children than the fathers of heterosexual respondents]. Their parents' roles were not equal and there was lack of helpfulness between siblings. Most of these students had experienced separation from their families (either residing at [boarding] school or in private dormitories) and their closest friends were in the main homosexual. (Sujitra, 1991, Dissertation Abstract, no page number)

These findings reinforced the stereotypical pathologisation of homosexuality as being "caused" by supposedly dysfunctional families and the influence of homosexual peers. Sujitra also reported that the following factors were significantly related to homosexual behavior among male students.

> Most of them were the youngest siblings and [they came from families where] the number of brothers was greater than the number of sisters . . . Their parents were weak and submissive, and they usually had major conflicts with their fathers. Their mothers often treated them like a daughter, and always argued and quarrelled with their husband. Furthermore, their mothers had more power and decision-making authority in their families, and their mother's occupation usually related to management or administration. Most of their close friends were homosexual. (Sujitra, 1991, Dissertation Abstract, no page number)

The various MA dissertations cited here had numerous deficiencies. None provided a copy of the questionnaire used in the study or a clear statement of how it was administered. However, indirect references in the texts suggest that the questionnaires were administered in face-to-face interviews. The key findings were reported in terms of rates of "homosexual behavior" (*phreutikam rak-ruam-phet*) and the "risk of engaging in homosexual behavior." However, neither of these variables is precisely defined, and appear to involve subjective assessment by the interviewer. For example, Nanthirat Khunakorn (1989) reported that she assessed students to be at risk of engaging in homosexual behavior on the basis of "the characteristics of the opposite sex [that the interviewee had reported they expressed] when a child," which she determined by unstated "indirect questions." Nujari Techapanya-chai (1989) assessed whether students had a "high tendency towards expressing homosexual behavior" on the basis of her own perceptions of effeminacy in males and masculinity in females, with an assumed "wrong-genderedness" (*khwam-phit-phet*) taken as implying homosexual tendency.

While the lack of a clear statement of methodology and the subjectivity of some assessments make the results of this set of studies questionable, the reported results are nevertheless consistent. One of the most interesting findings was the consistently greater reported prevalence of female than male homoerotic experience among adolescents. This suggests the possibility that Thai female sexual culture, at least among middle class students, may differ significantly from that in the West, where all quantitative studies have reported lower rates of same-sex experience among women than men. Overall, the studies found higher rates of homosexual experience among girls in girls-only schools than among boys in boys-only schools or among either girls or boys in co-educational schools. There were no significant differences in boys' rates of homosexual experience between single-sex and co-educational schools, but girls from girls-only schools had significantly higher rates of homosexual experience than girls from co-educational schools. Both male and female students in single-sex schools were reported as having more positive attitudes towards homosexual behavior than those in co-educational schools, and all the studies reported that female students had more positive attitudes towards both male and female homosexuality than male students. Chalorsak (1991) also found that non-Muslim (i.e., Buddhist) students had more positive attitudes towards both male and female homosexuality than Muslim students. However, his was the only study to report on differences between religious groups.

The Udomsin studies also reported higher perceived risk of engaging in homosexuality among females than males. Nanthirat reported that she assessed 24.4 percent of female students but only 8.5 percent of male students of being at "a high risk of engaging in homosexual behavior," while Nujari reported that 9.2 percent of female students and 7.4 percent of male students had "a high tendency towards expressing homosexual behavior."

Summarising the results of all the studies conducted in the research program led by Professor Udomsin, Sujitra (1991, p. 143) concludes that "Thai society and customary ways of child raising in Thai families appear to promote greater rates of homosexual behavior among females than males." These consistently higher rates of female homosexuality among teenagers counter findings on rates of female homosexuality in the whole population (Werasit, 1992b).[3] While the majority of researchers were female, at least one male researcher, Chalorsak (1991), also found higher reported rates of homosexual experience among female students than male students. This suggests that the results do not reflect a possible biasing effect due to the gender of the interviewer. One possible explanation is that class factors are involved. Only the Thai middle and upper classes can afford to educate their children, whether male or female, to senior high school or college level. It may be that female homoerotic activity is more common among adolescent females from the numerically small Thai middle class than among the general female population, thus explaining the apparent contradiction between Werasit's whole population study (see Table 3) and these sectoral studies.

Tawesak et al. (1991, pp. 24-25, Table 21) have reported the results of two further surveys of male homosexual experience among high school students (see Table 3), but do not describe the methodologies of these additional surveys, and the author has not been able to obtain copies of the original papers cited.[4] In a survey of 289 16-17 year old boys studying in senior high school years four to six in Bangkok, Suphak and Khajit (1990) reported that 1.4 percent had a homosexual experience. Also in 1990, Khemika et al. reported that 3.6 percent of a sample of 2,123 high school boys in Bangkok with an average age of 14.7 years reported that they had a homosexual experience. While the Suphak and Khajit figure is comparatively low, Khemika's result is of the same order as those reported in the series of studies sponsored by Udomsin.

TABLE 3. Usual Sex of Partners by Respondent's Sex (as a Percentage of Sexually Experienced Respondents)

	% Male (n = 983)	% Female (n = 1285)
Female only	96.6	0.9
Mostly female/some male	2.8	
Equally male/female	0.2	0.1
Mostly male/some female	0.1	0.2
Male only	0.2	98.9
	100.0	100.0

(Source: Werasit et al., 1992b, p. 2)

EPIDEMIOLOGICAL STUDIES

In the 1990s a second series of surveys of sexual behavior were undertaken in response to concerns about the explosive spread of HIV infection. These studies sought to gauge rates of sexual behaviors considered to be associated with the risk of transmission of HIV infection. Most of the epidemiological studies focussed on younger men, who were assumed to be more sexually active and at greater risk of sexually transmitted HIV infection. A significant number of the studies were also limited to the northern region of the country, which in the early 1990s reported much higher rates of HIV infection than other regions, and where the need for HIV/AIDS interventions was considered to be more acute. Because heterosexual contact was found to be as great if not greater a source of new HIV infections than same-sex activity, the epidemiological studies questioned men on all forms of sexual behavior, with questions related to same-sex behavior being just one component of broad surveys.

One of the most consistent results to emerge from the surveys is the influence of class on rates of homosexual experience, with significantly higher reported rates of same-sex contact among less educated working class and rural males than among middle class urban men. Kinsey et al. (1948) reported a similar finding in their research. However, the various surveys report significantly different rates of homosexual experience, even among men from similar class backgrounds. These widely disparate results appear to reflect the effect of different methodologies. The epidemiological studies are considered here in order of increasing reported rates of homosexual experience, rather than strictly chronologically, as this permits a clearer understanding of the impact of methodology on results.

A Whole Population Study

In 1992 Werasit et al. (Werasit et al., 1992b) reported on a nationwide survey of partner relations and risk of HIV infection. The questionnaire was administered in "confidential . . . structured interviews" (Werasit et al., 1992b, p. 1) and stratified random sampling techniques were used to select a sample of 2,801 Buddhist males and females aged 15-49 nationwide. Of the males sampled, 15.2 percent had no sexual experience, while 25.6 percent of the females sampled were sexually inexperienced. One question in this large survey asked respondents to characterize their lifetime sexual experience in terms of the gender of their partners in response to the question, "The gender [*phet*] of your spouse or regular partner who is your most frequent sexual contact" (Werasit et al., 1992b, p. A-7). The term *phet* used in the survey instrument may mean either "sex" (i.e., male or female) or "gender" (i.e., masculine or feminine), with these two concepts not being clearly distinguished in Thai. Werasit's published report quoted here is in English, being a translation of an original unpublished Thai manuscript. Werasit variously translates *phet* as "gender" and as "sex." The responses to this question are reproduced below.

This question did not ask about sexual behavior but rather the sex (*phet*) of the person whom the informant regarded to be their regular partner. As such, the questionnaire was poorly designed to detect rates of actual same-sex contact. Indeed, the authors noted that rates of homosexual and bisexual preference among men as well as rates of anal intercourse reported in response to a subsequent question in this survey were low compared to Tawesak et al.'s (1991) study of military recruits (see below). The authors explained these differences by saying that their survey enquired about "general sexual orientation" not "lifetime sexual behavior," adding that, "Given the very low level of social sanctions for and guilt over male-male contacts in Thailand, it is possible that the actual levels of male-male sexual behavior may be higher" (Werasit et al., 1992b, p. 32).

Commenting on this study, Beyrer et al. (1995) noted that self-administered questionnaires result in higher reported rates of homosexual experience among Thai men, and that Werasit's findings that "3.3% of Thai male adults described themselves as homosexual or bisexual, may be considered an underestimate of the numbers of Thai men engaging in same-sex behavior" (Beyrer et al., 1995, p. 173). Significantly, however, the Werasit survey found that rates of all types of sexual experience were much lower for females than for males.

Surveys Comparing Occupational and/or Class Differences in Rates of Same-Sex Experience

A number of studies have provided data on differential rates of same-sex experience between various occupational and class groupings. Tawesak et al. (1991) compared his own group's findings with the results of four other surveys of Thai men's sexual behavior: Khemika et al. (1990), Pharadorn et al. (1991), Sompol (1990) and Suphak et al. (1990). The results are shown in Table 4. A dash (–) indicates that a question was not asked in the particular survey.

The results of these additional surveys were provided without comment in Tawesak's paper, and no attempt was made to explain the divergent results. The average age of the high school students surveyed by both Suphak and Khemika is considerably lower than that of respondents to the other three studies, and for this reason the Suphak and Khemika studies are not comparable to the other studies cited by Tawesak.

It is possible that methodological differences account for the significant disparity between Sompol's findings and the more consistent results presented by Tawesak and Pharadorn. Nevertheless, there appear to be systematic differences in reported rates of all types of sexual experience between the less-educated and presumably poorer, rural army conscripts interviewed by Tawesak and Pharadorn and the better-educated and presumably more affluent, urban medical students studied by Sompol. Sompol's medical students reported higher rates of masturbation, while the men in the other two studies reported higher rates of homosexual experience as well as higher rates of heterosexual experience, both with prostitutes and with female friends or lovers. The picture that emerges is of higher rates of sexual experience, both heterosexual and homosexual, among rural, less-educated men than among better-educated, urban men, suggesting that socio-economic background is an important factor influencing rates of all forms of sexual experience. This finding is confirmed in a 1993 study conducted by VanLandingham et al., which compared rates of heterosexual and homosexual activity among unmarried men working in a range of occupations in Chiang Mai, northern Thailand, using a self-administered anonymous questionnaire. Tables 5 and 6 summarize the group's findings.

The authors observe that the greater sexual experience of soldiers and construction workers and the lesser sexual experience of students, "reflect the relative socio-economic status of the . . . groups" and supports "U.S.-based studies indicating a negative association between sexual experience and social class" (Kinsey et al., 1948; Vener et al., 1972) (VanLandingham et al., 1993, p. 303).

TABLE 4. Summary of Class and Occupational Group Surveys

Survey Team Leader:	Tawesak	Pharadorn	Sompol	Suphak	Khemika
Year:	1991	1991	1990	1990	1990
Sample Population:	Army Conscripts North Region	Army Conscripts Central & NE Region	Medical Students	Bangkok High school Years 4-6	Bangkok High sch. Years 1-6
Sample Size:	202	435	633	289	2123
Average Age:	21	21	21.7	16-17	14.7
Percent reporting having had a homosexual experience:	25.6%	31.5%	13%	1.4%	3.6%
Age of first homosexual experience:					
<14	1.6%	—	1.9%	—	—
>14 < 16	9.4%	13.6%	3.7%	—	—
>16 < 20	21.9%	25.5%	8.7%	—	—
% reporting having masturbated:	88.4%	—	98.4%	—	41.2%
Age of first masturbation:					
<10	1.1%	—	3.6%	—	—
>10 < 16	68.9%	—	87.2%	—	—
>16 < 19	86.7%	—	97.3%	—	—
Percent reporting having had heterosexual intercourse:	97%	—	61.2%	22.7%	12%
Age of first heterosexual intercourse:					
<16	53.9%	39.1%	8.4%	15.7%	—
>16 < 20	97%	93.2%	50.1%	—	—

(Source: Tawesak et al., 1991, pp. 24-25, Table 21)

TABLE 5. Background and Personal Characteristics of Never-Married Men in Northern Thailand

Occupation:	Tertiary Students	Dept. Store Workers	Soldiers	Municipal/ Construction Workers	All Groups
	(n = 514)	(n = 111)	(n = 360)	(n = 49)	(n = 1034)
Average Age	19.7	24.0	21.8	24.3	21.1
Rural Background	44%	73%	83%	81%	62%
Completed Secondary School	100%	65%	27%	11%	67%

(Source: VanLandingham et al., 1993, p. 301, Table 1)

TABLE 6. Sexual Experience: Never-Married Men in Northern Thailand

Occupation:	Tertiary Students	Dept. Store Workers	Soldiers	Municipal/ Construction Workers	All Groups
Ever had heterosexual intercourse (% of total sample)	34%	80%	90%	86%	61%
Ever visited a female prostitute (% of sexually experienced)	82% (n = 171)	74% (n = 89)	97% (n = 323)	98% (n = 42)	90% (n = 625)
Ever had sex with a man (% of sexually experienced)	11% (n = 169)	11% (n = 82)	15% (n = 323)	20% (n = 41)	14% (n = 615)

(Source: VanLandingham et al., 1993, p. 302, Table 2)

Surveys of Royal Thai Army Conscripts

Research teams headed by Beyrer and Tawesak conducted numerous surveys of sexual behavior among young military conscripts in northern Thailand during the first half of the 1990s. In Thailand men are conscripted between the ages of 21 and 23 and are selected by a compulsory national lottery based on the drawing of pieces of red and black coloured wood from a barrel. All conscripts have a compulsory medical check upon enlistment and the Beyrer and Tawesak teams included anonymous HIV testing and a survey of sexual history as part of this process. Most of the surveys reflected the men's sexual experiences prior to entering the army, and the results do not reflect possible situational homosexuality in an all-male military institution, which might have increased the figures for this sexual behavior. Neither HIV-positive status nor homosexual activity are grounds for exclusion or expulsion from the Thai armed forces, and the research teams secured the support of the Royal Thai Army in these surveys. Most military conscripts are from poorer, rural backgrounds, as young men from wealthier families are often able to avoid conscription. For example, attending military cadet training for a number of years during high school exempts a boy from the draft, but as most rural youth do not attend high school this option for avoiding conscription is not available to them. Also, in some circumstances it is possible to buy one's way out of the draft through bribing officials. Again, a poorer rural youth is less likely to have the resources to pay a bribe. The following studies therefore probably include only a small number of middle or upper class urban youth, with the majority of respondents being poorer men from rural and urban working class backgrounds.

In 1995 Beyrer et al. reported on a study of same-sex behavior among two cohorts of northern Thai military conscripts and one cohort of recently discharged conscripts. A total of 1047 men was studied, with 134 (6.5 percent) reporting one or more male lifetime sex partners. Of this subgroup, 130 (97 percent) had also had at least one female sex partner while 4 (3 percent) had exclusively had male partners. The authors commented on their study as follows:

> 9.3% of discharged men, who had returned to civilian life, reported same-sex behavior, while only 6.5% of men still in the military did. These [discharged] men are 2 years older, on average, than the men in the new conscript groups. They were also interviewed by civilian interviewers in civilian life. Thus, older age, longer sexual history, and an increased willingness to report same-sex behavior in a civilian context may all play a part in accounting for this difference . . . the MSM [men who have sex with men] in our sample also reported an earlier age of sexual

debut, more mean lifetime partners of either sex, more female and male commercial partners . . . our data suggest a pattern of men who are at higher risk [of HIV infection] in general, with same-sex behavior only one component of their more active sexual lives. (Beyrer et al., 1995, p. 175)[5]

An earlier study (Nelson et al., 1993) of military conscripts by the same research group found self-reported lifetime rates of same-sex behavior to be 3.02 percent among 2417 men. In their report the group also summarized a 1991 study (published in Nopkesorn et al., 1993) of army conscripts in Phitsanulok in the lower north (200 km south of Chiangmai), in which 11.3 percent of men reported a lifetime history of anal intercourse with another man, with 10 percent reporting insertive and 4.1 percent reporting receptive intercourse. Beyrer et al. (1995, p. 172) accounted for these disparities by suggesting that survey techniques in the second study may have led to under-reporting. In the 1993 Nelson et al. study, medical students and Royal Thai Army (RTA) paramedics conducted the interviews, and RTA camp locations were used in which men may have feared that their answers may not have been completely confidential. However, in the 1995 Beyrer et al. study, 9 young northern Thai men, all civilian health educators, conducted the interviews, and Beyrer et al. (1995, p. 175) observe that, "Reporting of same-sex behaviors in this population appears to vary significantly with data collection techniques . . . Self-administered questionnaires may help overcome under-reporting of same-sex behaviors, although these require literate subjects."

Indeed, two other surveys of young conscripts which used self-administered questionnaires both reported higher rates of same-sex experience than those found by Beyrer's teams. In 1993 Tawesak et al. reported a study conducted between January and March 1992 at the Chiang Kham army base in Phayao Province in the far north of the country. A total of 157 conscripts responded to a self-administered questionnaire, with 13.6 percent of the young men reported having engaged in insertive anal intercourse with a *kathoey*, 3.2 percent reporting insertive anal intercourse with a non-*kathoey* male and 3.3 percent reporting receptive anal intercourse with another male.

In 1996 Suchai Kitsiriphornchai reported on one of the most comprehensive surveys of RTA recruits conducted to date, a national survey of draftees conducted jointly by the civilian Ministry of Public

Health and the Medical Division of the Royal Thai Army.[6] Question-naires were administered to 4904 21-year-old conscripts from the country's four main geographical regions–the central, northern, north-eastern and southern regions. This sample group constituted 17 per-cent of the total national draft intake of 28,705 conscripts in 1996. Respondents were allowed anonymity. Respondents were advised not to include any information on the questionnaire form that might iden-tify them. A total of 350 questionnaires were administered in each of the sample army bases selected and an average of 272 questionnaires were returned from each centre. A little over half (58 percent) of respondents had only a primary education, indicating that the majority of men were from lower class backgrounds.

The majority (87 percent) of respondents reported having had sexu-al intercourse, with either a woman or a man, with 17 percent (714 of the 4210 who responded affirmatively to this question) having had sex with another male. Of this latter subgroup, 68 percent (484 of the 709 respondents or 11 percent of the total) replied affirmatively to the question, "Are you still engaging in this behavior?" Reported rates of same-sex experience differed significantly between individual prov-inces, from 9 percent for Phayao in the far north to 31 percent for Songkhla in the far south. However, the figure for Songkhla is excep-tionally high, being 50 percent above the next highest result and three times the result obtained from another southern province, Nakhonsri-thammarat, where only 11 percent of recruits reported having had a same-sex experience. These variations make the Songkhla result sus-pect, as figures for all other provinces across all regions vary within a much smaller range, suggesting greater reliability. Indeed, averaged rates for the four regions of the country vary to a much less significant degree. However, there does appear to be a trend for higher reported rates of same-sex experience in the more urbanized central and south-ern regions than in the more rural northern and northeastern regions, suggesting the existence of significant differences between male sexu-al culture in rural and urban areas. The results from each provincial sample location to the question asking about lifetime same-sex experi-ence are listed in Table 7.

It should be noted that while 4892 men responded to the question asking their age and 4786 responded to the question about their level of educational achievement, only 4210 replied to the question "Have you ever had sexual relations (*phet-samphan*) with a man (*phu-*

TABLE 7. Army Recruits' Reported Rates of Homosexual Experience, by Province

Home Province	Ever Had Homosexual Experience (%)
Central Region	
Bangkok	20
Saraburi	13
Ratchburi	20
Kanjanaburi	18
Nakhonsawan	14
(Central Region Average 17)	
Southern Region	
Nakhonsrithammarat	11
Suratthani	21
Ranong	16
Songkhla	31
(Southern Region Average [Excluding Songkhla] 16)	
Northeast Region	
Nakhornatchasima	10
Ubonratchathani	13
Khon Kaen	17
Udonthani	18
Sakolnakhon	14
(Northeast Region Average 14.4)	
Northern Region	
Chiang Mai	13
Phayao	9
Chiang Rai	12
Phitsanulok	17
(Northern Region Average 12.75)	

(Source: Suchai, 1996)

chai)?" Furthermore, 48 supplied an answer to the question
"Have you ever had sexual ... ations?," not specifying the sex of the
partner. This suggests that e... in self-administered questionnaires
the question of homosexual e... rience is sensitive and may still be
under-reported.

Perhaps the highest reported ... e of same-sex experience among
males in Thailand (excluding ... Songkhla result above) emerged
from a 1990 survey of the sexual ... ha vior of 199 21-year-old conscripts from northern Thailand wh... was reported by Tawesak et al.
in 1991. Most interviewees were fr... a rural background and the
survey was conducted anonymously ... ith respondents completing
the questionnaire in private and one qu... ter (25.6 percent) reporting
ever having had a homosexual experie... e. Results from the 1990
survey questions relating to homosexu... b havior are shown in
Tables 8, 9 and 10.

Just over one tenth (11.9 percent) of a ... b-group of 192 of the
conscripts also reported being sexually arouse... when presented with a
picture of a naked man with an erection. Tawes ... noted that Kinsey et
al. (1948) reported a 13 percent response to ... hi stimulus among
American men.

Note that the key question asked in this survey w... s, "Have you ever
had a homosexual experience (prasopkan rak-rua... p'et)?" In Thai
the expression "homosexual experience" would ... e likely to be
construed as including a wider range of same-sex e... u ters than the
expression "homosexual intercourse," as many men ... u'd be likely
to interpret this latter expression more narrowly as ... ning having

TABLE 8. Age of First Homosexual Experience (n = 192, 7 non ... plies)

	% of total	% of homosexually experienced
12-13 yrs	1.6	16.3
14-15 yrs	7.8	30.5
16-17 yrs	7.3	28.5
18-19 yrs	3.1	12.1
20-21 yrs	3	11.7

(Source: Summarised from Tawesak et al., 1991, Tables 17, 18, 19 on pages 19 and 20.)

TABLE 9. Method Used When Havi... mc sexual Intercourse (n = 192, 7 non-replies)

(Multiple answers possible)

	% of total	% of homosexually experienced
Used hand or rubbed sexual organs	15.6	60.9
Used mouth	4.5	17.8
Had anal sex	14.5	56.6
(insertive/receptive not specified)		

(Source: Summarised from Tawes... ...t al., 1991, Tables 17, 18, 19 on pages 19 and 20.)

TABLE 10. Ex... ie...ce of Homosexual Anal Intercourse

(Multiple answers possible)

	% of total (n = 199)	% of homosexually experienced
Ever Had Homosexual A...al Sex	14.5	
Role Taken in Ana... ...e...		
Insertive	9	62
Receptive	1	6.9
Alternative insert... ...r...ceptive	3.5	24.1
No response	1	
Reason f... E...gaging in This Behavior		
Wanted to...	9	62
Because ...r.k	3	20.7
For mo... /	2.5	17.2
Encou... ...d to	1	6.9
No re... ...onse	1	
V...ether or Not Enjoyed the Experience		
...njoyed (*mai chorp*)	8.5	58.6
...oyed (*chorp*)	3.5	24.1
...reply	2.5	17.2

(Source: Summarised from Tawesak et al., 1991, Tables 17, 18, 19 on pages 19 and 20.)

anal sex with a man. Significantly, this survey's response rate is considerably higher than those reported in the 1992 Werasit study (3.3 percent), the 1995 Beyrer study (6.5 percent) and the 1996 Suchai study (17 percent). Tawesak's higher response rate can no doubt be attributed to the fact that, unlike in the Werasit study, respondents were asked about homosexual experience, not self-perceived sexual orientation, and, unlike in the Beyrer study, the survey instrument was a self-administered questionnaire rather than a questionnaire completed at an interview. While Suchai used self-administered anonymous questionnaires and tabulated his findings as reported rates of "homosexual experience," the actual survey instrument enquired whether the men had ever engaged in "homosexual intercourse." It is therefore possible that this wording led to some men failing to report some sexual activities such as mutual masturbation or oral sex with another man.

AN IN-DEPTH QUANTITATIVE STUDY OF HOMOSEXUALLY ACTIVE MEN

In the majority of studies reported above, data on same-sex experiences have emerged in the context of broader population surveys of sexual experience. Very little quantitative research has focussed specifically on homosexually active men, De Lind van Wijngaarden's study of male sex workers in Chiang Mai in this volume being an exception. Perhaps the first in-depth study of a local network of homosexually active men in Thailand was conducted in March 1991 when Werasit et al. (1992a) undertook a survey in a large northeastern Thai province in order to gain more detailed information to assist in devising locally appropriate HIV/AIDS interventions.

The target population was "men who have sex with men" (MSM), regardless of their self-identification as gay, bisexual, transsexual or heterosexual. However, in places, this survey did begin to draw a distinction between homosexual behavior and homosexual or transgender identity, especially in questions relating to sexual partners and relationships. The sample of 157 men ranged in age from 15 to 57. Of the group, 150 were never married, three were married and four were either separated or divorced. 33.8 percent were tertiary students, 16.6 percent were labourers, 14 percent worked in commercial or retail occupations, 10.8 percent were government employees, 9.6 percent were beauticians or hair dressers and 5.1 percent were farmers. The majority lived in the province's main town or in nearby suburban areas.

At the time of the survey the main town had no bar or other venue catering for a predominantly or exclusively homosexual clientele. However, some "mixed" entertainment venues were more popular with homosexual men than others. While there was no gay commercial sex establishment, freelance male sex workers worked on a casual basis from a large central park at night. This park, together with some other localities such as the college swimming pool, were also popular cruising areas for non-commercial casual sex. The town had a number of distinct networks of homosexually active men, including loose groups of mostly younger gay-identified students at the college and *kathoeys* (cross-dressing males, some but not all of whom lived as women) who worked in beauty parlours, dress-making shops and other small businesses. Rural and urban working class men who cruised or sold sex from the town park formed a looser network. These different groups tended not to interact socially and indeed some mutual hostility existed between them. For example, the mostly middle class gay students disparaged the poorer men who frequented the park as "dirty" and undesirable, while the *kathoeys* often felt that the students were "stuck up" and refused to socialize with them. While Werasit's study provided little further ethnographic detail, focusing as it did on gathering data considered relevant to devising HIV/AIDS interventions, it nevertheless provides an insight into a relatively complex and structured series of networks of homosexually active and gay-identified and *kathoey*-identified men in a town far removed from the tourist centres of Bangkok, Chiang Mai, Pattaya and Phuket. Thus it provides a partial snapshot of a distinctively Thai subculture.

IMPLICATIONS FOR THE PROVISION OF SOCIAL SERVICES

Studies of rates of homosexual experience have contributed to two distinct public debates in Thailand which have impacted on the provision of social services to homosexually active men and women. The first debate focussed on an anxiety deriving from a perception that rates of same-sex experience among both male and female Thai youth were undergoing explosive growth. Discussion on this issue was common in the Thai psychological literature in the 1980s (see for example

Apha, 1985; Wanlop, 1988), and became a matter of public concern when academic seminars on the topic were widely reported in the local press. This anxiety and the associated public debate had a decidedly negative impact on the provision of supportive and non-judgmental social services to both homosexual men and women. This was because much discussion focussed on how the presumed explosion in youth homoeroticism could be stemmed or prevented, with service providers such as psychologists, doctors, school counsellors, sex educators and family planning workers often being more concerned to treat or cure homosexuality than to provide supportive services.

While a number of studies (e.g., the series sponsored by Udomsin) sought data to substantiate anecdotal observations that an epidemic of teenage homosexuality had hit Thai high schools in the 1980s, the studies in fact found relatively low rates of same-sex experience among this group. Indeed, while the focus of concern in the 1980s was homosexuality among middle class secondary and college students, rates of same-sex experience in these groups are in fact much lower than among young Thai people from lower class backgrounds. With a few exceptions, public anxiety about a supposed epidemic of youth homosexuality has tended to subside in recent years with fewer calls for anti-homosexual interventions. However, the decline in anti-homosexual rhetoric has not been paralleled by any rise in the provision of support services for homosexual youth and such services are all but non-existent. In these debates the sexual behavior of poorer youth who had left school and joined the workforce was rarely an issue, indicating a middle class bias and perhaps reflecting a distinctively bourgeois anxiety about sexuality that is not representative of the much larger populations of rural and urban poor. In summary, the psychological studies failed to provide data that could be used to support the calls of educators and psychologists for interventions in families and schools to stem the supposed rise in "wrong-gendered" behavior.

Quantitative studies also contributed to policy and program development for the provision of HIV/AIDS education for MSM. In Thailand the first deaths from AIDS occurred among homosexually active men. Furthermore, as in many Western countries, in the mid-1980s MSM were stigmatized as the supposed "sources" of HIV/AIDS by the press, media and even by Thai medical and health authorities. However, by the late 1980s HIV/AIDS had become a concern to the heterosexual population, to such an extent that by the mid-1990s

MSM were almost completely ignored as a target group for both government and non-government organisations' prevention programs. The HIV programs for homosexually active men reported by Borthwick and De Lind van Wijngaarden in this volume are among a few rare exceptions to the exclusion of these men from Thai HIV prevention and care programs. Despite the 1980s anxiety about a supposed "homosexual epidemic" among youth, MSM remained all but invisible in most government-sponsored HIV programs in the 1990s. In part this stemmed from a belief that in Thailand transmission via heterosexual intercourse and intravenous drug use were much greater risk factors than same-sex activity. However, it also stemmed from a perception among public health officials, as always concerned to maximize the impact of a restricted health budget, that only relatively small numbers of Thai men engaged in same-sex activity. Ironically, the statistics on rates of same-sex experience that some psychologists had hoped would demonstrate the existence of a supposed "homosexual epidemic," were interpreted by epidemiologists and public health officials as showing low rates of homosexual experience across the Thai population. However, as shown above, more methodologically sound studies of sexual experience among young Thai males indicate that about one fifth of this section of the population report having had a same-sex experience. These findings indicate the omission of MSM as a target group in HIV prevention to be a serious deficiency in recent Thai policies. The consistent finding of higher rates of same-sex experience among poorer, less educated men than among better off and better educated men also indicates that there is a particularly urgent need for HIV interventions among rural and urban working class men.

CONCLUDING NOTE: CROSS-CULTURAL COMPARISONS

As noted in the introduction, it is exceptionally difficult to make valid comparisons of rates of same-sex experience between societies with significantly different cultural patterns of sexuality and gender. Nevertheless, in both popular and academic debates on homosexuality in Thailand, the results of North American and British surveys are often used as benchmark figures against which Thai data are compared. These comparisons assume a genuine discursive importance in Thai debates even when methodological and cultural factors undermine the validity of such comparisons. In the context of these debates, it is perhaps important to point out that even taken as raw data devoid of any culturally specific meanings, the results of quantitative research in Thailand taken as a whole do not indicate any greater prevalence of homosexual behavior or any higher rate of homoerotic interest among Thai men or women than Kinsey's team found among Americans in the immediate post-War period. However, the Thai results are higher than the rates of homosexual experience that have been found in more recent Western studies. In other words, rates of same-sex experience among Thai males and females fall *within* the range found in Western studies conducted since the end of World War II. This means that the Thai data should not be used to argue that same-sex experience is more common in Thailand than the West. At the same time, however, the Thai results indicate that significant minorities of Thai men and women engage in same-sex eroticism, and that the interests of these people should not be dismissed by unsympathetic service providers and social policy makers with spurious claims that homosexually active people represent an insignificant section of the population whose welfare needs can or should be ignored.

NOTES

1. I here use expressions such as "same-sex interest," "same-sex experience" and "same-sex preference" to refer to homoeroticism. I have tried to avoid using the term "homosexuality" too much because of its strong western cultural resonances.

2. The authors and dates of the studies on the various regions are listed below.

Educational Region 1 (includes three provinces near Bangkok: Nakhonpathom, Pathumthani, Nonthaburi), by Nanthirat Khunakorn (female), 1989.

Educational Region 2, by Chalorsak Laksanawongsri (male), 1991.

Educational Region 4 (includes five southern provinces of Ranong, Phuket, Phang-nga, Krabi and Trang), by Sujitra Usaha (female), 1991.

Educational Region 5, by Thatsani Thanaprachum (female), 1989.

Educational Region 6, by Chawani Jannoi (female), 1990.

Educational Region 7, by Rangrorng Ngamsiri (male?), 1989.

Educational Region 9, by Thanthip Tansalarak (female), 1990.

Educational Region 10 (includes 7 Northeastern provinces: Nakhonphanom, Roi-et, Ubonratchathani, Mukdahan, Kalasin, Mahasarakham, Yasothon), by Nujari Tejapanyachai (female), 1989.

Educational Region 11, by Watchara Imjit (female), 1989.

Educational Region 12, by Suphaphorn Pradapsamut (female), 1989.

This list is incomplete, as only four dissertations have been sighted by the author (Nanthirat, 1989; Suijitra, 1991; Nujari, 1989; Chalorsak, 1991). The details and findings of the remaining studies have been collected from cross-references made to other studies in the four dissertations viewed.

3. Note that Wiresit and Werasit are the same person. This author spells his name differently in different publications cited in this paper.

4. The journal collections of the National Library of Thailand in Bangkok and of all university libraries in the country are incomplete. The author has attempted to obtain copies of all sources relevant to this paper on several visits to Thailand. However, several original articles have not been able to be located and are cited here only as secondary sources.

5. This group of highly sexually active and behaviourally bisexual men sounds very similar to Chiang Mai male sex workers whom De Lind van Wijngaarden reports as self-labelling as *seua bai* or "bi-tigers." See De Lind van Wijngaarden in this volume.

6. The author wishes to thank Lt. Col. Tawesak Nopkesorn, MD, for providing a copy of the unpublished report of this survey.

7. A total of 73.4 percent of the sample group reported having had their first sexual experience with a female sex worker, 11.5 percent with a female lover (*khu-rak*), 7.5 percent with a female friend (*pheuan ying*), 2 percent with their wife and 2.5 percent with an unspecified woman. A total of 97 percent of the conscripts had sex with a female sex worker.

REFERENCES

Note: In citing language publications it is customary for lists of Thai names to be arranged alphabetically by first name, not surname. All Thai publications are dated using the Buddhist Era calendar, which began in 543 B.C. Buddhist Era (BE) publication dates are included within parentheses after the equivalent Christian Era year.

Apha Jantharasakun. (1985, BE 2528). Are *tom-tut-dee* really a social problem? [*tom-tut-dee pen panha sangkhom jing reu*]. *Warasan Seuksasat Parithat, 1* (2), 69-83.

Beyrer, C., Eiumtrakul, S., Celentano, D.D., Nelson K.E., Ruckphapunt, S. & Khamboonruang, C. (1995). Same sex behavior, sexually transmitted diseases and HIV risks among young northern Thai men. *AIDS, 9* (2), 171-176.

Chalorsak Laksanawongsri. (1991, BE 2534). *Sexual behaviors and attitudes of adolescent students: A case study on homosexual behavior in educational region two* [*Phreutikam thang-phet lae jettakhati khorng nak-rian wai-run: korani seuksa phreutikam rak-ruam-phet nai khet kan-seuksa 2*]. Dissertation, MA in Clinical Psychology, Mahidol University Graduate College.

Foucault, M. (1980). *The history of sexuality, volume 1: An introduction*, (trans. Robert Hurley). New York: Vintage Books.

Goddard, Martyn. (1994). Surveys: How many of us are there? *Outrage No. 131*, 6-7.

Jackson, P. A. (1997) Thai research on male homosexuality and transgenderism and the cultural limits of Foucauldian analysis. *Journal of the History of Sexuality, 8* (1), 52-85.

Khemika Yamarat, Nikorn Dusitsin et al. (1990, BE 2533). *Attitudes of students and teachers to knowledge about sex and sex education in secondary schools–Research report of WHO grant* [*Thatsanakhati tor khwam-ru reuang phet lae phet-seuksa khorng nak-rian lae khru nai roong-rian mathayom-seuksa*]. Bangkok: Chulalongkorn University.

Kinsey, A. C., W.B. Pomeroy, & C.E. Martin. (1948). *Sexual behavior in the human male*. Philadelphia: W.B. Saunders.

Nanthirat Khunakorn. (1989, BE 2532). *Sexual behaviors and attitudes of adolescent students: A case study on homosexual behavior in educational region one* [*Phreutikam thang-phet lae jettakhati khorng nak-rian wai-run: korani seuksa phreutikam rak-ruam-phet nai khet kan-seuksa 1*]. Dissertation, MA in Clinical Psychology, Mahidol University Graduate College.

Nelson, K., Celentano, D., Suprasert, S., Wright, N., Eiumtrakul, S., Tulvatana, S., Matanasarawoot, C. (1993). Risk factors for HIV infection among young adult men in northern Thailand. *JAMA (Journal of the American Medical Association), 270*, 955-960.

Nopkesorn, T., Mastro, T., Sangkharomya, S., Sweat, M., Singharaj, P., Limpakarnjanarat, K., Gayle, H. & Weniger, B. (1993). HIV-1 infection in young men in northern Thailand, *AIDS, 7*, 1233-1239.

Nujari Techapanyachai. (1989, BE 2532). *Sexual behaviors and attitudes of adolescent students: A case study on homosexual behavior in educational region ten* [*Phreutikam thang-phet lae jettakhati khorng nak-rian wai-run: korani seuksa phreutikam rak-ruam-phet nai khet kan-seuksa 10*]. Dissertation, MA in Clinical Psychology, Mahidol University Graduate College.

Pharadorn Phanthumabamrung & Buntoem Saengdisth. (1991, BE 2534). *Sexual behavior of soldiers on active military service in Bangkok Province* [*Phreutikam thang-phet khorng thahan korng prajam-kan jangwat Krungthepmahanakorn*]. Bangkok: Research Report of Division of Disease Prevention for the Army Department of Medicine.

Prachan Wanliko. (1988, BE 2531). Sexually deviant behavior: Thailand has among the most in the world [*phreutikam biang-ben thang-phet: Thai tit andap lok*]. *Nittayasan Kan-tha-reua, 35* (365), 37-40.

Sompol Pongthai. (1990). Sexual experience and sexual orientation among Ramthibodi medical students. *Journal of the Medical Association of Thailand, 73* (Suppl.), 81-86.

Suchai Kitsiriphornchai. (1996, BE 2539). *Observing and preventing HIV risk behaviors among 21 year old Thai males* [*Kan-fao-rawang phreutikam siang tor kan-tit cheua et nai klum chai Thai ayu 21 pi*]. Unpublished internal report for the Royal Thai Army forwarded to the author by Tawesak Nopkesorn, M.D.

Sujitra Usaha. (1991, BE 2534). Sexual behaviors and attitudes of adolescent students: A case study on homosexual behavior in educational region four [*Phreutikam thang-phet lae jettakhati khorng nak-rian wai-run: korani seuksa phreutikam rak-ruam-phet nai khet kan-seuksa 4*]. Dissertation, MA in Clinical Psychology, Mahidol University Graduate College.

Suphak Wanitseni & Khajit Chupanya. (1990, BE 2533). Attitudes and knowledge about AIDS among teenagers [*Thatsanakhati lae khwam-ru kiaw-kap et nai klum wai-run*], *Warasan Rok-et [AIDS journal]*, 2(2), 76-80.

Tawesak Nopkesorn, Suebpong Sungkarom, Rungkan Sornlum. (1991, BE 2534). *HIV prevalence and sexual behaviors among 21 year old Thai men in northern Thailand* [*Khwam-chuk khorng kan-tit cheua rok-et lae phreutikam thang-phet khorng chai Thai ayu 21 pi nai phak neua*]. Bangkok: Thai Red Cross Society Program on AIDS and Kai Somdej Pranaresuan Hospital (Royal Thai Army), Third Army, Research Report No. 3.

Tawesak Nopkesorn, Sweat, Mike D., Sathit Kaensing & Thiang Theppha. (1993, BE 2536). *Sexual risk behaviors for HIV infection in young men in Phayao province* [*Phreutikam thang-phet thi siang tor kan-tit cheua et khorng chai num nai jang-wat Phayao*]. Bangkok: Thai Red Cross Society, Program on AIDS, Research Report No. 6.

Udomsin Srisaengnam M.D. (1978, BE 2521). *Klai Mor* sex, homosexuals (1) [*phet Klai Mor torn homosekchuan (1)*]. *Klai Mor–A Family Health Magazine*, 2(4), 83-86.

VanLandingham, Mark J., Somboon Suprasert, Werasit Sittitrai, Chayan Vaddhana-phuti & Grandjean, Nancy. (1993). Sexual activity among never-married men in northern Thailand. *Demography*, 3(30), 297-313.

Vener, A., Stewart, C. & Hager, D. (1972). The sexual behavior of adolescents in middle America: Generational and American-British comparisons. *Journal of Marriage and the Family*, 34, 696-705.

Wanlop Tangkhananurak (*Khru* Yui). (1988, BE 2531). *Thai society's forgotten children* [*dek thi thuk leum nai sangkhom Thai*]. Bangkok: Mulanithi Sangsan Dek.

Weeks, J. (1991). *Sexuality and its discontents: Meanings, myths and modern sexualities*. London: Routledge.

Werasit Sittitrai, Chuanchom Sakondhavat & Brown, Tim. (1992a). *A survey of men having sex with men in a northeastern Thai province*. Bangkok: Thai Red Cross Society Program on AIDS, Research Report No. 5.

Werasit Sittitrai, Praphan Phanuphak, Barry, Jean & Brown, Tim. (1992b). *Thai sexual behavior and risk of HIV infection–A report of the 1990 survey of partner relations and risk of HIV infection in Thailand*. Bangkok: Thai Red Cross Society & Institute of Population Studies, Chulalongkorn University.

Wiresit Sittitrai, Brown, Tim & Sirapone Virulrak. (1991). Patterns of bisexuality in Thailand. In Rob Tielman, Manuel Carballo & Aart Hendriks (Eds.), *Bisexuality and HIV/AIDS–A global perspective* (pp. 97-117). Buffalo NY: Prometheus Books.

Note: Werasit and Wiresit above are alternative spellings of the same name.

HIV/AIDS Projects with and for Gay Men in Northern Thailand

Prudence Borthwick

SUMMARY. In this paper I look at three HIV/AIDS projects which were run by and for gay men, transsexuals and men who have sex with men (MSM) in northern Thailand in the early 1990s. These three projects were very different in format and in context, ranging from a rural village AIDS association to an urban drag beauty contest. The projects were located in settings as different as gay bars and cruising areas, shopping malls and rural villages. Aspects of the three Thai projects have important implications for those working in HIV/AIDS prevention and in the care and support of people living with HIV/AIDS (PLWHAs) across cultures, particularly in relation to education, outreach and counselling programs. *[Article copies available for a fee from The Haworth Document Delivery Service: 1-800-342-9678. E-mail address: getinfo@ haworthpressinc.com]*

INTRODUCTION

In this paper I look at three HIV/AIDS projects which were run by and for gay men, transsexuals and men who have sex with men (MSM) in northern Thailand in the early 1990s. I have chosen not to use the real names of some of these projects due to the sensitive nature

---

Address correspondence to: Prudence Borthwick, 26 Holmesdale Street, Massrickville NSW 2204, Australia.

[Haworth co-indexing entry note]: "HIV/AIDS Projects with and for Gay Men in Northern Thailand." Borthwick, Prudence. Co-published simultaneously in *Journal of Gay & Lesbian Social Services* (The Haworth Press, Inc.) Vol. 9, No. 2/3, 1999, pp. 61-79; and: *Lady Boys, Tom Boys, Rent Boys: Male and Female Homosexualities in Contemporary Thailand* (ed: Peter A. Jackson, and Gerard Sullivan) The Haworth Press, Inc., 1999, pp. 61-79; and: *Lady Boys, Tom Boys, Rent Boys: Male and Female Homosexualities in Contemporary Thailand* (ed: Peter A. Jackson, and Gerard Sullivan) Harrington Park Press, an imprint of The Haworth Press, Inc., 1999, pp. 61-79. Single or multiple copies of this article are available for a fee from The Haworth Document Delivery Service [1-800-342-9678, 9:00 a.m. - 5:00 p.m. (EST). E-mail address: getinfo@haworthpressinc.com].

of the topics I discuss. In writing this paper and reflecting on these projects I found that I was not only comparing the three projects with each other, but also with my experience of having been involved in HIV/AIDS projects targeting gay men and men who have sex with men in Australia, as well as with my knowledge of AIDS projects in other western countries and the "gay scene" as I knew it in Australia. While there are significant differences between the Thai and Australian projects, to my mind, aspects of the three Thai projects have important implications for those working in HIV/AIDS prevention and in the care and support of PLWHAs across cultures, particularly in relation to education, outreach and counselling programs. I was involved with the Northern Thai projects primarily as a worker with an AIDS prevention and care program. However, my own close relationship to Thai culture and to gay and lesbian culture both in Australia and Thailand have undoubtedly played a significant part in my understanding of the projects and the issues they raised. I hope the following brief biographical notes will elucidate my own position.

Note that the borrowed term "gay" has a number of meanings in Thailand. Amongst gay-identified men, "gay" means a masculine, gay-identified homosexual man and is clearly distinguished from transgender persons or *kathoey*, as well as from predominantly heterosexually identified men who may have sex with other men. However, in the general community, and even among some *kathoey*, "gay" is often used indiscriminately to mean all homosexually active men, whether or not they identify as gay and whether they are masculine-identified or transgender.

BACKGROUND–A PERSONAL PERSPECTIVE

I completed my primary schooling[1] in Thailand in the 1960s when my father was posted to Bangkok with what was then the Australian Department of External Affairs (now called the Department of Foreign Affairs and Trade). My parents' philosophy of education was that their children should assimilate into the local culture wherever they were posted. This meant that my siblings and I were sent to Thai government schools. We were invariably the only *farangs* (Caucasians) at these schools, and as a consequence we were sometimes a target for abuse and ridicule from the other children. Initially, I spent recess being followed around the schoolyard by twenty classmates chanting as one, *"Farang khi nok, hok bai saleung!"* ("Bird shit *Farangs*, six for a penny!"), a childhood taunt. The Thai word for the guava fruit is the same as the term for a Caucasian person, *farang*. A very small, almost worthless variety of guava is colloquially called *farang khi nok*, literally "bird shit guava." This taunting play on words thus had strong derogatory connotations, implying that Caucasians, like "bird shit guavas," were virtually worthless.

I was often in trouble at primary school because as a child I was a "tomboy." I probably would not have stood out so much in Australia, but in Thailand, where cultural norms of "proper" (that is, demure) female behaviour are much more important, I was always the subject of comment and rebuke–from my own teachers, from teachers in other grades, from the parents, guardians and *phi liang* ("nannies") who came to pick up their kids after school. I do not know how many times I heard the reproving remark, "Prue is just like a boy, not sweet and decorous like her little sister, Jessie. Jessie is a real little girl."

I did eventually assimilate but at the end of 1965 had to return to Australia with my family, where I completed my education. After a period of activism in the Australian gay and lesbian communities, I began work in Sydney with Streetwize Comics, a community orga-nisation which produced health education resources for disadvantaged groups. I first worked on a community AIDS education project in 1985. After working there for eight years, I conducted an AIDS educa-tion project with Thai female sex workers in Sydney and realised that this project brought together linguistic and cultural skills and experi-ences that I had not thought I would ever be able to utilise. In 1993 I began work as Project Development Specialist with NAPAC, the Thai-Australian Northern AIDS Prevention and Care Project, a bi-lateral aid project originally funded by the Australian Government and based in Chiang Mai.

As a worker at Streetwize Comics and in my personal life I had been involved in various aspects of AIDS education and support in Australia. When I arrived in Chiang Mai, I found the AIDS "scene" there very different. I realised that the history of the HIV/AIDS pre-vention and care movement in Australia had been built on the achieve-ments of that country's urban social movements of the 1970s and 1980s, in particular, the gay movement and women's liberation. In contrast, in the north of Thailand I found that non-government orga-nisations with a background in rural community development were the most active players on the health education scene. I also found that my western preconceptions about the nature of the epidemic and about the right ways to undertake prevention and care were continually challenged by the radically different geographic, historical and cultural context in which I found myself.

THE MISS ANGEL KATHOEY BEAUTY CONTEST

In Australia I had accepted certain principles as essential to AIDS management. These included: the rights of HIV positive people, including their right to organise on their own (a battle fought by a range of politico-social movements from lesbian separatists to indigenous movements), to confidentiality and to privacy; the use of non-judgmental harm reduction principles in HIV/AIDS prevention which sought to reduce the risks associated with intravenous drug-use or sexual activity rather than require people to abstain from these activities; "sex-positivity" which presented sexuality in a positive light and often involved the use of explicit sexual images and language to promote safe sex; and the valuing of egalitarianism in informal education which promotes peers as the best educators. However, when I was working on AIDS projects in Thailand, the issues that emerged seemed to challenge the universality of some of these "essential" principles.

Not surprisingly, during my time in northern Thailand, I was drawn to projects that felt familiar, especially projects that reminded me of home: where the gay community or the queer nation (whichever way you like to look at it) had drawn on its own resources to raise awareness about HIV/AIDS issues. But even in the Thai projects where I worked with gays, trannies[2] and men who have sex with men, I found myself confronted by cultural difference. As it happened, the very first gay event I attended in Chiang Mai presented many challenges to my thinking.

This was the "Miss Angel" drag beauty contest, held in Chiang Mai at the Tantraphan Shopping Mall in October 1993. The contest was part of a three-day AIDS education event organised by a Bangkok-based Non-governmental organisation (NGO), which I will call Goh, in conjunction with another NGO, which I will call Koh, which ran one of Chiang Mai's first anonymous clinics for HIV testing and counselling. Established in the late 1980s, Goh was also one of the first NGOs in Thailand to be involved in HIV/AIDS education. Goh was the only organisation which had targeted gay men for education and prevention messages over the decade following Thailand's first recorded death from AIDS in 1985, a gay man who had returned from the US, where he had been studying for his doctorate. Goh ran AIDS awareness and information sessions, often including performances by their dance troupe. This jazz dance troupe was trained by the convener of Goh and performed dances on HIV/AIDS education themes. Goh also conducted education activities at beats[3] or cruising areas with their "Cruise Squad" of gay male "volunteers." (The term "volunteer" in Thailand often includes people who receive a small payment or other benefits in exchange for regular part-time community work).

The Miss Angel contest was sponsored by a number of contributors from the private sector, including the owners of Tantraphan Department Store where the event was held, while NAPAC supported the fares of the White Line Dance Troupe to travel from Bangkok.

I suppose the first major point of difference from HIV/AIDS education activities in Australia was the location of the event in a large shopping mall. Remember that this event took place in October 1993, well before the international release of the Australian film "Priscilla Queen of the Desert." The event kicked off with a formal opening ceremony, attended by the grandmother of the owner of the department store, a group of *kathoey* contestants and local school children who had participated in a competition to write AIDS education slogans in rhyming couplets. The general acceptance of drag as entertainment for the whole community was one obvious aspect of gay events in northern Thailand. I observed that the large audience for the final stage of the contest included groups of gay men, families and heterosexual couples. There were also some solitary men who shifted uncomfortably or walked hastily away when I attempted to engage them in an on-the-spot program evaluation. These, I suspected, were men who had sex with men but who preferred to keep a low profile.

The heats and final contest afforded many valuable opportunities to provide AIDS education in an entertaining format. In traditional beauty contest format, aspiring Miss Angels had to tell the audience their "interests." "The environment" was one of the most popular stated "interests," perhaps amazing, in view of the amount of CFCs released into the atmosphere by the large volume of hair spray used by contestants. Some Angels included in their speeches appeals for recognition of the rights and talents of the "third sex" (*phet thi-sam*), of *gays* (using the English word) and of *kathoey*, a Thai word which variously means transsexuals, transvestites and sometimes gay or effeminate men. In fact, in addition to the ambiguities in usage of the word *kathoey* there seemed to be a little confusion around the proper nomenclature to describe those participating, with some contestants using all three terms–"the third sex," *gay* and *kathoey*–to describe the group, including themselves. Contestants also had to answer questions about AIDS, such as, "How would you react if a friend told you he was HIV positive?"

Off stage there were cultural differences that were harder for me to come to terms with. Members of the NGO Goh had decided to encourage contestants to have HIV tests, partly hoping to demonstrate that the lingering scapegoating of gays or transsexuals for spreading AIDS was groundless. Members of the general public attending the event were also encouraged to have tests. These were all carried out on the spot after counselling by members of NGO Koh in booths set up in the shopping mall. A number of the contestants decided not to take the test, and it was suggested to me by people attending that these were the ones who thought themselves most "at risk." Eighteen *kathoeys* and *gay* men decided to take the test, together with about 50 members of the public. Two of the former group tested positive as did three of the latter group. These numerical results were announced from the stage by the Goh convener during the first heats in a bid to ensure that those who had been tested contacted Koh for their results. Naturally, this considerably increased the level of tension for some of the competitors. Initially I was alarmed by the seemingly casual treatment of the whole issue of testing.

In following up the outcomes, I found out that both the *kathoeys* who tested positive had been in regular contact with Planned Parenthood Association's anonymous clinic for counselling and follow-up health care and were also members of a PLWHA support group run by the clinic. A few of the general public had made contact with the clinic to obtain their results, but not the three people who had tested positive.

Clearly, there were a lot of issues to address here. Combining an elaborate and innovative stage event with HIV tests for contestants and the general public was a difficult task. At that early stage of the epidemic in the North, even health professionals had little experience of the issues around HIV testing. The entire region was on a steep learning curve and at the time little discussion had taken place on the ramifications of testing. Goh was an organisation that had a demonstrated commitment to assisting people with HIV at a time when these people's needs were not yet well known. The Miss Angel organisers considered that the event would be an opportunity to encourage people who were ordinarily hard to reach to take the HIV test. They clearly felt the task they had set themselves was well within their capabilities. After all, testing was to be voluntary and anonymous. The only compulsory aspect of the event was that contestants were required to attend two education sessions on HIV/AIDS beforehand. Pre-test counselling was provided on the spot in a little booth in the mall and people were to receive their test results at the NGO Koh clinic in Chiang Mai.

My experience in Australia had made me think of confidentiality as one of the primary issues in HIV testing. In an Australian context shopping malls would probably not be seen as appropriate places for even pre-test counselling as part of a special event to raise awareness of HIV/AIDS. Making public even the totals of test results would probably have been viewed in Australia as a breach of the right to privacy of those who had been tested. It may well be that other organisations and individuals active in northern Thailand in the HIV/AIDS area at the time of the Miss Angel contest would have approached the testing issue differently. I commended the clear commitment of the organisations concerned with the contest to assisting people with HIV and raising community awareness and acceptance of people with HIV. However, I felt uneasy about the testing arrangements, perhaps partly because of my prior sensitisation to the anxiety that participants were likely to feel when waiting for test results. But perhaps some of my unease was also due to differences in underlying values relating to confidentiality, privacy, and personal and public space.

In northern Thailand most people still live communally. Personal activities such as bathing are often carried out in full view of others, albeit the bather is always modestly clad in a sarong or loincloth. Families sleep together with children in the same room as parents. The importance that Westerners attach to privacy and personal space is often inappropriate in the northern Thai context, where to be alone is often seen as an anxious, lonely state in which one is vulnerable to being haunted by ghosts. In regard to HIV/AIDS, this is an important issue for counsellors. The need for confidentiality in regard to test results arises from a concern to protect the person with HIV from possible discrimination or forced disclosure. In the West confidentiality protects a person's right to disclose or not to disclose, as they choose. It protects their right to privacy. In Thailand the government has supported voluntary and confidential testing in conjunction with counselling since 1991. Yet, in a Thai communal context it may be impossible to hide illness within the family. It may also be hard to hide a positive diagnosis. In these contexts the whole notion of confidentiality becomes more complex.

The medical professionals I met in Thailand also seemed to have different views about confidentiality. For example, in the early 1990s it was still common practice for a family member to be told of a relative's cancer diagnosis before or instead of the affected person themself. Doctors generally commanded considerable respect and expected (and were expected) to make informed decisions in the interests and on behalf of their patients in most health areas. Initially, some doctors expected that they would be the ones to decide who to inform of a patient's positive HIV diagnosis, and some families, especially parents caring for a seriously ill adult child, felt that they should be the first to know. Furthermore, in many hospitals the pressure on space was such that the locations in which counselling was conducted afforded about as much privacy as a shopping mall.

This is not to say that Thai AIDS agencies accept the idea that the HIV status of positive people should be broadcast far and wide without their consent. I heard much discussion of the fact that counselling can and does occur in different settings from those in the western countries, although these comments were more often made about village settings rather than urban ones. There has certainly been a commitment to the need for confidentiality in HIV testing and counselling in HIV/AIDS agencies, by both government and non-governmental organisations. The Thai Coalition of NGOs Against AIDS working party on discrimination has expressed the greatest concern about the not uncommon practice where employers arrange for private clinics to test employees for HIV as part of a medical check-up and then ask for the test results to be returned to them. In practice, however, it is acknowledged that confidentiality is particularly difficult to maintain in small communities where everyone knows everyone else's business.

Another factor in the inclusion and encouragement of HIV testing during the three-day Miss Angel event may have been the importance given to education and "teaching by example." This was consistent with the aim of the whole event, which was to provide AIDS education in a novel format. Organisers explained to me that the contestants who took the test had been a good example to those who did not test. They had "taught" their friends something. A couple of months later I had the opportunity to talk to a contestant's friend about the Miss Angel pageant. This young gay man conceded that the timing of the announcement had made it a tense weekend for the eighteen who tested, but he supported the testing in the context of the beauty contest, "They would never have had the test otherwise," he said, "and it's better that they know."

For me, the location, organisation and conduct of the Miss Angel contest demonstrated many of the unique features of the Thai scene for gays and transsexuals, and of Thai approaches to AIDS. Firstly, there was confusion around terminology, which may have reflected confusion around issues of sexual and gender "identity." Some contestants seemed to be identifying both with gay men and transsexuals, whereas in Australia these two groups tend to be clearly distinguished. Secondly, there was the inclusivity of the event, the involvement of school children and the elderly, of the judges who were respected members of Chiang Mai society, and of the general public. And thirdly, there was the culturally distinctive valuation of issues of privacy and confidentiality, values that were markedly different from those I had experienced when working in Australian HIV/AIDS agencies.

A GAY GROUP IN A RURAL VILLAGE

Throughout the Miss Angel event the contestants remained a highly conspicuous group in terms of their self-presentation, behaviour, clothing, and hairstyles. The setting in a recently constructed and thoroughly modern mall, and the glamorous image the contestants presented with their big hair dos and elaborate outfits, together underscored the urban nature of the event. The Miss Angel Drag Beauty contest was quite different from community education projects targeting gays in rural northern communities, as I found when I visited the village which I will call Ban Coh.

I first heard about Ban Coh in 1993 when the village received TV coverage as the first village in Thailand to have a local AIDS Associa-

tion, the Chomrom Tan AIDS, literally the "Resist-AIDS Association" or "Anti-AIDS Association." I subsequently found out more
about the group when Ms Tippapon Apsarathanasombudh,[4] a staff
member from Chiang Mai's Sexually Transmitted Disease Centre,
presented an action research project carried out in the village by the
STD centre as part of a seminar held to mark the opening of the
NAPAC office in Chiang Mai city. Ms Tippapon's presentation included discussion of the role of a local gay group in the village's
Anti-AIDS Association. As a member of the Northern AIDS Action
Committee, I visited the village with Thailand's Assistant-Minister for
Health in 1995 and heard a brief account of the history of the Anti-
AIDS Association. This account was presented by the Association's
president, who concluded his talk with a "big thank you to the village
women's group and the gay group for doing such a good job on the
flower arrangements." On this occasion I was introduced to the Association's deputy president and head of what was locally called the
"gay group."

At first sight Ban Coh looks like an unlikely spot for a gay project.
It is a farming community and local crops include garlic and *lamyai*[5]
fruit. Ban Coh is not particularly close to a main road but it is a big
village by local standards, with 2,000 inhabitants, of whom about 60
to 70 are said to "be gay" (*pen gay*). This is not a migrant population,
and most of the gays in the village were local men who were born
there. The oldest member of the gay group was in his late fifties. These
villagers chose to describe themselves as "gay" rather than using the
old Thai term *kathoey*. I was told by a non-gay villager on the Anti-
AIDS Association that "gay" is a more fashionable word and that was
why it was preferred. From my observation of members of the gay
group who spoke at various conferences I subsequently attended, it
seems that they did not cross-dress and chose to dress as men, at least
on these formal, public occasions. On asking Khun Bun, the official
leader of the gay group, if they ever had drag events to assist in AIDS
education, he smiled and shook his head saying, "We don't do that
kind of thing. Our 'girls' (*sao*) aren't pretty enough."

The gay villagers of Ban Coh would probably have carried on as
one of many small social cliques in the village as they have for the past
forty-odd years had it not been for AIDS. Ban Coh came to the attention of the STD Centre and its parent agency, the Office of Communicable Disease Control (CDC) Region 10, at around the same time. The

STD Centre had been notified that some village youth had STDs, and at the same time it also became apparent that some of the gay villagers were ill with AIDS.

At this point CDC and the STD centre were contacted to provide some community education on AIDS and STDs for the village, and in turn this led to an action research project to develop a participatory community AIDS management model conducted by Ms. Tippapon Apsarathanasombudh from the STD Centre in consultation with Dr. Chaowalit Nathpratanh, Director of CDC Region 10. Focus group discussions were held with all groups in the village, including male and female householders, youth, school students, and the gays. From the discussion groups it was decided to set up a local Anti-AIDS Association with headquarters in the local village temple. The aim of the Association was to raise funds to help villagers sick with AIDS and their families, and to conduct prevention activities such as handing out condoms.

The Association had a committee with elected office bearers–president, deputy president, secretary, treasurer, and so on. All Association members were from the village, and around one third were gay. Members of the gay group had been active in the work of the Association, in caring for sick villagers and their families, peer education, condom distribution, joining the "lecture circuit"[6] to speak about the work of the Association, and in doing the flower arrangements for all formal functions presided over by the Association's committee. The main problems of the Association were those common to villagers all over the North of Thailand, namely, how to care for the steady stream of people–gay and straight–who were falling sick and dying from AIDS, and how to provide for their families.

Again, Ban Coh challenged some features of group organisation that I had assumed were integral to HIV and gay scenes. Despite the best efforts of gay groups organising in country areas, and of HIV/AIDS projects to reach gays and men who have sex with men in out of the way places, gay culture and HIV/AIDS culture in Australia remain largely urban phenomena. In rural or isolated communities in Australia it is not usually acceptable to be gay. Many young people who identify as gay or lesbian take the first opportunity to leave for the nearest city when they leave school. While this is also becoming the case in Thailand today, it seems that it was not always so. Many people I spoke to about "gays" in the course of my work in Chiang

Mai said they remembered *kathoeys* in their home village or town. The President of the Anti-AIDS Association told me that the gays were an accepted part of Ban Coh's village community. The unusual thing about Ban Coh in Thai terms was the size of the gay group and its prominence in village affairs. When it came to organising the village's AIDS education and care effort, there seems to have been an emphasis on inclusion rather than exclusion. Gays and heterosexuals worked together on the committee to raise funds and conduct the work of the Association. When I left Thailand in 1995, the committee was seeking funds for a home care scheme to look after the sick and dying. The members of the village had not split up into HIV-positive versus HIV-negative, or gay versus heterosexual groups in their community response to HIV/AIDS.

I found that this sense of inclusion was a feature of northern Thai social organisation which contrasted with my experience of social movements in Australia. The Australian gay movement, the women's movement and the PLWHA movement each drew their political strength from organising around their separate forms of oppression, and then building alliances with other sympathetic groups (at least in theory). In northern Thailand, the AIDS Widows group ended up including AIDS widowers as well as widowed women's new husbands. At events for HIV-positive people, the positive people invited neighbours and friends to come along. At a weekend camp held for over 70 PLWHA in northern Thailand in January of 1995, there was a transsexual (conspicuous for her numerous changes of attire, each more splendid than the previous) and two distinctively effeminate young men in stunning black. Only one of the young men was HIV-positive they explained to me; the other was a friend from the same village who had come to keep him company.

CHAI CHUAY CHAI – "MEN HELPING MEN"

If Ban Coh represented the point of greatest difference for me, immured in my Sydney-based understanding of gay and HIV/AIDS issues, then the third project I wish to discuss, Chai Chuay Chai ("men helping men"), probably provided the point of greatest similarity. Chai Chuay Chai was a little different from the previous two projects in regard to its location, target group and project design, being an outreach project to gay men and men who have sex with men in

Chiang Mai city. The setting for the project was largely, but not entirely, the commercial gay scene, often characterised by heterosexually identified male sex workers providing sexual services to gays or bisexual men for cash. A detailed account of male sex workers in Chiang Mai city can be found in Jan Willem De Lind van Wijngaarden's paper in this volume.

Chai Chuay Chai was set up jointly by De Lind van Wijngaarden and a Thai colleague who had worked previously with NGO Goh's Chiang Mai branch but was originally from Central Thailand. A Chiang Mai gay man also worked with the project, which was supported by both government and academic agencies working on AIDS in Chiang Mai. Consequently, Chai Chuay Chai had some direct western inputs into both the design of interventions and the project's philosophy.

The Communicable Diseases Centre Region 10 was involved with the project as an offshoot of some of the AIDS education work the organisation was doing in local bars as an adjunct to the sentinel surveillance program of the Thai Department of Health. The National sentinel surveillance program regularly conducts "anonymous de-linked testing" for HIV positivity among five groups, including military conscripts and male and female sex workers. At the time the Chai Chuay Chai project submission was developed in mid 1995, the sentinel surveillance program was being cut from six monthly to annual blood testing of the samples from the target groups. This had the effect of reducing the funds that were available for HIV education in the bars taking part in the program. At the same time these cuts were being implemented in early 1995, figures indicated an alarming increase in the incidence of HIV among male sex workers in Chiang Mai, being somewhat higher than the incidence rate of HIV among female sex workers. It appeared that in the years which had elapsed since the mid-1980s–when gays had been blamed for starting the epidemic–AIDS awareness and condom use amongst male sex workers had fallen to lower levels than among female sex workers.

The Chai Chuay Chai project used an intervention design similar to the approach which had been used by Goh's Chiang Mai branch, and elsewhere, in 1993-1994. In this approach, gay peer educators provided HIV/AIDS education and condoms to men frequenting gay bars and beats or cruising areas such as the city's public parks. In the case of Goh, bar education took the form of a stage show, while the beats had been reached by a "cruise squad." Chai Chuay Chai continued these efforts minus the stage show. The small project also aimed to build up a sense of community among gay and *kathoey* workers and bar-goers in Chiang Mai. To contribute to a sense of community, they produced a regular newsletter. Also as part of their "community building," Chai Chuay Chai hosted a gay and lesbian fund-raising party at the 3rd Asian and Pacific Conference on AIDS, which was held in Chiang Mai in September 1995.

Chai Chuay Chai confronted a problem at the second stage of the project, when they planned to undertake outreach education and condom distribution to young men working in what are locally called Chiang "boy brothels." The "boys" in this case were teenagers, many of whom appeared to work on a casual basis as a means of gaining additional income to support senior high school or college studies. The venues they worked from were not bars, but rather ordinary houses or shop-houses and were often locally called simply *ban* ("house"), being clearly distinguished from the more formal venues with full-time male sex workers that were always called *bar* or *bar gay* in Thai, using the English words. De Lind van Wijngaarden's study in this volume looks at full-time workers in Chiang Mai's gay bars. It seems that, unlike the young men working in the gay bars, some of whom identified as *gay* or *kathoey*, this group of sex workers almost entirely identified as heterosexual (*phu-chai*). The project team then had to consider the question of whether gay-identified educators would be accepted by this group of male sex workers and how to recruit new peer educators from this group's ranks.

Another question that arose in the first few months of Chai Chuay Chai's activities was whether "peer education" as such was appropriate for the Thai context, particularly for teenagers doing casual sex work at the "boy brothels." At this stage the project managers thought it would be better to engage slightly older men as educators who, it was assumed, the younger workers would admire and respect. In this regard, the kind of educational relationship selected was a "*phi* education" model rather than a peer education model, with an older sibling figure (*phi*) caring for a younger sibling (*norng*). This is a common model for social education in Thailand. For example, Thai parents often reprove their children with such reprimands as, "Big sister, it's your job to teach your little sister (not set her that bad example as you are now doing by being naughty)."

This *phi-norng* relationship is one of the building blocks of Thai society. In Thailand trust and mutual responsibility are invoked with the *phi-norng* relationship, where age is the deciding factor in determining the desired pattern of a relationship. Even lovers (of all genders and sexual orientations) in their most intimate moments use *phi* and *norng* as personal pronouns when talking with each other, that is, as terms both of address ("you") and self-reference ("I"). This inbuilt structuring along age and family lines pervades almost all relationships in Thailand. In the West, terms such "sisterhood" or "brotherhood" are used to invoke the desired relationship of solidarity and equality, and the divide is often along gender lines. Within these gender categories the levelling power of these "sisterly" or "brotherly" relationships is seen as a valuable social tool in programs based on peer education in Western countries. However, I suspect that "peer education" as such is a product of societies where people operate most comfortably with those they perceive as equals, rather than of a society such as Thailand, where most relationships are expected to be structured by a fundamental difference rather than equality. Chai Chuay Chai varied the western "peer education" model by engaging an older gay man who was effeminate and very non-threatening, and had been a member of Goh's original cruise squad, to work with the male sex workers. This man was often seen affectionately as an "auntie" (*pa*), by the young men whom he advised. Perhaps in Thailand we need to think of community HIV/AIDS projects being based on model of "pa education" rather than peer education.

In a session on homosexuality at the 3rd Asian and Pacific Conference on AIDS in Chiang Mai in September 1995, overseas researchers raised questions about the apparent imposition of "western" notions of "gay identity" and related HIV/AIDS management in an Asian context where the gay scene or gay community may not resemble that in the West. Similar questions could also be asked in relation to Chai Chuay Chai. For example, community building was initially an aim of the project. In the West it is becoming generally accepted that gays and lesbians have their own communities. In the gay HIV/AIDS arena it is often suggested that gay men who are identified with the gay community or who are in contact with the gay community are at less risk of contracting HIV/AIDS on the assumption that they have greater access to information and services and a higher self-esteem than homosexually active men who are more isolated. Whether this is or could become the case in northern Thailand is hard to say. As I left Thailand before the project finished, I am in no position to assess whether Chai Chuay Chai achieved this aim (although they did host a great party). However, it would equally be a mistake to assume there was no local sense of community beforehand, or that the population reached by Chai Chuay Chai and its predecessor Goh represented the entire homosexually active population of Chiang Mai.

Another component in Chai Chuay Chai that could be thought of as an import from the West was beat outreach. Some of the sex negotiated at beats in Chiang Mai was non-commercial. The educative efforts of gay-identifying Thai and non-Thai project workers using a model used widely in the West seem to have been well received in these locations. From reports of conversations of beat-educators with beat-goers (see Krissara, 1995, pp. 16-18), it seems that these informal, nonthreatening exchanges are as culturally appropriate in Chiang Mai as they are in the West. Each exchange involves a delicate mix of complex ingredients–interrupting a beat-goer's search for a sexual partner; establishing the purpose of the discussion; engaging the man's attention and interest (or otherwise)–and all this is dependent on a host of variables relating to the mood and personality of the educator and beat-goer and the timing of the encounter.

However, the outreach to Chiang Mai's gay bars was more dissimilar to the Australian experience, as a considerable number of the "bar boys" are not gay, but just there for a while to make money. Furthermore, in the boy brothels, which are located in private houses and rely on word of mouth rather than press advertising or neon signs to attract clientele, almost the entire population of workers is made up of heterosexually identified young men who engage in sex work strictly for commercial gain. For De Lind van Wijngaarden (personal communication), this last occupational group was the most dissimilar to the gay community and men who have sex with men that he knew from his home country of the Netherlands. For me, perhaps one the most striking features described by De Lind van Wijngaarden in his paper in this volume is his account of how young heterosexually identified men accept their homosexual sex work as simply being one of the services that the powerless provide to the powerful in a highly stratified society, a service that is unrelated to the sex worker's sexual orientation or gender identity and which they would no longer provide once they themselves had acquired a bit more money, status and power. De Lind van Wijngaarden also describes the workers' progression over time from sex work which involves higher risk practices for relatively little money to less high-risk practices for more money. While the group of Chiang Mai male sex workers appear to have behaved according to values for which there is little counterpart in the West, it is difficult to assess the degree to which this difference hindered the educational aims of the Chai Chuay Chai project.

CONCLUSION

The projects I have looked at in this paper suggest something of the variety of the gay and *kathoey* scenes in Thailand. It seems to me that there are some similarities with western social patterns, but also some significant differences. Perhaps the three main areas in which the northern Thai gay projects raised questions for me were:

1. exclusivity, in terms of the rights, desires or needs of people (whether gays, HIV-positive people, women or men-who-have-sex-with-men) to organise separately, as separatists within existing communities with strong community identities;
2. the assumptions about rights to privacy and personal space that underpin the notion of confidentiality in regard to HIV testing and counselling; and
3. egalitarianism as a basis for education.

To my mind, the imposition of western ideas in these three areas seemed more challenging to existing norms than the increasing use of the word "gay" or even the promotion of "gay identity." I find problematic the tendency of some westerners to decry all forms of "westernisation" in developing countries. In this age of globalisation it is inevitable that there will be some westernisation. But my experience is that Thai culture is extremely resilient and quite liable to reshape "western" inputs to suit local Thai needs. Visible westernisation is everywhere in Thailand, from clothing styles to industrialisation. However, fundamental and persistent "Thai-ness" is often invisible to Westerners. Everywhere I worked amongst Thai people I heard of projects, lifestyles, sexuality, evaluations, counselling, patterns of work organisation, manners of speech, expectations of punctuality, and other phenomena all being compared in terms of Thai ways and

Western ways. Almost invariably in these conversations, for something to be described as "western" or *farang* was a negative judgement. A common characterisation of Western societies was that they were characterised by an attitude of *khorng khrai khorng man* or "every person for themselves." However, such unfavourable opinions are not generally discussed with Westerners, and are usually kept for private discussions between Thais. Moderation and restraint are prized in most areas of Thai society. A culture that values restraint and subtlety of expression will not be easily accessible to outsiders whose cultural background requires them to see situations and emotions expressed plainly and strongly in order to notice them. This may mean that Westerners can be left to assume quite wrongly that (from computer games to psychiatry) all western inputs in Thailand are all equally valued.

It seemed to me that Thai social patterns were informing the outreach work of Chai Chuay Chai and subtly changing the expected model of "peer education." However, both Thai and Western men who were gay-identified did have a rapport with beat-goers and bar workers. In these urban centres created by industrialisation and maximally subject to globalisation, it seemed that gay identity was not out of place, and apparently overlapped the *kathoey* category in some areas, as the Miss Angel aspirants indicated.

In Ban Coh, however, it seemed that local geographic community ties were as strong as the gay social networks. While the government-funded CDC action research project acknowledged the gays as a separate group, the local Anti-AIDS Association worked for and represented the whole village, not just one segment of it. This seemed to reflect the desire for inclusivity that I observed more generally in northern Thai communities. Related to the inclusivity issue was the difference in some Thai approaches to confidentiality and privacy around counselling and testing.

Western gay men working in HIV/AIDS are sometimes criticised for assuming that gay subcultures are the same across the world. However, in my experience, HIV/AIDS projects designed by western gay men aimed at gay, transsexual and bisexual men have been successfully transferred across cultures. In contrast, other project designs or models (such as individualist personal development modules used with children from traditional communal societies) have been transferred less successfully yet subject to less critical attention. To my mind we have to strike a balance between being overly anxious about the finer points of subcultural difference and the misplaced confidence of funding bodies and "experts" who assume that once an approach has the status of a "model" it sheds its society of origin and becomes fully transferable to any other culture.

NOTES

1. Called "elementary school" in the United States.

2. In Australian idiom, transgender persons commonly refer to themselves and preferred to be referred to as "trannies," a self-chosen informal and non-judgmental term I will also use here to refer to Thai transgender persons, who locally are usually called *kathoey.*

3. In Australian gay idiom a gay cruising area is called a "beat" and cruising men for sex is called "doing the beat."

4. I am indebted to Ms. Tippapon Apsarathanasombudh from the STD Centre and Dr. Chaowalit Nathpratanh, Director of CDC Region 10, for their assistance in providing some of the background information and local contacts who assisted in the preparation of this paper.

5. Lamyai is a sweet variety of stonefruit a little smaller than a lychee and which is grown in the cooler upland areas of northern Thailand.

6. The Association's focus on AIDS prevention education meant that a wide range of community education activities were conducted. HIV-positive speakers, counsellors and NGO AIDS workers regularly appeared as guest speakers for AIDS education groups in northern Thailand.

REFERENCES

Borthwick, P. (1995). A first in community AIDS work: Dong Luang village AIDS association and gay group. *NAPAC Newsletter, 2* (2), 25-26.

Krissara Chiemcharoen. (1995). Gay anecdotes. *NAPAC Newsletter, 2* (2), 16-18.

Tippapon Apsarathanasombudh, Tim Piyano & Srisamon Mulchai. (1992). *Research and development project model development for community prevention and control of HIV/AIDS and STDs in Dong Luang Village, Pasang District, Lampoon Province Centre for Sexual Diseases and AIDS, Region 10.* Chiang Mai: Office for Communicable Disease Control Region 10.

Increasingly Gay Self-Representations of Male-Male Sexual Experiences in Thailand

Stephen O. Murray

SUMMARY. With Thailand's economic development, urbanization (especially the rapid growth of Bangkok), growing contact between Thais and non-Thais, an increased availability of representations of homogender homosexuality (i.e., masculine men being sexually penetrated), and international AIDS discourse, male homosexuality not structured by differences in age, gender or class has become more apparent. Three sets of stories and letters sent by Thai men to Thai gay magazines show a decline in a gender-stratified conception and enactment of homosexuality in Thailand, paralleling the heterogender-to-gay transformation of homosexuality elsewhere in the world. The highly developed commercial venues for males who have sex with males in Bangkok are little mentioned in these texts and suggest the need for the development of other kinds of community infrastructure such as telephone advice lines (providing information about the basic mechanics of safe sex and other aspects of male-male relationships). Males who have sex with males in Bangkok, in particular, need a community center in which to discuss issues of power, gender, and sexuality. *[Article copies available for a fee from The Haworth Document Delivery Service: 1-800-342-9678. E-mail address: getinfo@haworthpressinc.com]*

Address correspondence to: Stephen O. Murray, El Instituto Obregon, 1360 De Haro Street, San Francisco, CA 94107-3239 USA.

The author gratefully acknowledges comments on earlier drafts by Eric Allyn, Badruddin Khan, Gerard Sullivan, and two anonymous reviewers.

[Haworth co-indexing entry note]: "Increasingly Gay Self-Representations of Male-Male Sexual Experiences in Thailand." Murray, Stephen O. Co-published simultaneously in *Journal of Gay & Lesbian Social Services* (The Haworth Press, Inc.) Vol. 9, No. 2/3, 1999, pp. 81-96; and: *Lady Boys, Tom Boys, Rent Boys: Male and Female Homosexualities in Contemporary Thailand* (ed: Peter A. Jackson, and Gerard Sullivan) The Haworth Press, Inc., 1999, pp. 81-96; and: *Lady Boys, Tom Boys, Rent Boys: Male and Female Homosexualities in Contemporary Thailand* (ed: Peter A. Jackson, and Gerard Sullivan) Harrington Park Press, an imprint of The Haworth Press, Inc., 1999, pp. 81-96. Single or multiple copies of this article are available for a fee from The Haworth Document Delivery Service [1-800-342-9678, 9:00 a.m. - 5:00 p.m. (EST). E-mail address: getinfo@haworthpressinc.com].

INTRODUCTION

As in much of the world, until recently, homosexuality was largely invisible in the kingdom of Thailand.[1] Generally, gender variance tends to be more visible than private sexual behavior, and in Thailand, as in many other societies, the popular conception of masculine persons (of both sexes) penetrating feminine ones (of both sexes) has camouflaged homosexuality that is not structured by one partner's gender non-conformity. Almost certainly, there have been sexual aspects to some patron-client relations, especially those involving age disparities, and also relationships between equals, especially unmarried men in Thailand. The three recurrent social organizations of homosexuality–age-stratified, gender-stratified, and egalitarian–often coexist within a given society, although one of these is usually the main cultural conception and social organization, that is, the dominant discourse in a particular time and place.[2] Thus, although in ancient Athens the primary idiom of male-male eros was pederastic, there was also a (derogatory) conception of effeminate, sexually receptive adult males (the *kinaidos*). In contemporary Latin America the primary idiom of homoeroticism is in terms of gender non-conformity (male *maricones*, female *manfloras*), but there are also age-stratified, class-stratified, and egalitarian same-sex sexual relations; and in contemporary "Western" cities on three continents (Europe, North America, Australia) the primary idiom is of egalitarian or gay relations, although there are pederasts and drag queens in the same cities.[3] Males who recurrently engage in sex with males in many places know of the modern Western model of homosexual relations between males of similar age, status, and masculinity in which it is not obvious who is the "top." The term *gay* has been borrowed into Japanese, Portuguese, Spanish, Thai, Turkish, and other languages to label a way of being openly and exclusively homosexual without the flamboyant effeminacy that traditionally signalled sexual availability in many cultures.[4] The application of such terms as *moderno* (in Peru), *internacional* (in México and Guatemala), and *quing* (in Thailand, a combination of the English words "*queen*" and "*king*") to those who both penetrate and are penetrated also indicate the prestige of gay homosexuality.[5] It seems to me that what is "modern" and "international" is the attitude that being penetrable has nothing to do with gender (that is, self-presentation as masculine or feminine) but rather is more related to patterns of actual sexual behavior. Moreover, sexual "versatility" does not preclude preference for a particular position in a particular kind of sex (e.g., liking to be fellated), or require anything approaching a perfect balance between taking insertive and insertee roles.

What is not modern and international–what is "old-fashioned" and "unsophisticated" in these societies–is the distinction between masculine inserters who are not considered homosexuals and feminine insertees who are. The sexually passive, effeminate *kathoey* role in Thailand resembles the Latin American *maricón* role. A *kathoey* takes the subordinate ("woman's") role in what we might call gender exogamy with Thai "complete males" (*phu-chai tem tua*), just as does the *maricón* with real *hombres*. In their widely recognized womanly inferiority, the *maricón* and the *kathoey* visibly reinforce gender stratification. They perpetuate men's fear of appearing effeminate and the equation between being sexually penetrated and being like a woman in other ways. Those privately involved in receptive homosexuality, but who maintain a masculine public appearance, are obviously unwilling to forgo male privileges,[6] and have a vested interest in ensuring that the stigma remains on effeminacy rather than on homosexuality. As in Latin America, the homosexuality of effeminate Thai men has been taken for granted, and the men who fuck them have not been stigmatized as "homosexual." Many young and poor men who consider themselves "100% male" lack wives. In Bangkok, as in Latin American capitals, men tend to marry a decade or more after puberty. Increasingly, for many landless rural-urban migrants in Thailand, marriage in the mid-20s–"if I can accumulate some money"–is an uncertain hope. McCamish reports such an attitude amongst young male sex workers in Pattaya in his study in this volume. The possibilities of sexual contact with the "good girls" who are the most likely candidates for future wives are extremely limited, so "bad girls," prostitutes, or effeminate men, provide culturally expected, quasi-legitimate sexual outlets, again, as in Latin America. Subject to possible correction by historical research, it appears that gender variance was what was noticed and that Thai homosexuality (both male and female) was primarily heterogender, that is, between same-sex partners who played out masculine-feminine gender roles. In particular, the male homosexual transvestite *kathoey* role was named, while it was not commonly considered that apparently masculine males might be sexually receptive. With Thailand's economic development, urbanization, and especially the rapid growth of Bangkok, there has been increased contact between Thais and non-Thais, especially European, North American, Australian and Japanese gay tourists. This, together with the fact more Thai gay men have been able to travel and study abroad, has led to increased access to representations of homogender homosexuality (i.e., masculine men being sexually penetrated). These representations are now widely available in Thailand via hard-core magazines and videos, the non-hard-core Thai print media, and within the increasingly prevalent international AIDS discourse. As a consequence "modern" gay homosexuality has become more apparent in Thailand.

A striking transformation from *kathoey* to gay assumptions is visible between Pisan Archaraseranee's 1985 film *Phleng Sut-thai* ("The last song") and his 1986 sequel, *Rak Thoraman* ("Tortured love"). The first film shows an unhappy female impersonator distraught about losing his lover to a woman. In the final scene, he cuts off his long hair and shoots himself on-stage at a Pattaya *kathoey* revue. The second film involves the dead man's masculine identical twin seducing his brother's fickle lover in a complicated story of revenge. In one scene in *Rak Thoraman* the avenging twin rolls around beside a swimming pool with his brother's former lover. The twin, whose occupation is stereotypically masculine (he is a mechanic), is asked if he is a *king* or a *queen*. He responds, "I am *gay*," confounding the expectations of his brother's errant "husband" (and presumably of much of the viewing audience) of gender-dichotomizing role separation.

Lacking survey data about the organization of homosexual behavior in Thailand over time, or even at present, I here draw on three collections of Thai male writings about same-sex eros to support the argument that modern/egalitarian/gay homosexuality has become increasingly plausible to Thai males. Anthropologist Herbert Phillips (1987, p. 3) recommended treating Thai writings as "embodiments of culture" and as "noetic expression of a social and cultural milieu." He stressed that, in contrast to most social science data, what is written by Thais to be read by other Thais is not question-dependent or shaped by alien audiences, and therefore provides more direct access to native concerns than do interview data.[7] Of course, "native representations" are still representations that may not be accurate records of typical encounters but, in understanding sexualities, representations of desire are at least as important as records of behavior. Moreover, the records of sexual behavior–in any culture–are self-reports,[8] not naturalistic observation of actual, quotidian sexual behaviour. With the exception of some video-recordings, the available data on what people do sexually is what they say they have done (whether they say it in conversations, interviews, or on the page on which they write).

Like Jackson's (1989/1995) collection of letters to the advice columnist "Uncle Go" (the pen name of Pratchaya Phanthathorn), *The Dove Coos*[9] collections (Allyn, 1992, 1995) provide English translations of indigenous Thai gay materials. In the first volume of *The Dove Coos*, two gay magazine editors, Somboon Inpradith and Nukul Benchamat, translated sexual autobiographical narratives from three gay Thai magazines (*Weekend Men, Midway, Neon*).

These materials are more recent (1988-90) than the letters to "Uncle Go" translated by Jackson, which date from the period 1980 to 1984).[10] Thai editors of the gay magazines *Horng Ha Liam* ("Five-sided room"), *Neon, Midway*, and *Violet* originally selected a range of stories for translation and inclusion in the second *Dove Coos* volume, although editor Eric Allyn, with advice from the pseudonymous translator and the Thai magazine editors, selected the final list of included stories. Allyn states (personal communication, 11 March 1996) that he wanted to include some stories involving *farang* (Caucasian) sexual partners of Thai men, but the main selection criterion was the quality of the writing, not any of the attributes of the characters in the personal narratives.

None of these three books includes discussion of selection criteria, either for inclusion in the English-language books or for the Thai magazines in which they originally appeared. For first-person stories to gay magazines, and especially for letters to a heterosexually identifying advice columnist in a general circulation, sensationalist magazine, what gets published may not be typical of what gets written. Those who problematize sexual identity and/or sexual encounters and write questions about them are not likely to constitute a random sample of Thai men who are sexually involved with men, and those who write to gay magazines at the very least know something of gay cultural institutions.[11] Although caution should be exercised in generalizing about male homosexuality in Thailand on the basis of these sets of native texts, these books contain relatively unmediated native representations that seem to me to be valuable cultural materials and to convey much about Thai attitudes.

As in Boyd Macdonald's compilations from the US (the closest analog), in *The Dove Coos* it is difficult to distinguish fantasy from "objective" reporting of what happened–as one-after-another desired man seduces one-after-another narrator, and as pain turns to rapture as "cobras," "doves," "dragons," "locomotives," "swords," "spears," "riders," etc., penetrate previously tightly shut "back doors" (sometimes exalted to being "heaven's gate"). Forced by press censorship to use metaphors for sexual parts and acts, the authors pound away relentlessly within whatever metaphorical set they have chosen. Martial metaphors abound.[12] However, a recurrent metaphor for ejaculation–"the dove stretches its neck when it coos"–does not seem very bellicose to me (in contrast to say, eagles or, for neckiness, the cranes that winter in Thailand), perhaps because it signifies the imminent collapse of the erection outlasted by whatever orifice it has visited. "Dragons" and "tigers" returning to "caves" they have found pleasant seem to me metaphors of more dominant, less fragile phalli.

KATHOEYS, FARANGS AND COMMERCIAL VENUES

None of the stories in *Dove Coos I* and only two in *Dove Coos II* involve the overtly gender-variant *kathoey*, and one in the latter involves anal-insertive *kathoeys*. The writer of "A *gatuhy's* [i.e., *kathoey's*] grand entrance" was "amazed that his [the *kathoey's*] 'little brother' [penis] was much larger than mine . . . Since then, I've played with at least ten different *gatuhys* and that all had bigger 'brothers' than me, and many like being a *king* and a *queen*" (Allyn, 1995, pp. 92-3), i.e., playing insertive as well as receptive sexual roles.

Only one of the stories involves (and indirectly at that) a commercial sex venue. Similarly, only one of the letters to Uncle Go (#6) mentions a commercial sex venue. In story 22 in *Dove Coos I* two friends from the Northeast are "auditioned" by a gay bar owner. Two stories in *Dove Coos II* involve *farang*, an Australian (in story 2) and a pair of Japanese tourists (in story 24). One story in *Dove Coos I* involves a threesome with a French photographer and his Thai lover. In these representations, all four non-Thais are hungry for (i.e., readily orally receptive to) Thai penises. Two of the three narrators reciprocate by fellating the *farang(s)*, but none are anally penetrated by any of the *farang* (one Thai is anally penetrated by a compatriot), and only the Australian is anally penetrated by one of the Thai males. Like Western gay hard-core videos and the scene from the local film *Rak Thoraman* referred to above, the encounter with the Australian challenged assumptions about gender indicating sexual role:

> I couldn't believe that a guy like Kerry, who was "all man" and came better equipped than me, was the one to receive pleasure like that instead of giving it. It was an important thing for me to learn: the guy with the most masculine appearance and the biggest weapon was not always the aggressive player. (Allyn, 1995, p. 24)

INCREASINGLY "GAY" HOMOSEXUALITY

The "gay" breakdown of the equation of relative masculinity with sexual role is also evident in both the earlier letters and later observations in Jackson (1995). In one response (which I suspect is later than most of the others), Uncle Go counsels Athit, who had resisted anal penetration and whom Go classifies as "bisexual," to relax and be modern (*than samai*),[13]

> If your heart was a bit warmer you would probably let someone come in your back gate, too. Because these days the words 'gay queen' don't mean the guy only takes it. The world is evolving, the gay queen can be an active gay king, too. (Jackson, 1989, p. 160; 1995, p. 168)

This acknowledgment that mores were changing was supplemented from the other direction by Pratchaya Phanthathorn (a.k.a. Uncle Go) telling Eric Allyn in 1989 (see Allyn, 1990), that "nowadays *gay queens* often think they can be a *king* too" (from an interview included in Jackson, 1995, pp. 117-8).

The norm in the "true life experiences" in the two *The Dove Coos* collections is for both partners to "reach heaven" (often in close synchronicity, if not simultaneously). Reciprocity in manual and/or oral sex is common, being mentioned in 10 of 34 stories in the first collection and in 18 of 37 in the second collection.[14] Alternating roles in anal sex is uncommon, occurring in only two stories from the first collection and in six from the second.[15] However, those being anally penetrated in 19 of 34 stories in the first collection and in 18 of 37 in the second collection also ejaculate either spontaneously or from manual stimulation (including all but one of the narrators in the first collection who recall being anally penetrated).[16] There is no sexual reciprocity in the two stories involving *kathoeys*. In one the *kathoey* is exclusively insertive (Vol. II #17), in the other he is exclusively receptive (Vol. II #8).

Fewer of the authors in the (earlier) letters to Uncle Go mentioned reciprocity. In sixteen of the sexual encounters related in the letters translated by Jackson, both partners "reach heaven" with some sort of aid of their partner's hand, mouth, or rectum.[17] Seventeen only mention their partner getting off,[18] and seven mention only themselves getting off.[19]

There are two passing mentions in *The Dove Coos I* of Buddhist motivations for satisfying another's desire (which is more pressing than one's own)–"I thought it would be a sin to give up and deny him this pleasure" (Allyn, 1992, p. 70); "If you're so horny, why not just tell me? I'll do it for merit" (Allyn, 1992, p. 96). However, generally both insertee and inserter receive pleasure from anal penetration. All told, 30 of the 34 stories in the first collection include anal sex, 27 include oral sex. In the second collection, 28 of 37 include anal penetration, and 35 of 37 include oral sex (in one of the other two stories a tongue precedes a penis into an anus).

COMPLAISANCE: NOT TAKING THE INITIATIVE

Usually (in 23 of 32 instances of sexual encounters in the first volume of *The Dove Coos*, in 32 of 40 in the second volume, and in 32 of 36 instances in Jackson 1995), the narrator attributes the initiation of sexual behavior to his partner, not himself.[20] In recollections of first homosexual and heterosexual experiences gathered in a pretest of a survey in 1993 of those engaged in same-sex sexual behavior in Thailand, I have also found this to be the case–regardless of the relative age, relative status, whether the initial act is insertive or receptive, and even the sex of the partners. I think there is a tendency for Thais to attribute sexual and other kinds of behavior to what someone else wants (or what they think someone else wants). Notably, complaisance is inseparable from preferring to attribute responsibility, including responsibility for one's own action, to others.[21]

RELATIVE SOCIAL STATUS

Those writing stories of their sexual adventures (in the letters to Uncle Go and in the Thai gay magazines translated in the two volumes of *The Dove Coos*) did not always mention the occupation or status of the sexual partner (in some instance, they probably did not know it), or their own occupation or social status. For those whose relative status can be coded from the information they supply, in the two volumes of *The Dove Coos*, sexual partners are generally peers such as fellow students and co-workers or else somewhat older and more affluent. The eroticization of the working class that is common in American –and even more so in British–representations of same-sex encounters is not evident.

Table 1 suggests a decline over time in the (reported or desired) social status of partners. However, the temptation to take the more balanced distribution in *The Dove Coos II* as an indication of increasing egalitarianism is militated against by the lack of change in the "equivalent status" column for the three volumes considered. That is, over time there is an increase in reports of sex with lower-status partners, but little change in the proportion of encounters with status equals. (I do not think that the relative status of partners was a criterion applied by Jackson or Allyn in selecting which representations to translate.)

TABLE 1. Relative Status of Sexual Partners in Three Collections of Thai Sexual Experiences

	Higher	Equivalent	Lower
Dear Uncle Go (Jackson, 1989) (N = 44)	57%	34	9
Dove Coos I (Allyn, 1992) (N = 27)	44%	41	15
Dove Coos II (Allyn, 1995) (N = 29)	31%	35	35

Table 2 details the statuses of sexual partners coded as higher, equal, or lower in Table 1, so that readers may assess for themselves my codings of relative status.

In quoted dialogue in the *Dove Coos I*, but not in the sequel volume, the narrator is frequently addressed as *norng* ("younger brother"), i.e., as someone who should defer to what the male of higher (senior) status wants.

AMBIGUITIES OF THE GAY LABEL

Although Allyn has argued that *gay* in Thai has taken on connotations of effeminacy to such an extent that it is not a polite term (contrasting with the decorous expression for homoeroticism *mai pa diaw-kan*–"trees together in same forest"),[23] narrators refer to themselves as *gay* in *The Dove Coos I* on pages 47, 49, 84, 102, and (arguably) pages 20, 29, 66, and 122 (along with typification of the narrator as gay by a gay sexual partner on page 96).

Narrators on pages 22, 37, 55, 79, and 94 of *The Dove Coos I* distinguish at least their past selves (before the relationship they are writing about) as being aware of but distanced from the category of *gay*, and another three attestations, on pages 55, 61, and 76 neither embrace nor reject the term. The same corpus shows some men distinguishing *gay* from *kathoey*, e.g., "I had sex with some gay guys and a few *gatuhy*" (Allyn, 1992, p. 55); the recollection that earlier "I didn't know what was 'gay' and couldn't imagine what the 'gay life' was like. I only knew about effeminate men, the so-called *gatuhy*" (Allyn, 1992, p. 61); the distinction between a *kathoey* "sissy type" and more butch "closety type" (Allyn, 1992, pp. 76, 96) for masculine-appearing non-*kathoey* gay men who enjoy being penetrated.[24] These provide additional evidence for Jackson's (1995, pp. 186-7) conclusion: "Gay men in contemporary Thailand are in the process of negotiating this ambiguous psycho-cultural space and, in general, are attempting to overcome the stigma that attaches to homosexuality by aligning themselves with the gender-normative status of 'men' and distancing themselves from gender-deviant *kathoeys*."

Some of those who wrote to Uncle Go during the early 1980s asked if they or their male sexual partner was *gay*, and, if so, what kind (i.e., *king* or *queen*). Two of the letter-writers described themselves as *gay*

TABLE 2. Relative Status of Sexual Partners in Three Collections of Thai Sexual Experiences

Dear Uncle Go (1989) (letter number(s))	Dove Coos I (1992) (story number(s))	Dove Coos II (1995) (story number(s))
Higher Status Partner		
doctor (13,19)	boss (21)	older neighbor (9, 33)
headmaster (15) providing housing (24)	doctor (1)	landlord's nephew (18)
father's friend providing housing (14)	banker (10)	administrator (19)
boss's son (3)	boss's son (3)	teacher (26, 26)
teachers (18, 21)	foreigner (5, 30)	Japanese tourists (24, 24)
headmaster's son (15)	elder (13, 17, 28, 31?, 34)	Australian tourist (2)
uncle (33)	older brother's friend (27)	
adult patron (31)		
elders (5, 16, 29, 29, 34)		
adult neighbor (6B, 19, 26, 27)		
stepmother's lover (8)		
older sister's boyfriend (7)		
schoolmate's older brother (6B)		
policeman (32, 37)[22]		
Equal Status Partner		
schoolmate (2, 6A, 7, 12, 18, 28, 34)	schoolmate (12, 18, 19, 24)	schoolmate (13, 16, 17)
co-workers (3, 6B, 8, 22, 25)	co-worker (9, 20, 22, 26)	lover (4)
army mate (26)	teammate (4)	friend (4, 25, 36)
friend (23, 35)	army buddy and future brother-in-law (16)	friend's brother (27)
		neighbor (30)
		assistant to factory owner (7)
Lower Status Partner		
younger (1, 20, 22)	student (6)	work trainee (35)
students of teacher (17)	younger friend (11)	construction worker (32)
	temple boy (14)	worker (14)
	(kick) boxer (15)	bus driver (28)

TABLE 2 (continued)

Dear Uncle Go (1989) (letter number(s))	Dove Coos I (1992) (story number(s))	Dove Coos II (1995) (story number(s))
Lower Status Partner (continued)		
		taxi driver (31)
		ice-cream vendor (6)
		son of father's employee (10)
		younger schoolmate (29, 34)
		farmworker/servant (20)
Indeterminate Relative Status of Partners		
strangers (1, 8, 15, 21, 22, 37)	video shopkeeper (33)	
	policeman (23)	
	traffic cop (8)	
	restaurant captain (25)	
	Singaporean (29)	
	strangers (2, 7)	

(letter 6 a *gay queen*, letter 27 unsure of the kind of *gay*). Go labelled nine correspondents as *gay*, plus one semi-bisexual as a *gay king* (letter 29), and three as *bisexual* (letters 16, 21, 23). Of those he labelled *gay*, he judged five to be *gay kings* (letters 5, 22, 24, 26, 29), three *gay queens* (letters 7, 19, 33), and two *king-queens* (letters 6 and 20).

CONCLUSION

Although it is impossible to know how much can be generalized from the material in Thai gay magazines, such material does provide an alternative source of insights to the rhapsodies of Western sex tourists based on experiences (including conversations) in Bangkok commercial venues.[25] Together, the two collections of *The Dove Coos* and the two editions of Jackson's book (1989, 1995) indicate both a lot of what is represented (by the Thai authors) as complaisance to the desires of others,[26] and a decline in gender-stratified conception and enactment of homosexuality in Thailand, paralleling the gender-to-gay transformation of homosexuality elsewhere the world. The word *gay* is diffusing around the world and a referent for it, the homogender model of homosexuality, is developing and becoming more prominent in many places, not least in Thailand.

NOTES

1. This paper does not presume any knowledge about Thai culture. For those seeking to learn more about general Thai patterns of conduct, Mulder (1985) provides a readable account. Phillips (1987) provides a useful collection of Thai literature in translation. Allyn (1991), Jackson (1995, pp. 226-80), and Morris (1994) all address changing Thai conceptions of homosexuality; Morris focusing on females and on gender among both males and females rather than sexuality (as is typical in anthropology: see Murray, 1997). For overviews of Southeast Asian history see Coedès (1966, arranged chronologically, 1968, arranged geographically) and Keyes (1995).

2. On this typology, see Murray (1998, 1995a, pp. 3-32) and Adam (1979). On visibly effeminate males making it easier for others to engage recurrently in homosexuality without being noticed, see Trumbach (1977), who was writing specifically about "mollies" in London at the end of the 17th century. Morris (1994) discusses the visibility of gender-variant females and males as advertising for (gender-conforming) sexual partners in Thailand. Enacting gender nonconformity has been a venerable strategy to advertise homosexual desire in the US and elsewhere. Murray (1996a, pp. 150-6) discusses unlearning these stereotypes in contemporary North American lesbian and gay settings in which gender nonconformity is not necessary, and is often devalued.

3. See Winkler (1990), Murray (1998) on Greece; Murray (1995a) on Latin America; Murray (1996a) on North America.

4. Not everyone who is *gay* is exclusively homosexual. Butch-femme role dichotomization seems much more prevalent among lesbians than among gay men in the West, perhaps in part because of the fragility and evanescence of lesbian identity for many women (see Murray 1996a, pp. 158).

5. See Murray (1992, 1995b, 1998).

6. Thais generally accept each other "at face value" and smooth interaction is highly valued. Introspection (self-scrutiny) and, still more, public discussion and criticism of stigmatizing information (public scrutiny) are generally avoided. Early in life Thais learn to keep their feelings to themselves, and to hide behind the impersonal, unemotional presentation called *jai yen* (lit. "a cool heart"). "Whatever is to be found deep down in the self is a Thai secret about which one often knows little oneself," but as long as people do not challenge the rules in public, "there is room for some tolerated individual deviation from the rules," as Mulder (1985, pp. 64, 71, 82) wrote. This makes affirmation of a gay or a lesbian identity difficult to achieve, as Morris (1994, pp. 36-7) discussed.

7. As Sullivan and Leong (1995, p. 2) have noted, "Much of the literature on homosexuality in Asia and the Pacific has been written by Western scholars and trav-

ellers. Many of these have noted the lack of legal proscriptions against the behavior and the presence of transgendered individuals who, in contrast to many Western societies, are integrated into their communities and have a positive status. From this and other evidence the conclusion has often been drawn that these societies are tolerant and accepting of homosexuality. . . . While there may be an absence of criminal sanctions, there are often overpowering social pressures which compel people to marry and procreate. While homosexuality in private may be tolerated, public displays of this status can be strongly disapproved." Although my focus is not on social acceptance, this background is relevant to Thailand, and a wish to get beyond how aliens experience Thai homosexuality is the reason for turning to Thai writings.

8. This includes anthropologists' attempt to draw on their own inter-cultural sexual experiences: see Murray (1996b) on epistemological problems with such "observational" data.

9. In Thai idiom, "the dove coos" (*nok-khao khan*) is a euphemism for an erection.

10. Nevertheless, it is of course possible that the events related in *The Dove Coos* stories may have occurred years before writing and publication.

11. Are writers anywhere ever typical? This surely has some implications for the current thrust away from behavioral data to literary texts of both lesbian/gay studies and anthropology. Practitioners of both increasingly consider everything to be "representations" and all "representations" to be equal without any concern about representativeness.

12. Story 10, "Chinese Battle Strategy Defeats the Dragon" is the best example in the first *The Dove Coos*.

13. Compare, *moderno* is the term in Peru for someone involved in homosexuality who is neither *activo* nor *passivo* (Murray 1995a, pp. 105, 139-41).

14. *The Dove Coos I*: 2, 6, 9, 11, 14, 21, 25, 28, 29, 30; *The Dove Coos II*: 1, 2, 3, 4b, 5, 7, 10b, 11a, 14, 15, 16b, 18a, 21, 22b, 24, 26a, 31, 36.

15. *The Dove Coos I*: 5, 15; *The Dove Coos II*: 1, 3, 19b, 20, 30, 33.

16. *The Dove Coos I*:1, 3, 6, 7, 8, 10, 11, 12, 16, 18, 19a, 20, 21, 23, 26, 27, 30, 31, 32, and *The Dove Coos II*: 6, 10a, 11b, 12, 13, 16a, 17, 18b, 19a, 22a, 23b, 26a, 27, 28, 29b, 31, 34, 37. The narrator of story 25 in *The Dove Coos II* says his turn is coming.

17. Jackson 1995: 3a, 6a, 14, 17, 20, 21, 23, 25, 26a,b, 27d, 29a,b, 32, plus the account on p. 240.

18. Jackson 1995: 3b, 6Ab,c, 6Ba,b, 7a,b, 11a, 15, 16a, 19, 24, 27a, 35-38.

19. Jackson 1995: 12, 13, 16b, 22, 27b, 30, 31.

20. However, making the first move does not seem to be related to differences in role, i.e., *gay kings* are no more likely than *gay queens* to make the first move. Looking only at *The Dove Coos II*, of those who reported initiating sex, 37.5 percent began with insertive sex. Of those who attributed the first move to others, 33 percent were insertive in the first sexual intercourse (with another 26 percent beginning with reciprocal oral sex; if these were excluded, 45 percent of the non-initiators who began insertive or receptive began insertive). Similarly, relative social status does not account for taking the initiative. *The Dove Coos II* narrators made the first move on three (of

nine) higher-status males, three (of ten) males of equivalent status, and two (of ten) of lower status.

21. An anonymous reader suggested that those writing letters would be more likely to attribute motivation to others. I think that writing a letter or a "true-life account" takes some initiative, so if there is a bias from the kind of data, it would be toward initiative not toward passivity.

22. Because policemen have some power to protect narrators in the situations they were first encountered, I consider them patrons of sorts, rather than working-class sexual partners.

23. *Gay* has been "increasingly used by the public for *gatuhy*. . . . Even the Thai gay magazines have confused *gay* and transvestite. . . . A Thai of the lower classes may deny that he's *gay*, associating it with it getting fucked (as one expects of *gatuhy*). He may, in fact, respond 'I am a man'–meaning he is the inserter or *gay king*. A *farang* gay's claim that he's a 'gay man' is often met with bewilderment, as the two words together to him are illogical" (Allyn, 1991, p. 144; also see Jackson, 1995, pp. 229, 278; Wiresit et al., 1991, p. 107). A similar oozing of old gender meanings into the stigma-challenging new container "gay" in Latin America is discussed in Murray (1995a, p. 138-44, 1995b).

24. Typifications as gay, bisexual, etc., are largely lacking from the more recent *Dove Coos II* collection. Excluding the introductions, there are 6 uses of the term "gay," 2 of "gay magazines," and one of "gay queen" (Eric Allyn, personal communication 29 August 1996 e-mail, reporting a computer search of the text).

25. I agree with Allyn (1991) that these venues are primarily for Thais. If they depended upon farang patronage, even those in the Patpong district of Bangkok would be out of business, judging by the paucity of Japanese and Western customers I observed there in 1993 in what should have been the peak time for tourism, December.

26. A number of those who wrote to Uncle Go sought replicas of the man who introduced them to the pleasure of male-male sex. In particular the writers of letters 13, 15, and 32 seem imprinted on their first sexual partner's occupation.

REFERENCES

Adam, B. D. (1979). Reply. *Sociologists' Gay Caucus Newsletter, 18*, 8.

Allyn, E. (1990). *An interview with "Uncle" Goh Bhaknam*. Bangkok: Bua Luang. Excerpted in Jackson (1995, pp. 33-36, 116-120).

Allyn, E. (1991). *Trees in the same forest: Thailand's culture and gay subculture*. Bangkok: Bua Luang.

Allyn, E. (Ed.). (1992). *The dove coos: Gay experiences by the men of Thailand*. Bangkok: Bua Luang.

Allyn, E. (Ed.). (1995). *The dove coos II: Gay experiences by the men of Thailand*. Bangkok: Bua Luang.

Coedès, G. (1966). *The making of Southeast Asia*. Berkeley: University of California Press.

Coedès, G. (1968). *The Indianized states of Southeast Asia*. Honolulu: East-West Center Press.

Jackson, P.A. (1989). *Male homosexuality in Thailand: An interpretation of contemporary Thai sources.* Elmhurst NY: Global Academic Publishers.

Jackson, P.A. (1995). *Dear Uncle Go: Male homosexuality in Thailand.* Bangkok: Bua Luang.

Keyes, C.F. (1995). *The golden peninsula: Culture and adaptation in mainland Southeast Asia.* New York: Macmillan.

Morris, R.C. (1994) Three sexes and four sexualities: Redressing the discourses on gender and sexuality in contemporary Thailand. *Positions, 2*(1), 15-43.

Mulder, N. (1985). *Everyday life in Thailand.* Bangkok: Duang Kamol.

Murray, S.O. (1992). The "underdevelopment" of gay homosexuality in urban MesoAmerica, Peru and Thailand. In K. Plummer (Ed.), *Modern homosexualities* (pp. 29-38). London: Routledge.

Murray, S.O. (1995a). *Latin American male homosexualities.* Albuquerque: University of New Mexico Press.

Murray, S. O. (1995b). Stigma transformation and relexification in the international diffusion of *gay.* In W. Leap (Ed.), *Beyond the lavender lexicon: Gay and lesbian language* (pp. 236-260). New York: Gordon & Breach.

Murray, S.O. (1996a). *American gay.* Chicago: University of Chicago Press.

Murray, S.O. (1996b). Male homosexuality in Guatemala: Possible insights and certain confusions of sleeping with "natives" as a source of data. In E. Lewin & W. Leap (Eds.), *Lesbian and gay ethnography* (pp. 236-260). Urbana: University of Illinois Press.

Murray, S.O. (1997). Explaining away same-sex sexuality when it obtrudes on anthropologists' attention. *Anthropology Today, 13*(3), 2-5 .

Murray, S.O. (1998). *Homosexualities.* Chicago: University of Chicago Press.

Phillips, H.P. (1987). *Modern Thai literature* Honolulu: University of Hawaii Press.

Sullivan, G., & Leong, L. (1995). *Gays and lesbians in Asia and the Pacific.* Binghamton, NY: The Haworth Press, Inc.

Trumbach, R. (1977). London's sodomites. *Journal of Social History, 11*(1), 1-33.

Winkler, J.J. (1990). *The constraints of desire. The anthropology of sex and gender in ancient Greece.* New York: Routledge.

Wiresit, S., Brown, T., & Virulrak, S. (1991). Patterns of bisexuality in Thailand. In R. Tielman, M. Carballo & A. Hendriks (Eds.), *Bisexuality and HIV/AIDS: A global perspective* (pp. 97-117). Buffalo, NY: Prometheus.

Masculinity and *Tom* Identity
in Thailand

Megan Sinnott

SUMMARY. Thai lesbian women engage local cultural meanings of masculinity in the creation of personal identities. Lesbian identity in Thailand is largely framed in terms of "butch-femme" gender role-playing, with the masculine woman referred to as *tom* and the feminine woman *dee*. According to informants, the dynamics between *toms* and *dees* differ from the normative expectations and experiences of heterosexuality for Thai women. Although Thai *toms* express their identity in terms of being "like men," they often differ from typical Thai male attitudes in terms of attitudes towards female sexuality, masculine sensitivity, and expectations from women in terms of long-term relationships. I conclude that Thai *tom*-identity is positioned against both normative Thai femininity and masculinity. This paper addresses the feelings towards sexuality and self-identity of many Thai lesbians, and seeks to help health and welfare professionals be sensitive to cultural nuances of gender identity, and attitudes towards relationships and sex among lesbian Thai women. *[Article copies available for a fee from The Haworth Document Delivery Service: 1-800-342-9678. E-mail address: getinfo@haworthpressinc.com]*

INTRODUCTION

In contemporary Thai, *tom*[1] is a term derived from the English word "tomboy" and refers to masculine-identified women who have sexual

---

Address correspondence to: Megan Sinnott, Anthropology Department, 5240 Social Science Building, 1180 Observatory Drive, University of Wisconsin, Madison, WI 53703 USA.

[Haworth co-indexing entry note]: "Masculinity and *Tom* Identity in Thailand." Sinnott, Megan. Co-published simultaneously in *Journal of Gay & Lesbian Social Services* (The Haworth Press, Inc.) Vol. 9, No. 2/3, 1999, pp. 97-119; and: *Lady Boys, Tom Boys, Rent Boys: Male and Female Homosexualities in Contemporary Thailand* (ed: Peter A. Jackson, and Gerard Sullivan) The Haworth Press, Inc., 1999, pp. 97-119; and: *Lady Boys, Tom Boys, Rent Boys: Male and Female Homosexualities in Contemporary Thailand* (ed: Peter A. Jackson, and Gerard Sullivan) Harrington Park Press, an imprint of The Haworth Press, Inc., 1999, pp. 97-119. Single or multiple copies of this article are available for a fee from The Haworth Document Delivery Service [1-800-342-9678, 9:00 a.m. - 5:00 p.m. (EST). E-mail address: getinfo@haworthpressinc.com].

attraction towards and relationships with feminine-identified women, who are called *dee* (from the English word "la*dy*"). I will examine the ways *toms* interpret and express masculinity as a form of self-identity. From information provided by informants and from personal observation, and newspaper and magazine articles, it is clear that women identifying as *tom* and *dee* are found throughout the country–in rural villages as well as urban centers. The recent emergence of visibly identified lesbians, the *toms*, has been fodder for sensation-seeking Thai tabloids, which have covered the topic regularly for roughly the past fifteen years. The tone of these articles has, until recently, been almost entirely negative, ill-informed, and aimed at shocking the reader. For example, the following statement occurred in an article in a Thai women's magazine in 1984,

> [T]he world of fashion is the source of this problem. The *tom-dee* fashion is disseminating everywhere. Many young women are leaping onto the new fashion band-wagon. Today, it doesn't matter where you turn, you will see the bizarre phenomenon that some people call 'perversity.'[2]

The media coverage of the existence of *tom-dees*, while not providing accurate information about the lives of these women, charts the emergence of *tom-dee*-ism on the Thai cultural landscape. Female homosexual behavior has been part of Thai life throughout history, evidenced by representations in Buddhist temple murals, and court poetry describing sexual activity between women in royal harems, as well as the existence of Thai expressions referring to lesbian-sex such as *len pheuan* (Matthana 1995). However, the appearance of a culturally recognized category of women who publicly declare their lesbianism in the form of dress and appearance seems to be a relatively recent phenomenon. *Tom-dee*-ism has been a recognized cultural phenomenon for around fifteen to twenty years according to most informants' recollections.

The *toms*' outward expression of masculinity is what makes *tom-dees* a recognized cultural phenomenon. Yet, as I will argue, *toms*' masculinity, as defined by *toms* and *dees* themselves, is in marked contrast to normative conceptions of masculinity for Thai men in terms of attitudes towards sexuality, romantic relationships, and social status. Furthermore, I contend, *toms*' masculinity is a selective appropriation of Thai expectations of both normative masculine and feminine genders, and has several points of significance for the women concerned. Firstly, association with masculinity allows *toms* sexual agency that is typically denied to Thai women. Secondly, *toms'* continuing association with femininity allows feminine-identified women the freedom to engage in relationships with *toms* free of the onerous moral restrictions placed on heterosexual Thai women's sexuality.[3]

My argument that *toms* have a culturally recognized masculine gender, which is distinct from normative Thai models of masculinity, is framed in terms of an understanding of gender as a context-dependent field of culturally specific meanings. Anthropologists, such as Mead (1949) and Benedict (1934), have convincingly argued that what Westerners perceived to be natural distinctions between males and females are actually culturally specific values that define and proscribe attitudes and behavior for men and women. Foucault's (1978) focus on "discourse" in social analysis, has led to a shift in approaches to the study of gender. Rather than assuming gender accurately reflects what men and women do or think in a particular society, scholars have examined the ways that masculinity and femininity are fields of meaning employed in strategic ways to support or subvert power relations (see Ong & Peletz, 1995; Errington, 1990). The analysis of gender as a flexible, context-dependent spectrum of meanings has led to insightful historical and anthropological studies of phenomena which on the surface might appear to have little to do with biological sex, such as supporting colonial systems, right-wing militant nationalism, and even leftist social movements (see Mosse, 1985; Stoler, 1991).

The use of masculinity as a basis for self-identity by Thai *toms* illustrates the fluid, contradictory, and historically specific nature of cultural systems and understandings of gender, and the variability of expressions of gender within a given society. I will argue that Thai masculine behavior is commonly defined by both male and female Thais as drinking, smoking, "womanizing" and gambling. Thai masculinity is also identified with strength, leadership, as well as spiritual potential. These definitions of masculinity contain inherent contradictions, and either set of definitions cannot be assumed to accurately describe what a given Thai man, or *tom* does. Keyes (1984) and Kirsch (1985) have pointed out that femininity in Thailand embodies a spectrum of values: virginal purity, untamed sexuality, worldly attachment, and motherly goodness. The difficulty in pinning down a singular referent for masculinity or femininity, or showing perfect opposing symmetry in meanings between masculine and feminine in a *yin-yang* way, has led to a flurry of debate over the "status" of women in Thailand. Looked at in one way, women are valued, especially as mothers, and as bread-winners. From another perspective, women are devalued as embodying sexual desire and sensual excess, and as being incapable of high spiritual achievement such as is embodied in the highly revered (male) Thai Buddhist monk. Van Esterik (1982) points out that discourses of gender often manifest on the level of metaphor, and should not be taken to mean that these discourses are accurate descriptions of what men and women are or do. When I use the term "normative" models of gender, I am referring to what people, in general, based on accepted codifications of cultural meanings, think men or women should do, or typically do, and the values that are attached to these acts. The multiple symbolic associations of femininity and masculinity support Joan Scott's claim that gender is an essentially unstable and contradictory field of meaning,

> [G]ender identification, although it always appears coherent and fixed, is, in fact, highly unstable. As meaning systems, subjective identities are processes of differentiation and distinction, requiring the suppression of ambiguities and opposite elements in order to ensure (create the illusion of) coherence and common understandings. (Scott, 1988, p. 38)

Following Scott's lead, an analysis of "gender" in a particular society would examine the discursive field of contradictory, and contested meanings of masculinity and femininity. The meanings of gender that an individual or group–whether *tom*, heterosexual male or other groups such as male transvestites or male sex workers–will employ depend on social context, and contain the possibility of multiple interpretations by the actors themselves. *Toms*, as a "transgender" identity, exemplify the contradictory and constructed bases of gender.

"Transgender" refers to the practice of people labelled as biological males assuming a feminine persona, or vice-versa, either for a temporary period, such as in the case of spirit mediums, or on a more permanent basis, such as in the case of *toms*. Historically, research on transgendered identities has tried to explain to a Western audience how it is possible in different cultural contexts for a person to adopt a gender identity that seemingly contradicts their biological sex (see Blackwood, 1984; Gremaux, 1994; Nanda 1990). Other anthropological studies are not focussed directly on transgendered identities but nevertheless mention transgendered or related homosexual practices. In an excellent account of spirit mediums in Thailand, Irvine (1984, p. 320) notes female spirit mediums who transgress gender norms by dressing as men, "Mediums who negate the physiological facts of their sex and act like males, thereby becoming men for themselves and their adepts."

But do these women indeed *become* men? Do they really think of themselves as men? Studies, such as Nanda's (1990) and Jackson's (1995), reveal the contradiction that while transgendered people might be accepted as feminine or masculine beings, their status is not equivalent to women or men who live in accordance with their respective society's normative models of appropriate male and female identity and behavior. The example of the Thai *toms* will illustrate the uniqueness of transgender identity.

RESEARCH METHODS

Data for this paper are based on sixteen months (January 1996–August 1997) of dissertation research on the topic of lesbian identity and community formation in Thailand. Research has consisted of interviews with approximately seventy-five women from a variety of class and regional backgrounds. As anthropologists have long recognized, understandings of other societies and cultures often comes equally from daily interactions, friendships, informal discussions, and socializing, as from the formal interview, complete with tape-recorder and question lists. Such is the case here. All of the women I interviewed were introduced to me by friends or acquaintances. Some of the interviews led to friendships, long conversations over the months that followed, and further introductions. These interviews, and prosaic interactions, are the core of my research. Lesbian informants ranged from eighteen to fifty-eight years old, included rural and urban women, working class women (factory workers, vendors, construction workers), and middle and upper class women (students, professionals, housewives). I have also included interview material from non-lesbians, gathered as general background material, such as attitudes towards marriage, and sex. To provide a larger social context of lesbian lives in Thailand I have also collected magazine, newspaper, and academic journal articles on the topic of lesbians in Thailand covering approximately the past fifteen years.

THE THAI CONTEXT:
SOCIAL ATTITUDES TOWARDS SEXUALITY AND GENDER

Thailand is reputed to be a tolerant society in terms of personal behavior, including homosexual, as long as one does not "flaunt" or make such behavior apparent (see Jackson, 1995). "Coming-out," the verbal declaration of one's homosexuality, is not common in Thailand, even among women who are easily recognized as *toms*, and therefore lesbians. Almost all the *toms* interviewed said that their families knew that they were *toms*/lesbians, but very few *toms*, or *dees*, had actually had open discussions with their families about their lesbianism. Even in relatively supportive families, where a *tom* brought home her girl-friend to meet her family or live together, *toms* usually communicated their identity in non-verbal ways such as through their dress and behavior. As Jackson (1995) points out, there is very little open and frank discussion about the realities of sex, especially homosexual sex, in Thailand, as public revelations of what are perceived to be private and personal affairs are not considered proper. The closest that infor-mants came to having any formal sex education in schools were courses in "morality" in which the teachers warned the (female) stu-dents of the immoral nature of pre-marital or adulterous behavior. Easy recognition of *toms* in Thai society serves as a visual marker of a significant lesbian community in a society in which verbalizations and open declarations of female sexuality are taboo.

Social sanctions against homosexual behavior in Thailand do not usually take the official, legal forms found in the West (see Jackson, 1995). However, informants have described feeling that people malign them behind their back. Gossip and innuendo can be brutalizing in a society in which social appearance and "face" are highly valued.[4] Outdated Western medical theories that pathologize homosexuality have been imported into Thai academic discourse as well. However, homosexuality, like most other "vices," in Thai Buddhist discourse, is considered essentially a private affair, and not subject to extreme repression, as long as the behavior is kept discrete and private. Thus, many Thai lesbians are held hostage to the Thai "don't ask, don't tell" policy. They are tolerated as long as they do not make their identity or behavior obvious in discourse. Thai lesbians have often expressed feelings of crushing isolation and depression as there is almost no positive and informative discussion on what it is to be lesbian in Thai society. All that most lesbians have to identify with are the sensationalistic and overwhelmingly negative media portrayals of lesbianism.

Kot,[5] a *tom* in her early thirties living in a provincial town, explained how her girlfriend, Oy, would complain that Kot would dress too much like a man, and should not wear her hair so short. Oy claimed that if Kot looked too much like a man people would disapprove of her, saying Oy would drink and smoke. I interpreted this interaction to mean that Oy wanted to be less obvious about their relationship, veiling people's disapproval of *toms* as general disapproval of stereotypical negative male behavior. Kot said she had not told her mother that she was a lesbian, although her girlfriend lives with her and her family. She said her family knew, and there was no need to tell them directly. If she told her mother directly, Kot reasoned, her mother could forbid her. It is easy to hide the sexual relationships between women, Kot said, because nobody really thinks that two women together are lovers anyway.

Kot's comments imply that it is easy to hide lesbianism (see Took Took, 1994). Invisibility is a double-edged sword, however. It allows women to have some freedom to engage in homoerotic activities, but denies them access to information and the possibility of forming community connections. I argue this invisibility is in part due to Thai attitudes that female sexuality exists only in terms of men and heterosexual activity. Jackson (1995) explains that it is hard to find explicit prohibitions in cultural discourse on homosexuality for men, and the same is true for female homosexuality in Thailand. However, heterosexual female sexuality is much more restricted than heterosexual male sexuality in Thailand. Everyday conversations between village women I have spent time with, and urban working class women, are replete with anxiety over daughters' sexual behavior, fear of daughters being seduced or raped, and negative comments about other women's perceived promiscuity.

One discussion I had with several women villagers on the problems of drug abuse in Thailand quickly became focussed on the special dangers of moral misbehavior that drug use had for women because it made them sexually vulnerable. I had a hard time pinning the women down on whether they meant that drugs would lead to women being easier targets for rape, or the women would feel sexually excited and pursue sex with someone while under the influence–the distinction did not appear relevant. According to informants' conversations amongst themselves, unmarried women, in particular, are moral mine-fields, easily suspected of plotting to steal husbands, or attracting morally-threatening male attention. On the other hand, female same-sex activity is rendered near invisible by the Thai sexual ideology that women are by their nature devoid of sexual needs. Sex is something that men do, either to women or other men.

Thai discourses on sex consistently negate women as sexual agents. For example, the perpetual debates (in the media and in private discussions) about the situation of commercial sex work in Thailand often include a commonly held assumption that prostitution is a necessary moral evil because men's sexual needs are natural and in need of fulfillment (see Sanitsuda, 1991; Niramol, 1991). According to Kasem Adchasai, a well-known Thai journalist and editor of the Thai language daily *Bangkok Business* (*Krungthep Thurakij*), the common Thai practice of men having a minor wife is derived from a biological need for males to have "harems," and can "ensure greater variety in [men's] sex lives."[6] The writer claimed that "real Thai[s]" see polygyny as "heroic" and natural, as love and lust cannot be regulated by morality. The love and lust the writer speaks of are unquestionably applied solely to men. No mention is made of women's sexual drives, or their need for a variety of sexual partners.

A brochure promoting safe sex and AIDS prevention explains to women readers, "Women might want only to be close to their lover and just look into [his] face or hold hands, and will feel warm and contented already. But men want more and [to go] further than women . . . " (*Bangkok AIDS,* 1994).[7] Women are warned to make sure the man really loves them before they agree to any sex. A parallel brochure for men, on the other hand, explains that sexual feelings are natural for men, and sensibly warns them of the possibility of sexually-transmitted diseases. The brochure advises safe sex or masturbation for men, while no mention is made of the possibility of women wanting to have sex purely for pleasure (*Bangkok AIDS*, 1994) Women having "natural" and healthy sexual needs are rarely mentioned in mainstream discourse of sex in Thailand. Thais often find it difficult to even perceive of the possibility of female to female sex.[8]

Maew, a twenty-nine year old married middle-class woman, sitting in the lobby of her clean and spacious cosmetics shop, told me how much simpler it is to raise a boy than a girl. With a boy, she explained, you do not need to worry about whether they are having sex or not. I asked why she was not worried about her boy having sex, and she said, "Who would know? Nobody can tell if a man loses his virginity." I asked if she thought it would be dangerous for a woman to marry a man who might have been having sex, and possibly have contracted a disease, and she said "No, they could have a blood test first." Women's sexual behavior outside of marriage is highly stigmatized, and frequently discussed with abhorrence and disgust by both men and women. Almost every informant questioned perceived the separate standards for male and female sexuality as "natural."

Given that female heterosexuality is perceived to be a morally dangerous affair, and that female same-sex activity is negated as a likely possibility, many lesbians, with proper discretion, can engage in homoerotic activity free of much public notice. Same-sex friendships and intimacy are the norm in Thailand and, according to informants close companionship between girls, including hand-holding and spending the night together, is not presumed to be sexual. Non-lesbian informants told me of the common practice of school-girl crushes, calling each other *phi* and *norng* (kinship terms between older and younger siblings, but which are also used intimately between couples). *Tom-dee* couples are common among school girls, and according to informants, parents view these relationships as passing phases, soon to be replaced with a "natural" heterosexual relationship and marriage, a view commonly supported by magazine articles warning parents of the new homosexual "fashions."

Although accurate data are hard to find, from the stories that my informants have told me, and anecdotal evidence from other acquaintances, I believe that female homosexual activity is common, albeit not obvious to outsiders. Casual sexual activity between women, and crushes and even love affairs between girls and young women do not exclude the reality that most young women will marry and have families. Western concepts of two mutually exclusive categories of sexual beings, homosexual and heterosexual, are not widely held by Thais, especially concerning women. The gender-disruptive display of masculine-identified lesbian women, *toms*, makes female homosexuality more apparent, and therefore more disturbing, for the Thai discourse on female sexuality; hence, I believe, the rash of anti-*tom-dee* articles in the media.

There is a precedent to the gender-crossing *tom* in the Thai cultural discourse of gender–the *kathoey*. Tom informants recalled that when they were young they either heard of other girls or were themselves called *kathoey* due to their stereotypical male behavior, or preference for wearing male clothing. *Kathoey* is an historical third gender category that used to be applied to both men and women who transgressed gender norms. The common contemporary use of the term *kathoey* usually refers to cross-dressing homosexual men, although informants report that, especially in rural settings, *kathoey* is still used to indicate both boys' and girls' non-normative gender behavior. *Kathoey*, unlike *tom*, did not necessarily refer to the *sexuality* of the person referred to, but rather to their gender identity. *Kathoey* referred to the girls' typically un-feminine behavior, like the way "tomboy" might be used in Western societies, and not as a reference to their perceived (future) sexual orientation.

Som, a working class woman in her early thirties, grew up in several rural villages in Surin, a province in Northeastern Thailand. Som recalled how as a child of around twelve years old, she liked to wear male clothing,[9] cut her hair very short, and play rough games with boys. Som laughed as she remembered the villagers playfully calling her *pak-ham*, a Northeastern Thai term of endearment for young boys. Other villagers would call her the central Thai word *kathoey*. Som did not take these labels as a reference to her sexuality, and did not believe that others intended to imply she was a lesbian by calling attention to her masculine behavior. Later in life, Som had several sexual relationships with women, but did not consider herself to be a *tom*, or identify with the increasingly recognized term "lesbian," or link her sexual experiences with women with her earlier masculine persona. Som married when she was eighteen and soon had a child, like many of the other young village women. Sexual behavior between Thai women does not necessarily mean a self-consciousness of oneself as homosexual, or as being different from "normal" women.

While *kathoey* was essentially a third gender category, sexual activity between women was called *len pheuan*, glossed as "play a friend," (distinct from "play with friends," *len kap pheuan*). *Len pheuan* is now a somewhat antiquated expression, and not widely used any more. Homosexual *len pheuan* activity and *kathoey* transgender identity have now become conflated and transformed into the terms *tom-dee*, with both the gender-crossing *tom* and her feminine partner being discursively marked. *Dee*, however, is a much looser term than *tom*, and does not usually carry the same intense sense of personal sexual identity that *tom* does.

Toms often described *dees* as bisexual, or "normal" women in that they are attracted to masculine partners. Toy, a middle-aged professional urban *tom* gave a typical summary of older *toms'* perspectives on *dees*, "The *dees*, they are all straight women, that is why I am broken-hearted, because [the dees] are going to marry." I asked her if she knew of any *dees* that really wanted a long-term relationship with a *tom* instead of a man, and she replied, "I've never met one like that, nobody is like that." In fact, most *toms* told me that they thought being with a man was better for *dees* anyway, as it was more "natural." Toy said, "I am not selfish, if a woman says she can go on living a normal life with a man, I'll say, please go, to go is better, because I probably can't give her very much." Actually, many of the *dees* I spoke with were exclusively lesbian and wanted to find a *tom* to fall in love with and build a life together, or were already in long-term relationships with toms. Nevertheless, many *toms* perceive *dees* as only temporarily interested in homosexual relationships, which tends to correspond to general views of outsiders as represented in the media and conversations with non-lesbians. The ability of *dees* to cross-over into heterosexual relationships is a significant dimension of *tom-dee* dynamics, as *toms* have often described feeling that one day their partner might leave them for a "respectable" life.

Financial concerns, as well as desires for children, have influenced informants' decisions to maintain heterosexual relationships while still being romantically involved with women. Ot is a wealthy married woman in her late forties, elegantly dressed, and living a comfortable existence with a mobile phone and country-club memberships. Ot has maintained a fourteen-year relationship with a *tom*, Aa. Ot explains that she occasionally sleeps with her husband out of a sense of duty, but when Aa touches her she says she immediately feels aroused. Her husband is the economic anchor of the family and the father of Ot's child, and she says she could not leave him, but she insists her erotic, emotional, and romantic self is bound to Aa. Ot said that she decided to have a second child because Aa wanted to be a parent.

Not only *dees* consider financial issues when making decisions about marriage. Nit and Mot are both commercial sex workers in their twenties and have engaged in heterosexual relationships as part of their business, and sexual relationships with women for their own personal satisfaction. Nit identifies as a *dee*, and Mot as a *tom*, but they both have had long-term relationships with male clients and Mot is currently engaged to a Western man. Mot explains, "I have to think about my future," and describes her plan to study for three years while her husband supports her. Mot says that if the marriage does not work out she will still have a chance for a better future. The economic necessity of heterosexual relationships is not perceived as a contradiction to their personal interests in lesbian relationships.

TOMS AND MASCULINITY

Tom identity is a fluid concept structured by class, ethnic, and educational background, but the idiom of masculinity, or "maleness," is a consistent feature of being a *tom*. What being a *tom* means specifically is a topic of debate among *toms* themselves. For example, *toms* criticize other *toms* (in letters to *Anjareesan*,[10] in social interactions with other *toms*, and in interviews) for not taking responsibility for their "wives" and families, being too weak and vulnerable to *dees*, being too much like men in terms of aggressiveness, drinking, or vulgar speech and their behavior towards women. However, *toms* and *dees* I have talked to, as well as outsiders, usually agree that in some basic way *toms* "want to be men," are "like men," or even are "men."

In June 1995 a visiting American professor of psychology gave a talk at Thammasat University in Bangkok on the topic of current psychological theories of homosexuality. The professor's statement, "Some women have sex with other women but do not consider themselves as lesbians," was mistakenly translated with the word "man" (*phu-chai*) replacing "lesbian." After murmurings from members of the audience who understood English, and a discussion between the translator and speaker, the sentence was retranslated with the English word "lesbian" carried over into the Thai. Apparently "lesbian" was an untranslatable culturally specific term.

Responding to my question of, "How are *toms* like men?" informants replied in such a repetitive way that their answers soon became predictable: *toms* are strong, leaders, dress and act like men, are "womanizers" (*jao-chu*), and can or should take care of their "wives" (*mia, faen*). Mainstream society, and even *toms* and *dees* themselves, stereotype *toms* as engaging in activities that are widely held to be typical for Thai men, such a excessive drinking, smoking, gambling, and promiscuity. I believe that the use of these terms refers to cultural beliefs and expectations that Thai masculinity, as a conceptual category, is associated with sensual pleasures, and rough and tumble enjoyments. I have frequently heard *toms* criticizing other *toms* for these types of behaviors, saying that it is "acting like men." Thus, *toms* define themselves as being like men in that they are masculine, but at times will also criticize the ways *toms* are too much like men.

The inability to list a coherent and stable set of values defining the concept "masculinity" is evidenced in the frequent occurrence of *dees* defining *toms* in terms of "knavish" (*ke-re*) behaviors, and in the same breath, saying that their ideal *tom* does none of these activities. A woman wrote in a personal advertisement in a lesbian newsletter, "I want to meet a *tom* who is 100% *tom* in both her body and mind, who really dresses like a man, has short hair, and the personality of a leader . . . " (*Anjareesan* 1996, 3 (18), p. 31). The personal advertisement above also specifically requested a *tom* who does not engage in the baser masculine activities (smoking, etc.), indicating a belief on the part of the writer that many *toms* engage in these activities, but also that it is possible to find a "100% *tom*" who does not. I have interviewed many *toms* who do in fact gamble and drink a great deal, and who consider these behaviors as part of their *tom*-ness. Many women who claim a *tom* identity, and certainly many Thai men as well, do not engage in these activities, but these stereotypes are a code of culturally recognized masculine meanings that may be employed by *toms* as part of their self-identity. Or, alternatively, it might be reasoned that by virtue of their masculine identity, *toms* are granted more social freedom to engage in those activities that they find enjoyable than is possible for feminine women. While *toms* are clearly perceived to be "like men" in that both normative Thai men and *toms* are masculine, *toms*' masculinity differs from men's in terms of attitudes towards sexuality, and social dynamics between *toms* and *dees*.

TOM-DEE SEXUAL DYNAMICS

Sexual dynamics are an important part of *tom-dee* relationships, as they focus on both female pleasure and female sexual agency. Lesbian relationships in Thailand, like elsewhere, are also based on love, companionship, and partnership, and it would be incorrect to construe my focus on sexual dynamics as insinuating that Thai lesbianism is solely about sex. However, a review of the ways that sexual dynamics between *tom-dee*s differ from heterosexual dynamics is important for understanding some basic premises of *tom* masculinity. Both *tom*s and *dee*s consider *tom*s to be the "active" partner in sex. *Tom-dee* sexual relationships, according to both *tom* and *dee* informants, are based on the primary importance of the feminine partner's sexual satisfaction. *Tom*s pride themselves in being sensitive and intuitive to their partners emotional and physical needs, typical qualities that are valued for Thai women, not Thai men. *Tom*s and *dee*s have described the "untouchability" of many *tom*s, that is, either *tom*s or *dee*s refusing to let the *tom* be touched during sex. Some *tom*s do not undress during sex, and do not allow the *dee* to see them naked at any time. Masculine lesbians' untouchability is a phenomenon found in many lesbian communities throughout the world that have established gender role-playing identities, including the United States in the middle-part of this century and, particularly pertinent for the study of Thai lesbians, in other Southeast Asian societies (see Faderman, 1991; Kennedy & Davis, 1994; Reinfelder, 1996).

Feminists have criticized lesbian gender role-playing practices as imitating oppressive heterosexual patterns, especially the masculine partner who is perceived as appropriating male prerogatives. For example, criticizing masculine-feminine lesbian couples in the Philippines, and especially the masculine women's untouchability, Malu Marin (1996, p. 47) says,

> Many non-feminist lesbians insist on perpetuating male/female dynamics in their relationships. The butch partner, or *pars*, acts out the male role, while the femme partner, or *mars*, acts out the female role. Thus, the dynamics of their relationship are derived from heterosexist patterns, with the *pars* functioning as the provider, in terms of economic and financial support. This role is even more pronounced in the sexual aspect of the relationship. The *pars* play out the male (dominant) role more pronouncedly in

the sex act, priding themselves as the 'doers' or 'givers' in sexual intimacy. This means that they alone are responsible for the sexual pleasure experienced by the *mars*, and therein lies the power, that they can be as equipped as 'real' men in making love to women. One of the most sacred tenets of this dynamic is that *pars* do not allow themselves even to be touched by their partner. To allow this would mean becoming 'women' themselves, and as 'women' they would be stripped of their power over the *mars* in the relationship. The *pars* provokes awe while posturing as a man, with male privilege and power extended to her as part of the illusion.

It is not clear from this description if these are attitudes commonly held by Philippine *pars-mars* themselves, or are the views of the author. If these *are* attitudes of *pars-mars* couples themselves, their involvement in such relationships is perplexing. Why would the feminine women choose the *pars* as partners rather than men? I believe that the evidence from Thai *tom-dee* relationships demonstrates that lesbian role-playing relationships are not, and cannot, imitate the structural dynamics of heterosexual relationships. *Toms* are women, and although their status as *toms* grants them certain masculine privileges, they do not fill the social roles occupied by men in Thai society. Ting, a well-educated urban *tom* in her late-twenties, pointed out that *toms'* untouchability can stem from insecurity and embarrassment over their female bodies, and fear that their lovers do not want to be reminded that they are not with "real" men. Ting posed the question, "Do you think Thai men are that insecure over their body [that they would not allow it to be touched or shown to their partners]?"

Toms, by virtue of their masculine identity, and their lack of participation in heterosexual sex, are granted freedom from the moral restrictions applied to other women. *Toms* can positively value their own sexuality with enthusiasm, as can Thai men. Feminine women who brag about sexual ability, experience, and sexual needs would be speedily condemned as prostitutes, and slandered with one of the numerous Thai aphorisms for such a sexually experienced woman, e.g., *ee tua* ("prostitute," "slut"), *kari* ("prostitute," "slut"), *ee hee yet* ("fucking cunt"), *samsorn* ("promiscuous"). *Toms* talk with excitement among themselves about women they are attracted to, sexual techniques and experiences. *Toms* can pursue partners openly, brag about experiences, and express sexual needs openly. The trade-off of women gaining sexual agency as *toms*, explained Ting, is that *toms* who strictly adhere to the ideas of *toms'* untouchability provide sexual attention and pleasure to their *dees*, while their own sexual needs are left to their own devices. To break away from rigid feminine social roles, and be the one who pursues is a good feeling, said Ting, but the role you must play as a *tom* has its own rules.

What it means to be masculine is not only determined by *toms*, or men, but also by the feminine women who will judge them. *Dees* have often complained to me about how rigid *toms* are about their untouchability. *Toms*, on the other hand, have often expressed frustration with the pressures that *dees* put on them to be "real *toms*." Bang, a 34 year old *tom* from a working class background, confided to another *tom*, Com, how her past lover would ridicule her if she would ask her partner to perform for her sexually. Com, a well-educated Bangkok woman in her forties, sympathized with the humiliation Bang's lover caused, and related how one of her past lovers would ridicule her by saying that her other *tom* lovers were "real" *toms* and did not require the *dees* to be "men" for them.

According to both *toms* and *dees*, one of the most salient qualities of a *tom* is her ability to intuit her partners' needs, both emotional and sexual. *Toms* pride themselves on their ability to be sensitive to their partners' feelings. *Toms* and *dees* have both emphasized to me during interviews and discussions that a *tom*'s sensitivity is based on an appreciation for what women want. Jackson describes how some working class Thai men scarify and wear rubber bands on their penis in the belief that this is pleasurable for women, even though all the female sex workers interviewed in a safe-sex project reported these devices caused pain, not pleasure (Jackson, 1995, pp. 48-49). *Toms'* willingness to satisfy their partners sexually, without their partners even touching the *toms'* bodies, is only one dimension of *toms'* commitment to pleasing women. A group of *toms* sitting at a bar drinking and boasting about sexual exploits, reprimanded each other for not knowing how to please *dees*, "Do you notice if her drink is full?" they asked one. My own observations of families with their children, and the way grown women offer hospitality, support informants' claim that Thai girls, not boys, are taught to anticipate and be aware of others' needs constantly.

Toms openly acknowledged feeling that *dees* are with them because they know how to please and satisfy them, and that is what they had to focus on in order to compete with men who the *toms* felt could offer families and social respectability. *Dees* describe *toms* as soft, tender, intuitive, and understanding. Many *dees* have told me that toms have the ability to understand them in ways that men cannot, a sentiment often shared by *toms*. Kluay, a 24 year-old urban, middle class woman, says that she likes being a *tom* because she feels strong, like she can take care of her partner and give her sexual pleasure. *Toms* are better for women, says Kluay, because they are soft (*num-nuan*) and can understand a woman in ways a man cannot. Interestingly, Kluay described both being strong and soft as qualities that typify *toms*. Com complained that she feels she cannot be weak, and cry, for example, because she is a *tom*. Com has also expressed pride in sexual conquests, and pride in her ability to be extremely attentive and caring for her partners. Contradictions in definitions of ideal gender behavior are not unique to *tom* masculinity. Discourses on Buddhism and popular perceptions of Thai manhood describe men both as being more sexual than women (see above) and also more capable of spiritual renunciation of material, and sexual desires.

Not only is the sex between *toms* and *dees* different from heterosexual sex in terms of the former's focus on feminine sexuality and *toms'* willingness to be sensitive, lesbian sex in Thailand does not carry the same sexual taboos or restrictions on women's behavior that heterosexual sex does. Both lesbian and heterosexual women have explained that an advantage of having sex with *toms* is that one does not risk scorn for *sia*,[11] adultery, loss of virginity, or promiscuous behavior as a woman most certainly would face if engaged in sexual relationships with men. Ot, when questioned on how her husband reacts to her long-term relationship with her *tom* lover, says he accepts it and shows no interest or jealousy in their private lives. He even expresses sympathy for Ot when she goes through her periodic depressions over troubles with her and Aa's relationship. Before she was married, Ot had relationships with several men, and her husband (then boyfriend) at that time was indeed jealous. But since Ot is no longer involved with other men and has Aa to look after her, they have all reached an agreement. Ot's sexual relationship with Aa is not perceived as adulterous by observers, including Ot's husband, family, and friends, and is perhaps even seen as a guard against unacceptable adulterous behavior with other men. While Aa engages in many of the stereotypical behaviors of Thai men and *toms* alike, such as drinking and gambling, she also depends on Ot for financial support, and takes most of the responsibility for the care of Ot's child.

The burdens that heterosexual relationships place on Thai women were among the reasons women gave for enjoying relationships with *toms*. Bor, a 33 year old *dee* factory worker from a poor rural background, stressed her unwillingness to carry the burdens that relationships with men entail. She saw her friends and other workers get pregnant, married, and raise families, and the hardship in their lives increase. For Bor, relationships with *toms* have provided a way to explore love and sex free of the onerous responsibilities and risks that sexual relations with men are sure to involve.

Toms' masculinity is not a quality granted them by their bodies. For Thai men as well, masculine gender is a complex system of meanings that must be continually enacted in order to conform to social expectations.[12] Nevertheless, many *toms* see themselves at a disadvantage to Thai men in terms of presenting themselves as long-term partners for women, and usually explain this disadvantage in terms of their female bodies–the enduring reminder of their femaleness. *Toms* have often expressed insecurity that even though they are attentive and affectionate in ways that most Thai men are not, they still suffer a disadvantage in that the *toms* perceived women to be more willing to form long-term relationships with men, or prefer heterosexual sex. One *tom* reflected that she used to believe that her girlfriends wanted a lover with a male body, but experience has shown her that her lovers are very satisfied with her as a woman. Nevertheless, *toms'* insecurity over *dees'* commitments to lesbian relationships might be somewhat justified in that there is very little social support for long-term lesbian couples, and plenty of social pressure to marry.

Ban, an 18 year old factory worker from Surin, expressed excitement over her recent love affair with a woman, but when asked if she would ideally like to have a long-term relationship with a woman, she looked downcast. Ban said that she was too poor and would not be able to support her girlfriend like a man could, and "she would grow to hate me." "I don't think it would be possible to find a woman willing to be poor with me," Ban explained. Although poor men certainly worry about being able to support a wife, Ban entirely ruled out the possibility of being accepted as a woman's partner. It is not only poor *toms* who feel that they cannot provide for women as is expected of men. Kluay, with a college degree and professional employment, said that she does not feel that it would be possible to be in a long term relationship with a woman because she felt all women need to get married. A *dee,* over-hearing this conversation, challenged "Isn't she a woman? Why does she think she doesn't need to get married [but *dees* do]?" conveying a sense that *toms* do not always understand *dees'* commitments to lesbian relationships in that *toms* do not recognize that *dees* might want to be with a woman as much as a *tom* does.

There is a common perception among *toms* that *dees* only have relationships with *toms* because they want to have the sexual attention that *toms* provide, but do not take *toms* seriously as life partners. Kluay said that she would probably get bored with one person if they were together for a long time anyway. Kluay wanted to avoid becoming like some of the older *toms* she sees–so vulnerable to the *dees'* rejection. She does not cry over girlfriends, and will not be a victim of one, she asserts. In contrast to Kluay's bravado about not wanting to be tied down to one person, she sighed that if she was a man she could find somebody she really likes and get married.

Toms and *dees* creatively produce their relationships and home lives, often in ways distinct from typical Thai heterosexual patterns. Tuk is a *tom* in her late thirties who has been involved with a woman several years her senior for over ten years. They live together in Pattaya where her lover, Phoon, is a commercial sex worker in the bars that cater to foreign tourists. Five years ago Phoon had a child by one of the customers. Tuk raises the child as her own, providing most of the daily child care. She feels very strongly about her responsibilities to her family, and vows that no matter what happens she will stand by her wife (*mia*) and child. Tuk calls herself a man and uses masculine speech (using the masculine pronoun *phom* ["I"], and *khrap-phom*, a polite sentence particle used by men). Tuk combines familiar rhetoric about male responsibility to support wife and children with a non-conventional family arrangement. Both couples, Tuk and Phoon, and Ot and Aa (mentioned above), did not consider it contradictory that the *tom* in the couple was the one primarily responsible for child care (it is certainly atypical for men to be responsible for childcare in most Thai heterosexual relationships). In her own view, Tuk is both the masculine head of the family and lovingly responsible for the childcare of a girl fathered by an unknown client of her wife, while her wife earns the money to support the family. Tuk says, "This is Pattaya, we have our own society here."

CONCLUSION

I have argued that *toms* have created an identity in which they have appropriated certain aspects of normative masculinity (e.g., sexual and social freedom), and aspects of normative femininity (sensitivity to others' needs). In so doing, I contend that *toms* express an oblique opposition to normative Thai gender codes by rejecting social expectations that women will embody femininity, and providing re-interpretations for the enactment of masculinity. However, this opposition is only partial, as *toms* often expect other women to uphold the same codes of normative femininity that they have rejected in their own lives. Kep, a wealthy *tom* in her late 50s who lives alone, expressed concern that most young women will want to be with her mainly for her money, which makes her unwilling to pursue a stable relationship with anyone. She said that in the past she had on occasion visited go-go bars and paid female sex workers for sex, but she now discouraged other *toms* from doing so, for fear that they would get involved with the wrong type of woman. She says she needs a proper woman, well dressed and well mannered. Kep's attitudes towards women mirrored the general perception of mainstream Thai society that women should be pure and virtuous in order to be considered respectable partners.

Tom-dee identities provide an interesting site for the examination of the practice of gender as these identities are both derivative of stereotypical dominant Thai models of gender and unique formulations based on the specifics of lesbian practices and identities in Thailand. To refer to *tom-dee* practices as "role-playing" should not imply that these practices are somehow "artificial" in comparison to the ways that gender is employed by heterosexual men and women. Gender differences are used by both heterosexual and homosexual populations as erotic devices and social structuring mechanisms and neither practice is more "natural" than the other (see Butler, 1990; Newton, 1972).

NOTES

1. The unequivocal association of *tom* identity with lesbianism by *toms* marks a clear distinction from the English use of the expression "tom boy," which rarely directly implies lesbianism and is usually used in reference to children rather than adult women. I have therefore italicised *tom*, indicating that the term has been adopted into the Thai language with a unique meaning separate from the English root word.

2. "From gay to *tom-dee*: the strange world," *Pheuan Chiwit*, 1984, 2(6), 19.

3. According to informants' discussions of the positive aspects of their lives, being a *tom* is not solely determined by the desire for women sexually, but also by a desire for the independence and freedom afforded to men. Several *toms* said that their parents were even pleased to see their daughters as *toms* because they then would not have to worry about them being attacked at night or getting pregnant. A group of young women explained that in their all-girls boarding school there were so many lesbian couples that everyone had to decide at one point if they were a *tom* or a *dee*, and that most women chose to be *toms*, because, they said, who would want to be a *dee* and have to follow a *tom* around all the time? However, I have here chosen to focus on *toms*' sexuality because of the importance of sexual meanings to Thai definitions of masculinity.

4. In August 1995 a Thai newspaper carried the banner headline, "*Tom* Masters degree student kills herself [due to] relatives' ridicule" (*Thai Rath*, 8 August 1995, p. 1). In 1996 the same newspaper related the story of a *tom* who had committed suicide because of "teasing" ("Teased for being a *tom*, civil servant (grade 6) drowns herself") (*Thai Rath*, 17 December 1996, p. 1). Although I suspect these stories made their way into the notoriously trashy newspaper because of their sensationalist qualities (i.e., homosexuality and violence, a popular theme in Thai tabloids), they also reflect the reality of the extremely serious consequences of "loss of face."

5. All names of informants are pseudonyms.

6. Cited in "Of love, lust and human nature," *The Nation*, 21 April 1997, p. C1.

7. The brochure is produced by an association of Thai NGOs, including the Centre for Labour Information Service and Training (CLIST).

8. For example, a survey (Wiresit et al., 1991, quoted in Jackson 1995, p. 55) revealed that of almost three thousand men and women questioned, only 7.4 percent of men and 7.0 percent of women considered female-to-female caressing to be "sex," while 19.4 percent and 24.9 percent, respectively, considered the same acts between men and women to be "sex."

9. *Pha-khao-ma:* a patterned strip of sarong-like cloth wrapped around the waist and typically worn by men. Giving it a particularly masculine appearance, Som would twist one end of the *pha-khao-ma* and tuck it up between her legs.

10. *Anjareesan* is the newsletter produced by Anjaree, a Thai organisation which supports lesbians' rights and interests through the publication of a newsletter, group activities and lobbying. Anjaree is the only formal organisation in Thailand devoted specifically to supporting lesbians' rights.

11. Heterosexual sex is commonly referred to as *dai-sia*, where men "get" (*dai*) and women "lose" (*sia*).

12. See Butler (1990) for an analysis of gender as "performance."

REFERENCES

Benedict, R. (1934). *Patterns of culture*. Boston: Houghton Mifflin.

Blackwood, E. (Ed.). (1986). *Anthropology and homosexual behavior*. New York: The Haworth Press, Inc.

Butler, J. (1990). *Gender trouble: Feminism and the subversion of identity*. New York: Routledge.

Errington, S. (1990). Recasting sex, gender, and power: A theoretical and regional overview. In J.M. Atkinson & S. Errington (Eds.), *Power and difference: Gender in island Southeast Asia* (pp. 1-58). Stanford, California: Stanford University Press.

Faderman, L. (1991). *Odd girls and twilight lovers: A history of lesbian life in twentieth-century America*. New York: Penguin.

Foucault, M. (1978). *The History of Sexuality, Vol. 1*. London: Penguin.

Gremaux, R. (1994). Woman becomes man in the Balkans. In G. Herdt (Ed.), *Third sex, third gender* (pp. 241-81). New York: Zone Books.

Irvine, W. (1984, August). Decline of village spirit cults and growth of urban spirit mediumship: The persistence of spirit beliefs, the position of women and modernization. In *Spirit cults and the position of women in Northern Thailand* (pp. 315-24), *Mankind 14*(4), Special Issue 3.

Jackson, P. (1995). *Dear Uncle Go: Male homosexuality in Thailand*. Bangkok: Bua Luang Books.

Kennedy, E.L., & Davis, M.D. (1994). *Boots of leather, slippers of gold: The history of a lesbian community*. New York: Penguin.

Keyes, C. (1984). Mother or mistress but never a monk: Buddhist notions of female gender in rural Thailand. *American Ethnologist, 96*(3), 223-41.

Kirsch, T. (1985). Text and context: Buddhist sex roles/culture of gender revisited. *American Ethnologist, 12*(2), 302-20.

Marin, M. (1996). Stolen strands: The in and out lives of lesbians in the Philippines. In M. Reinfelder (Ed.), *Amazon to zami: Towards a global lesbian feminism* (pp. 30-55). London: Cassell.

Matthana Chetame. (1996). *Withi chiwit lae chiwit khrorpkhrua khorng ying rak ying*. [The lifestyle and family life of women who love women]. Master's thesis, Department of Anthropology, Thammasat University, Bangkok.

Mead, M. (1949). *Male and female: A study of the sexes in a changing world*. New York: Morrow.

Mosse, G.L. (1985). *Nationalism and sexuality: Middle-class morality and sexual norms in modern Europe*. Madison, Wisconsin: University of Wisconsin Press.

Nanda, S. (1990). *Neither man nor woman: The Hijras of India*. Belmont, California: Wadworth Publishing Company.

Newton, E. (1972). *Mother camp: Female impersonators in America*. Chicago: University of Chicago Press.

Niramol Prudthatorn. (1991). Prostitution: Attitudes are the problem. *Friends of Women Newsletter, 2*(1), 14-15.

Ong, A., & Peletz, M.G. (Eds.). (1995). *Bewitching women, pious men: Gender and body politics in Southeast Asia*. Berkeley, California: University of California Press.

Reinfelder, M. (Ed.). (1996). *Amazon to zami: Towards a global lesbian feminism*. London: Cassell.

Sanitsuda Ekachai. (1991). How did we get to this state of affairs? *Friends of Women Newsletter, 2*(1), 16-17.

Scott, J.W. (1988). *Gender and the politics of history*. New York: Columbia University Press.

Stoler, A. (1991). Carnal knowledge and imperial power: Gender, race, and morality in colonial Asia. In M. di Leonardo (Ed.). *Gender at the crossroads of knowledge: Feminist anthropology in the postmodern era* (pp. 51-101). Berkeley, California: University of California Press.

Took Took Thongthiraj. (1994). Toward a struggle against invisibility: Love between women in Thailand. *Amerasian Journal, 20*(1), 45-58.

Van Esterik, P. (1982). Laywomen in Theravada Buddhism. In P. Van Esterik (Ed.), *Women of Southeast Asia* (pp. 55-78). Dekalb, Illinois: Northern Illinois University Press.

Wiresit Sittitrai, Brown, T., & Sirapone Virulrak. (1991). Patterns of bisexuality in Thailand. In R. Tielman, M. Carballo, & A. Hendriks (Eds.). *Bisexuality and HIV/AIDS–A global perspective* (pp. 97-117). Buffalo, NY: Prometheus Books.

Transformations of Transgender: The Case of the Thai *Kathoey*

Han ten Brummelhuis

SUMMARY. Transgender males, called *kathoey* in Thai, are an ancient and widespread phenomenon in Asia and especially Southeast Asia. In this paper I consider Thai transgender males from a more contemporary perspective, focusing on changes in the definition and presentation of *kathoey* in the last two decades. These changes are related to alterations of the sex scene in western countries, the application of new medical technologies, and the development in Thailand of a new *kathoey* "career." I base my study on in-depth interviews conducted in Thailand and the Netherlands. I discuss the inadequacy of conceptualizing *kathoey* as a category of homosexuals, arguing that *kathoey* first and foremost have to be seen as women. From this perspective, *kathoeys'* relationships with the partners they prefer become more understandable. I also interpret *kathoeys'* preference for *farang* (Caucasian) partners, the meanings they ascribe to having a sex-change operation, and their sexual behaviour from the perspective of considering them as women. I conclude with recommendations for social service work among *kathoey* and a reflection on the theory of sexual and erotic excitement. *[Article copies available for a fee from The Haworth Document Delivery Service: 1-800-342-9678. E-mail address: getinfo@haworthpressinc.com]*

Address correspondence to: Han ten Brummelhuis, Department of Anthropology, University of Amsterdam, Oudezijds Achterburgwal 185, 1012 DK Amsterdam, The Netherlands.

[Haworth co-indexing entry note]: "Transformations of Transgender: The Case of the Thai *Kathoey*." Brummelhuis, Han ten. Co-published simultaneously in *Journal of Gay & Lesbian Social Services* (The Haworth Press, Inc.) Vol. 9, No. 2/3, 1999, pp. 121-139; and: *Lady Boys, Tom Boys, Rent Boys: Male and Female Homosexualities in Contemporary Thailand* (ed: Peter A. Jackson, and Gerard Sullivan) The Haworth Press, Inc., 1999, pp. 121-139; and: *Lady Boys, Tom Boys, Rent Boys: Male and Female Homosexualities in Contemporary Thailand* (ed: Peter A. Jackson, and Gerard Sullivan) Harrington Park Press, an imprint of The Haworth Press, Inc., 1999, pp. 121-139. Single or multiple copies of this article are available for a fee from The Haworth Document Delivery Service [1-800-342-9678, 9:00 a.m. - 5:00 p.m. (EST). E-mail address: getinfo@haworthpressinc.com].

121

INTRODUCTION

During my first visits to Thailand (1975-76) I became aware of the existence of transgender males or what Thai people variously called "lady-boys" or *kathoey*[1] in a way I never had been conscious of in my own society. The *kathoey* I saw did not reflect an atmosphere of pathology, and often looked quite attractive. They hassled tourists on the streets, but appeared to be part of the everyday scene of Thai society. Later I had the opportunity to talk to them and to learn more about their motivations, and I became less naive. In a sense, this paper is a reflection on my impressions and on my research data about Thai *kathoey*.

The study of sexuality has revealed and produced many sexual categories, with the rise of new categories and the deconstruction of older essentialist categories like "homosexual" and "heterosexual." A recent volume on bisexualities in different cultures demonstrates what a wide range of sexual identities accompany so-called bisexual behaviour. The editor concludes that these studies demonstrate the necessity of "in-depth study of the subjectivities of those involved" (Aggleton 1996, p. 2) when we want to understand and explain what actually takes place. This is an approach I wish to follow in this paper. I will describe and interpret my interview material with the intention to make the reader more sensitive to the categories we normally use when talking about Thai *kathoey*. I will especially point to the inadequacy of considering the *kathoey* in terms of notions of homosexuality. First, a few more words are required to introduce my subject.

My focus will be on the last two decades and I wish especially to clarify changes that have taken place in this period. I certainly hope to avoid an analysis in terms of a uniform Thai or Southeast Asian culture. This is not to deny, however, that in the last few years several publications have pointed to similar culturally supported models for male-to-female transgender roles elsewhere in Southeast Asia (see Coleman et al. [1992] about the *acault* in Burma; Oetomo [1991] about the Indonesian *waria*; and Tan [1995] about the *bakla* in the Philippines). Indeed, it is easy to unearth older observations of this phenomenon and to establish the wide acceptance and social integration of male cross-dressers in many parts of traditional Southeast Asia. *Kathoey*, for example, are reported to participate as a group in village festivals and in certain professional activities (e.g., hairdressing, cooking) and historical sources enable us to trace them back to earlier centuries. We have to be aware that there is a relevant Southeast Asian and South Asian (see Nanda 1990) cultural and historical context of the Thai *kathoey*.

I intend to travel an alternative itinerary, which departs from recent developments. Nowadays, Thai *kathoey* can be found in many cities in Europe. Migration networks have been established that connect the Thai countryside with places such as Amsterdam, Berlin, Paris, Rome, Dusseldorf and Copenhagen. Furthermore, *kathoey* are not part of the older transvestite scene in these cities, which in the past was connected with the local gay scene. Taking Amsterdam as an example, it is clear that Thai *kathoey* have managed to acquire a segment of the heterosexual prostitution scene. Striking in these developments is the connection between local Thai ambitions and cultural forms on the one hand, and the gratification of Western male desires on the other hand–a particular case of the globalization of local patterns. One of the results of this development is the creation of what I would provisionally like to call a global *kathoey* "career." Switching to the female sex offers opportunities to Thai village youths that are not available to them in other ways. In particular, it creates opportunities to leave a poor and boring countryside, to acquire some wealth and even to migrate to another country.

The category of *kathoey* is an elusive one, not only for a Westerner, but also for the Thai (see Jackson and De Lind van Wijngaarden in this volume). The term *kathoey* itself is ambiguous, even when used by *kathoey* themselves. In translation it is often rendered as "transvestite," "transgender" or "transsexual." In recent years there has been attention to *kathoey* in the popular Thai press and media and *kathoey* has also entered scholarly literature on sexuality (e.g., Herdt 1997, pp. 147-150). Confusingly, the term has often been translated as "homosexual" and it is also not uncommonly used for any kind of man who has some feminine characteristics. But with the coming into existence of a masculine gay identity in Thailand, the term is more and more used exclusively for male cross-dressers. However, in this circle it is not a particularly well-liked term that can readily be used in addressing persons. Indeed, *kathoey* can be a threatening term for persons who are trying to pass as females. People whom others label as *kathoey* often prefer to call themselves "a second type of woman" (*phu-ying praphet sorng*) or "a transformed goddess" (*nang-fa jam-*

laeng). We may also find certain regional, social, cultural and individual variations in the use of the term. My concern here is exclusively with born males who opt for the female gender role.

My data are based on different contacts over the years, but especially on a series of systematic interviews conducted over the last four years. The interviews took place in Thailand and in Amsterdam. In Bangkok and Chiang Mai I approached *kathoey* at tourist locations and tried to establish good conditions for a formal meeting on another day. In Amsterdam I met them at Thai shops, a Thai temple or through Thai friends. The core of the material consists of twenty systematic interviews that follow core themes, but I must admit that only eleven interviews addressed the questions which I consider most relevant. A further complication is that both the conception and the realisation of the *kathoey* role in Thailand have changed in the last two decades and my own perception has also been modified. I will present my thoughts from my current perspective and understanding, and speak about *kathoey* in the sense of persons who choose the female gender. Further, I will not differentiate systematically between migrant *kathoey* living in Amsterdam or Europe and *kathoey* living in Thailand. I do not pretend to present a representative study of the whole population for which the label *kathoey* may be used. My intention is to present a tentative interpretation of the "logic" of what I consider as an ideal type of the recent reconfiguration of the *kathoey*.

CHANGES IN THE KATHOEY ROLE

The changes regarding *kathoey* that have taken place since the last two decades relate to concepts and categories as well as to the realisation of the *kathoey* role in social life. From a word that originally covered all forms of more-or-less feminine male same-sex behaviour, it has developed into a word used almost exclusively used for males who prefer the female gender role, i.e., cross-dressers, transsexuals and varieties in-between. That is, *kathoey* has begun more and more to denote "transgender," although even in this usage it largely remains an outsider's qualification. There is no definitive meaning and definitions continue to be fluid. The changes in the last two decades are, for instance, reflected in the "conquest" by Thai *kathoey* of a substantial segment of the sex work market in Europe. At least three developments can be distinguished that have created differences between what it meant to be a *kathoey* when I first visited Thailand in 1975 and today in 1997.

First, there have been changes in the Western sex scene, which can be characterized as a masculinization of "gay" and homosexual men (Levine 1992). The result was a gradual–and possibly incomplete–shift of a type of transvestism or transgenderism from a homosexual to a heterosexual scene. Notably, migrant Thai *kathoey* and Latin American transvestites living in Europe took advantage of this development and at the same time intensified it. From presentations given at the International AIDS Conference in Yokohama in 1994 (Morelli et al. 1994; Serre et al. 1994) one gets the impression that Latin American, and especially Brazilian, transvestites tend to dominate the transgender sex work scene in Southern Europe, while migrant Thai workers dominate in the Northern European cities. In the last two years, however, Latin American transvestites have also begun working in some Northern European cities like Amsterdam. Most remarkable, however, is the fact that the space both groups exploit and the customers they attract, are no longer on the fringes of the gay scene, as once might have been expected. As concluded in an abstract at the 1994 Yokohama AIDS conference, " . . . most clients [of the transvestites] considered themselves as heterosexual" (Serre et al. 1994). This is a relevant observation and we will notice that it has implications for the conception of these "transvestites." The contradiction between homosexual and heterosexual cannot be solved adequately by defining broader categories like "bisexual" for the partners of transgender persons.

Second, the wide application of new medical technologies in the fields of surgery and endocrinology were instrumental in the creation of convincing–and highly marketable–examples of sex change. Applied to Southeast Asian males, the results seem to have been even more convincing. Many Thai, like some other Asians, appear to have no great reluctance to utilize the possibilities of cosmetic surgery now available. In addition, these developments gave cosmetic surgeons in Asia the opportunity to develop their practices at a greater speed than comparative Western specialists. Almost none of the twenty or so Thai transgendered persons I know in Amsterdam considered the possibility of utilizing the sex-change procedures available to them there, even under conditions of health insurance. They preferred to go back to Thailand to clinics that specialise in the reformation of individual body parts (e.g., head, nose, neck, breasts, genitals).

Third, in Thailand a kind of new *kathoey* "career" has developed. I refer here to a pattern of expectations that makes youths living even in remote provinces aware of the possibility of entering a new world by becoming a beautiful and well versed *kathoey*, often in a western-oriented market. It opens up a pathway with opportunities not imagined before (see the representation in the BBC documentary *Lady Boys*, produced in 1992 by Jeremy Marre). One stage of such a career has been documented in some of my interviews with cross-dressers in Thailand. For instance, the ambition to work with Westerners (or other "naive" but wealthy foreigners) or to find a Western partner, has been expressed as the underlying motivation for undergoing a sex-change operation and for the decision to migrate to a country where marriage registration as a female is possible. A later stage of this career can be observed in cities like Amsterdam, where some *kathoey* manage to acquire either high status and/or earn substantial amounts of money, some by selling sexual services, others by offering a sophisticated and self-conscious presentation of female beauty. At many places in Europe the Thai *kathoey* are often beauty "prizewinners." Their partners sometimes come from the higher classes (e.g., surgeons, lawyers, dentists, professors, etc.), and some who work in the sex business command higher prices than their female sex-worker counterparts. Such a global career witnesses a progress from a position that has been labelled as a cheaper prostitute (Jackson 1995, pp. 189-90) to the highest echelons of sex work in European cities.

ARE KATHOEY HOMOSEXUAL?

It is my conviction that the conceptualization of *kathoey* as a specific type of homosexual is misleading. Such a conceptualization is highly influenced by the western supposition of a dichotomy of two genders, and the assumption that a feminine role or the role of *kathoey* is preferred by homosexual men in societies that do not accept homosexuality. In other words, in this view the feminine role helps to make the sexual preference for men socially acceptable. Roles like *kathoey* are then seen as a modification of the homosexual role in a society that has difficulties with "straight homosexuality." I doubt the usefulness of this interpretation and abandon the conceptualization of *kathoey* in terms of homosexuality. In support of this I offer three arguments.

First, the assumption that Thai and other Southeast Asian cultures have great difficulty with "straight homosexuality" is not convincing. There is a general acceptance of close male relationships. There is little concern with what people do privately, although there is a low public acceptance of homosexual identities. It is difficult to find in these cultures examples of "homophobia" which are more familiar in Western countries. For instance, groups of males living closely together (such as on ships or in the army), are generally less obsessed with anxieties about homosexuality.

Second, it is extremely important to look at the partners of *kathoey*. They do not correspond to any image of a homosexual man. These men often have or have had girlfriends, and many return to having girlfriends after having had *kathoey* partners. It is no coincidence that Thai *kathoey* sex-workers in Europe locate their business within the precincts of heterosexual prostitution.

My third argument is personal, but not irrelevant. I must admit that I find some *kathoey* extremely attractive. When analyzing and reflecting upon this reaction, I cannot find a ground to conclude that they exploit hidden or unconscious homoerotic or homosexual feelings. On the contrary, they are capable of playing a feminine sexual role convincingly.

I conclude that *kathoey* in the first instance have to be seen as women. Their female gender explains more adequately why (and how) they love men, than their love for men explains their femininity. The possibility that some Thai become *kathoey* because they like men is more and more improbable. The changes over the last two decades have seen further feminization of *kathoey*. As we have seen, this development has been stimulated by the new possibilities of plastic surgery and endocrinology, by the rise of a gay movement and by opportunities provided in the global market.

INDIVIDUAL VARIATIONS AND "INNER DRIVE"

My description of a *kathoey* career reveals that there is a substantial leeway for variation in personal, social and cultural construction. *Kathoey* seems to be a Thai (or Southeast Asian) sexual category that shows a particular social and cultural elasticity. It is not rooted exclusively in internal motivations, let alone in biological scripts. Often, however, we come across the assumption that in the case of *kathoey* male-to-female transgender we see a clear failure in the biological sex script. It is beyond my capacity to discuss this, although I allow myself the space to at least ask whether this "failure" is uniform or allows again for many variations. Even if it is uniform, there must be many different ways to develop or deny it. I will concentrate on the other end: on the socially and culturally constructed form or career which allows for many individual variations.

The attraction of such a career has created a situation in which not all *kathoey* are motivated by even a strong, deep and identical psychological motive. One can sometimes hear *kathoey* complain about other *kathoey* who undergo a gender or sex change for money alone, and who are disparagingly called *kathoey thiam* or "artificial *kathoey*." An important question is, therefore, what proportion of persons are entering this career out of an inner motive and what proportion are acting more from an economic motive? In other words, do we find here something similar to what Ringrose described centuries ago as "males who became eunuchs not from an essential desire to have a female body . . . they sought the prestige and the privilege of the eunuch's position in the Byzantine court" (quoted by Herdt 1994, p. 38). The suggestion is therefore that some *kathoey* seek "the prestige and privilege" of getting access to new opportunities, becoming the registered wife of a western man, a citizen of a western country, or getting the chance to make money out of their newly acquired beauty. In several interviews this was a recurring theme. On the one hand, there was a desire to acquire female gender, while on the other hand there was an expectation of gaining access to new sources of wealth. Another source of individual differentiation between *kathoey* is in how far they are prepared to go in accepting physical or cosmetic changes.

If I am right in my assumption that being a *kathoey* is more about gender identity than about sexual orientation, then we could expect that sexual desire is not the dominant motivation for having a sex change. Outstanding is their ambition to be accepted or loved as a female. Sexual gratification is rather an instrument within strategies to reach this wider objective. My information on *kathoey* sexual behaviour is, on first appearance, quite confusing. Some *kathoey* only like to be embraced and be close to a partner and do not particularly like more specific sexual acts, only tolerating being penetrated and often seeing their penis as a source of embarrassment. Others insist on retaining the pleasure derived from their penis and sometimes like to penetrate their partners, as well as being penetrated. This seems to suggest further individual differences. A complicating possibility is that there may be quite a difference between the "public image" of *kathoey* and the individual lived realities. However, taking all this information into account, I consider my dominant impression that sexuality does not count that much to be reliable. Sexuality is accepted, since it is part of "the game." That her body is being admired and completely accepted as female is more important to a *kathoey*. One informant, Lek, even stated: "As soon as I am taken from behind [anally penetrated], all excitement disappears immediately."

PARTNERS OF KATHOEY

How are these transgendered males able to attract other men? The first part of the answer must be that the *kathoey*–at least some of them–are indeed beautiful. Among their partners is a category of men (mostly Westerners) who are unaware that they are going with a *kathoey*. Most *kathoey* I interviewed estimated that about twenty-five percent of their partners are not aware they are transgender males. Some of these men accommodate themselves during the experience when they find out during sex that their beautiful partner is not a woman, others become shocked. Then there is a group who are attracted to some of the *kathoey's* physical attributes (e.g., tough buttocks, boyish traits, etc.)

For the remainder of partners or customers there will be a great difference in the degree to which the *kathoey's* penis plays a role in their attractiveness. All *kathoey* have a technique for keeping their penis out of the game, making it invisible. Some partners do not mind being confronted with a penis, and some even like it. As indicated before, I cannot make any representative statements here, but several statements by *kathoey* lead me to doubt the assumption that an artificial vagina is often used in sex. One informant admitted that she never used it, another one tried to avoid using it.

Furthermore, it is important to be aware of some of the benefits that a relationship with a *kathoey* can have for some men, at least temporarily. It is a form of sex which is completely beyond reproductive sexuality, and it is also a play between a male and a female yet also among men. To some men, *kathoey* offer something extra: by offering heterosexual gratification within a homosocial environment or, differently expressed, gratification of heterosexual desires without the

tenseness and (unconscious) anxieties some men experience in a relationship with women. This can complement another sexual benefit in a
cultural environment where women are expected to be sexually passive.

The combination of a male-male social domain and male-female
sexual domain helps to avoid difficulties in coming to grips with an
"other" female world. To understand that this combination does not
necessarily spoil the sexual atmosphere, some reflection about the
character of sexual excitement is relevant. An essential element in the
production of sexual excitement is fantasy. In some sense, a man has
to work hard to imagine a perfect image and to hold off disturbing
influences in order to bring about stimulation. He has to objectify and
isolate his erotic object, and his sexually excited part is in a sense
split-off of himself (Stoller 1979). Evidence of this condition is the
often reported feeling of disillusionment or disenchantment immediately after satisfaction. One can learn to turn on or to influence this
mechanism of sexual excitement. It can be directed exclusively to the
femaleness of a *kathoey* and it can exclude any association with male
sex.

From a common sense perspective, the genitals are the core of
sexual excitement. Sexologists, however, have shown that the *gestalt*
of a female nude is most exciting to heterosexual men (from J. Wein-
rich in the "sexnet" e-mail list of August 6, 1996). Their more refined
physical features (and perhaps some psychological qualities) help
many Thai or Asian males to assume this female *gestalt* in the eyes of
Western heterosexual men and so to play the female role in the heterosexual game convincingly. What is decisive is whether the erotic *gestalt* "works," whether it is effective, not its inner characteristics.
Sexual excitement is about images, the presence or absence of a penis
can be bargained about or accommodated.

THE KATHOEY PERFORMANCE

I was impressed by *kathoeys'* descriptions of the capacities needed
to play the perfect woman during sex work: how stressful it is; the
necessity to command the voice; and especially to control body language. It was as if there was an "on air" or "on stage" persona. Lek
contrasted this with the way she felt when we were talking during our
interview or when she was at home. The latter was more relaxing to

her. There was also no pressure to conceal her sex when I addressed her as a *kathoey*. My speculation is that "in public" there is always an awareness of "on stage" and "behind stage." *Kathoey* often value sex work because it is a scene where they can prove their female qualities day after day. In some sense there always remains an awareness of the play or performance. This is shown, for instance, by the long make-up preparations required before they enter the scene. Or as Kung from Bangkok explained, "We are *phu-ying* (female), but since we are not real, we have to do everything better."

As was revealed in several interviews, most partners of *kathoey* expect "something new" from a sexual contact with a person who has an intimate knowledge of the male body, a knowledge with which many woman can never compete. Khan, a female Thai who has been involved in the business of the Amsterdam red light district for years, explained why many Thai *kathoey* earn more money than female prostitutes, "They have more to offer, behind, in front, and above. And they also sell themselves better. Look how they know to allure customers and talk them over." Lek from Chiang Mai clarified why she thought that so many *farang* or Westerners like Thai *kathoey*, "They want to try this. And the *kathoey* know better where the exciting parts of the body are located . . . they are able to use their mouth and they have a tight ass-hole, especially if you compare them with women who have had several children."

It is important for my argument not to look exclusively at *kathoey* as isolated individuals, but to see them in connection with the partners they look for, or attempt to attract. From such an investigation, a series of observations present themselves that show how inadequate it is to conceptualize these *kathoey* in terms of a homosexual orientation. Considering friends and partners of *kathoey* helps to answer the question of whether the game they play is a homosexual or a heterosexual one. (I am leaving out the option of "bisexuality" for their partners here.) Does the *kathoey's* partner accept that he is also "homosexual" or even "gay"? Does it mean that the partner also has sexual contacts with what *kathoey* call "real men"? Of course, *in sexualibus* everything is possible, but almost all of my *kathoey* informants indicated that they prefer a "real man." Many reacted outspokenly to the possibility of having a "gay" partner, "Oh no, no gay, certainly not." Several of them indicated that their fantasy is to get a man who is married in order to prove that they are better than his wife. Lek mentioned that she only wants men who are "one hundred percent men." She ended a relationship with a Thai man because she did not like his *tam-jai* (passive or submissive) attitude and behaviour: "The man has to be the leader." Lek's present Danish friend is 29 years old and works in a supermarket. She added that she allows him to have contact with women, but does not want him to hang around with other *kathoey*. She understands that she can never forbid her partner from contacting women. The actual threat to most long-term relationships for *kathoey* indeed seems to be women. *Kathoey* can prove that they are more attractive, they can keep a partner for a longer time, but there is a steady risk that the partner will return to "normal" after some time. In fact, this seems to be the common pattern among partners of *kathoey* in Amsterdam. It is a kind of paradox; while aiming to play a perfect female role, they never succeed in eliminating their partner's wish for a real woman.

Often, partner choice is functional to the gender wish of *kathoey*. Most partners are good looking men, sometimes even macho, and in many cases younger than the *kathoey* herself. The message seems to be, "Look at me with my perfect man." The more masculine her partner is, the more feminine a *kathoey* feels. In several countries, AIDS-inspired studies have led to detailed descriptions of groups that for a long time were simply seen as bisexuals or transvestites. A study in Costa Rica describes a group of "lovers of transvestites" that has a remarkable similarity with the *kathoey* and their partners (Schifter, Madrigal, & Aggleton 1996). It struck the interviewers of these "lovers of transvestites" that their gender construction was masculine. They did not find

> traces of resistance to rigid roles or to machismo. Their [the lovers'] lifestyle is similar to any other Costa Rican heterosexual: married, with children and attracted to feminine qualities. They do not remember, as children, feeling attracted to members of their own sex, or having any feeling of being 'different,' as occurs with many men who are gay. Few feel attraction towards men other than transvestites. (ibid., p. 114)

Most of them were blue-collar workers with low income and little schooling. Others were supported by transvestite partners. All expressed their preference for a transvestite over a woman, feeling that the transvestite is warmer, more passionate, sexier, and tighter than most women . . . the transvestite and his clients or lovers participate in a sexual culture in which gender takes on a very particular meaning. Transvestites feel like women and are perceived as such, with few exceptions, by their clients and lovers. Being a 'woman' means 'feminine,' and their sexual organs present no obstacle. (ibid., p. 115)

I learned about the above report after completing the first draft of my argument about *kathoey* in this paper. Some of the similarities between Thai *kathoey* and Costa Rican transvestites are remarkable. The above report was also based on in-depth interviews with transvestites and their partners, and it emphasized the importance of the relationship between transvestites and their lovers, which is interpreted as a heterosexual one. It stresses the prominence of gender and the notion that "the penis does not make the man" (ibid., p. 115).

FARANG PARTNERS OF KATHOEY

Many *kathoey* have the impression that their attractions work more convincingly in a *farang* or western environment. They are right in some sense, since many *farang* think in terms of only two rigid gender categories and do not allow for in-between variations. It is the way of thinking of the biological sex dichotomy, you are either male or female, or there is a "failure." To Thai *kathoey* the possibility offered in several European countries of obtaining a passport describing them as female has a great attraction. Thai law does not permit people to officially change the sex noted on their birth certificates, and the Thai passports of all *kathoey* record their sex as "male." *Kathoey* show pride when acquiring a foreign passport that describes them as "female." Lek explained that it was her ambition to get a Danish passport, and she gave an intriguing explanation, "It has a higher percentage [i.e., status]" (*mi persen mak kwa*). She then would not need a visa to travel to Italy or France, which she wanted to visit because she "liked old things" (*chorp khorng kao-kao*). It is fascinating to observe how in her case the reality of changing gender went together with the expectation of becoming a higher-class world citizen.

Often the preference for a *farang* partner is justified in moralistic ways. They are seen as being more trustful, honest and respectful.

Similar opinions are sometimes recounted by Thai women who intend to, or have actually, married a *farang*. However, the naivety of *farangs* is sometimes exploited. Unfamiliarity with Thai language and culture can make a *farang* man "stupid" or easy to manipulate. Other *kathoey* stress straightforwardly the possibility of earning more money with *farang*. When we look at individual cases, we will certainly find the whole spectrum, from *kathoey* who only exploit the better financial prospects offered by *farang* partners, to others for whom erotic or sexual attraction also plays an important role.

THE "OPERATION"

Important to all *kathoey* are questions related to whether or not to undergo a full sex-change operation. Why do some want it? Why do others like it only partially? Is it necessary to get rid of the penis to become a "complete *kathoey*," or is it possible to have a compromise? Most of the *kathoey* I know in Amsterdam underwent a full operation, inclusive of genitalia change. However, I have rarely met a complete male-to-female transsexual in Thailand. Obviously, in the first place, there is a financial consideration involved. The total cost of such surgery in Thailand easily amounts to 100,000 baht, a substantial amount of money. But I wonder whether other reasons also play a role. Is it that in Thai daily life more tolerance is shown towards persons who claim a position somewhere between the male and female gender?

It is hard to interpret my data about the wish to undergo a full sex change operation. A sex change is often considered to be the last step of a *kathoey* career. Often it coincides with the intention to migrate to Europe, or follows afterwards. My impression is that in the last few years, fewer and fewer *kathoey* are following this pattern. I have come across *kathoey* who claimed that they had full hormonal treatment but would like to keep their penis, since their partner liked it that way. Others were remarkably open in their answer to the question of whether or not they had an ambition to undergo sex-change surgery, "Only when my partner wants it." Laa explained that, "to have or not to have a penis is just a matter of fashion." She had promised her mother not to "throw this away," again an indication that having or not having a penis is not the most crucial issue to *kathoey* themselves. Nevertheless, to several *kathoey* their penis was the most regrettable part of their body. Naa, for instance, could not imagine keeping her penis. Lek was more indifferent, "I will ask my friend whether he intends me to undergo a sex operation. If he wants it, I am prepared to do it."

MIDDLE CLASS ATTITUDES

My descriptions and interpretations here are based on interviews with *kathoey*. This needs some emphasis, since the public discussion about *kathoey* in Thailand is determined by the opinion of middle class professionals such as psychiatrists and psychologists. Their attitudes are often anti-homosexual, anti-gay and pathologizing. Their discourse is often adapted from theories that prevailed in Western academia two or three decades ago (see Jackson in this volume). Although some *kathoey* belong to the middle classes, their lifestyle is certainly not in accordance with middle class perceptions. One has to be aware that, apart from the open, tolerant and flexible climate which is implicit in my descriptions, moralizing and hostile opinions also circulate in the public Thai discourse.

Recent publications about a *kathoey* volleyball team that represented Lampang Province in northern Thailand and won the national male volleyball championships, made clear how intriguingly varied opinions can co-exist. Let me illustrate three different attitudes to this team's win through citations from the same newspaper article published in the English language *The Nation* (3 July 1996). An official talking about two *kathoey* who were national level players stated, "Besides finding a job that interests them, the two can expect to receive more support from sponsors for their predominantly transsexual team in the future." This official saw new marketing possibilities. Asked if putting a team of transvestites on international courts would cause problems, a different view came to the surface and was voiced on condition of anonymity by another official of the Amateur Volleyball Association of Thailand: "I've heard them gossiping on the bench about how many men they get after a competition," said the official. "If we let them join the [national] team, what will happen to our real men players, who are still young and impressionable?" The highest expectation of negative foreign reactions came from one of the two top players, "We have to admit that we want to be beautiful–gear, make-up, long hair . . . So we know and accept that we cannot be in the national team and have to think about our country's reputation."

FINAL REMARKS

I have to admit that the above remarks are tentative and need to be followed by wider studies. Their modest contribution is in opening up an approach to *kathoey* that breaks with moralizing or pathologizing qualifications and does not subsume them automatically under the category of gay.

For health personnel, social workers, or activists, it is important to realize that treating *kathoey* as homosexuals or gay is inadequate. One does not have to exclude the possibility of bringing them under one common denominator with gays, but we have to be aware of the many differences. The assumption that they are gay easily leads to difficulties. It has to be accepted, for example, that they often want to enter a heterosexual world. They prefer to be approached as beautiful and graceful ladies. From some persons, this may require tolerance and flexibility. The going together of *kathoey* and gay is perhaps at least as difficult as cooperation between gay men and lesbians. Mansalansan (1996) describes the potential conflicts between expatriate Filipino gay men and *bakla* (who perhaps can be compared with *kathoey*) in New York City. The differences center on the issue of crossdressing and effeminacy. One *bakla* said that he and other men "who cross-dressed attempted to look like real women [. . .] he did not crossdress for shock value but for verisimilitude" (Mansalansan, 1996 p. 53). The *bakla* attracted non-gay men and they were accused of having illusions and being internally homophobic or self-hating. In Amsterdam we do not see such a conflict, since Thai expatriate gay men and *kathoey* live in separate social worlds within the city.

There are also problems specific for *kathoey*. *Kathoey* spend a lot of energy and money in order to become convincing females. However, the discrepancy between how they want to look and what they actually are is almost permanent. Women often fulfil the role of an intimate friend with whom personal worries and fears can be discussed.

Kathoey also meet particular health problems. They often use several drugs to stimulate their female characteristics or their beauty and often are not informed about unintended side-effects. There can also be unexpected effects from surgery, and the medical construction of a vagina can create unique medical problems. A health strategy of using the same approach as in the case of female vaginal complaints is not always the best one. Effective HIV prevention also has to be adapted to the specific risks encountered by *kathoey*, whether they engage in vaginal or anal sex. Depending on the place where they live, it is not uncommon for some *kathoey* to also use drugs that are illegal. In western countries *kathoey* are often in need of information about legal issues regarding marriage, visas and sex change.

There is very little information about older *kathoey*. I assume, however, that they enter a difficult period when age reduces their physical attractiveness. Do they find professions where their success is not dependent on beauty? I have come across persons who manage to alternate between a male and female role, between day and night; or who tried the *kathoey* role for a period and then moved back into a homosexual role. It is therefore extremely important to have information about how *kathoey* develop or change over the years. It is most common to see *kathoey* in their twenties, but more rarely in their forties and fifties. Is return to the male role considered seriously or is it seen as a form of betrayal? Recently, I heard that in the north of Thailand some older *kathoey* have started to act as brokers between women who offer sexual services and those who have specific sexual desires. This is a new and growing market for commercial sex since most visible and easily accessible brothels have been closed.

Kathoey in Amsterdam look for niches in Dutch society. They fear attention from the press and media, but they enjoy the atmosphere that allows them to move around freely and look for partners and/or clients. This is certainly related to the legality of their status as migrants.

I hope I have been able to show that the opening up of a foreign market plus a foreign demand for Thai *kathoey* has gradually transformed this traditional category. This development has not been planned by any formal agency. It has happened even without the understanding of the people involved. Through the logic of *kathoey* taking small steps to improve their lives, these changes have taken place. Their response to the new possibilities offered by foreign contacts and increased mobility is especially important. Globalization in this case has meant basically an opening up of new opportunities and adapting to these chances, the envisioning of a career, of a life prospect. The local changes are the most basic. Here, reality is actively transformed and new opportunities to grow in different directions are grasped.

Most of my information is from *kathoey* who were at least partially engaged in sex work. What are their differences from *kathoey* who do not earn a living from sex work? Can we identify *kathoey* for whom sexual activity is not important at all? It is my assumption that they do exist, since their essential characteristic is the ambition to live a life that reinforces the feeling of being female. We have, however, to also understand that sex work has the particular quality to prove day after day that a *kathoey* is as good or even better than a real woman.

In analyzing my material, I must also conclude that many other questions should have been asked in a more systematic way. For instance: What is a typical *kathoey* in the eyes of a *kathoey*? Is it a word they accept fully or do they also dislike it? Is there any other word they prefer themselves? What are the differences between *gay queen* and *kathoey*? It must be clear, however, that there are no definitive answers to these questions. *Kathoey* has enjoyed a wide range of meanings. Nowadays, its meaning is especially adapted by the development of a gay-homosexual, on the one hand, and the development of a feminine *kathoey*, on the other.

I have tried to organize my material in a way that makes sense to me, while at the same time withholding theoretical representations– but there is always theory, and the case of Thai *kathoey* is certainly relevant for sexual theory. Apart from issues related to constructionist versus essentialist perspectives of sexuality, I would like to point to its relevance for the nature of sexual and erotic excitement. *Kathoey* seem to be systematic specialists in heterosexual erotic attraction and excitement. They appear to take heterosexual eroticism out of the context of reproduction, marriage and male-female gender ideologies to focus it exclusively on the manipulation of its most effective fantasy mechanisms. By spelling out the partializing and objectifying mechanisms of sexual excitement, we start to understand how such a manipulation of erotic desire and excitement is possible. A further analysis of *kathoey* and their partners could contribute to our insight into the idiom of heterosexual desire and excitement. Especially pertinent is the observation that, in some relationships of *kathoey* and heterosexual males, the question of having or not having a penis has almost become an irrelevant matter.

NOTE

1. When talking with *farangs* Thai people may call transgender males by the borrowed expression "lady boys," while in Thai they will most likely use the local term *kathoey*.

BIBLIOGRAPHY

Aggleton, Peter (Ed.). (1996). *Bisexualities and AIDS*. London: Taylor & Francis.

Coleman, Eli, Colgan, P. and Gooren, L. (1992). Male cross-gender behavior in Myanmar (Burma): A description of the Acault. *Archives of Sexual Behavior* 21 (3), 313-321.

Herdt, G. (Ed.) (1994). *Third sex, third gender. Beyond dimorphism in culture and history*. New York: Zone Books.

Herdt, G. (1997). *Same sex, different cultures: Gays and lesbians across cultures*. Boulder: Westview Press.

Jackson, Peter A. (1995). *Dear Uncle Go: Male homosexuality in Thailand*. Bangkok: Bua Luang Books.

Levine, Martin P. (1992). The life and death of gay clones. In G. Herdt (Ed.), *Gay culture in America*. Boston: Beacon Press

Manalansan IV, Martin F. (1996). Searching for community. Filipino gay men in New York City. In R. Leong (Ed.), *Asian American sexualities. Dimensions of the gay & lesbian experience*. New York and London: Routledge.

Morelli, D., Cattorini, P., Maffei, C., Mauri, M.A., Palumbo, G. & Visintini, R. (1994). AIDS, prostitution and information. *Abstracts of the Tenth International Conference on AIDS*, Yokohama, Japan, 7-12 August 1994 (Abstract No. PD0609).

Nanda, Serena (1990). *Neither man nor woman. The Hijras of India*. Belmont: Wadsworth Publishing Company.

Oetomo, Dede (1991). Patterns of homosexuality in Indonesia. In Tielman, R. A.P., Carballo M. and Hendriks, A.C. (Eds.). *Bisexuality and HIV/AIDS*. Buffalo, N.Y.: Prometheus.

Schifter, J. and Madrigal, J. with Aggleton, P. (1996). Bisexual communities and cultures in Costa Rica. In Aggleton, P. (Ed.). *Bisexualities and AIDS*. London: Taylor & Francis.

Serre, A., Cabral, C., Castelleti, S., & De Vincenzi, I. (1994). Feasibility of preventive actions among transvestite/transsexual prostitutes in Paris. *Abstracts of the Tenth International Conference on AIDS*, Yokohama, Japan, 7-12 August 1994. [Abstract No. 395C]

Stoller, R.A. (1979). *Sexual excitement. Dynamics of erotic life*. New York: Pantheon.

Tan, Michael L. (1995). From *bakla* to gay. Shifting gender identities and sexual behaviors in the Philippines. In R. Parker & J.H. Gagnon (Eds.) *Conceiving sexuality. Approaches to sex research in a postmodern world*. (pp. 85-96), New York: Routledge.

Rehearsing Gender and Sexuality in Modern Thailand: Masculinity and Male-Male Sex Behaviours

Graeme Storer

SUMMARY. In this paper I draw on a series of interviews with gay-identified Thai men, and with male bar workers and their clients in order to chart the traditions, discourses, and institutional contexts contributing to the construction of gender and sexual identity in Thailand. I argue against the uncritical application of Western paradigms to the study of Thai sexuality and present a view of gender and sexuality that is "fluid and pragmatic." I consider difficulties associated with sexual choice and levels of acceptance and toleration, and look at examples of how sex work has been socially constructed. Finally, I discuss the attachment of Thai male bar workers to the "gay" community. *[Article copies available for a fee from The Haworth Document Delivery Service: 1-800-342-9678. E-mail address: getinfo@haworthpressinc.com]*

INTRODUCTION

In the Thai HIV/AIDS campaign and the discourse surrounding HIV/AIDS, homosexual practice has been a muted presence (see Lyt-

---

Address correspondence to: Graeme Storer, c/o Peter Jackson, Division of Pacific and Asian History, Research School of Pacific and Asian Studies, Australian National University, Canberra ACT 0200, Australia.

[Haworth co-indexing entry note]: "Rehearsing Gender and Sexuality in Modern Thailand: Masculinity and Male-Male Sex Behaviours" Storer, Graeme. Co-published simultaneously in *Journal of Gay & Lesbian Social Services* (The Haworth Press, Inc.) Vol. 9, No. 2/3, 1999, pp. 141-159; and: *Lady Boys, Tom Boys, Rent Boys: Male and Female Homosexualities in Contemporary Thailand* (ed: Peter A. Jackson, and Gerard Sullivan) The Haworth Press, Inc., 1999, pp. 141-159; and: *Lady Boys, Tom Boys, Rent Boys: Male and Female Homosexualities in Contemporary Thailand* (eds: Peter A. Jackson, and Gerard Sullivan) Harrington Park Press, an imprint of The Haworth Press, Inc., 1999, pp. 141-159. Single or multiple copies of this article are available for a fee from The Haworth Document Delivery Service [1-800-342-9678, 9:00 a.m. - 5:00 p.m. (EST). E-mail address: getinfo@haworthpressinc.com].

141

tleton, 1996) and Thai male sex workers must ascribe meanings and respond to HIV/AIDS campaigns largely directed at the "family man" or heterosexually active youth. This reticence to openly discuss homosexual behaviours serves to marginalise the male sex workers because, in order to understand the social contexts of male sex work, we need to be able to talk openly about both male-male sex and male prostitution. In addition, research on male sex work in Thailand has tended to focus on individual issues, such as demographics and the background of the sex workers; reasons for entering the work; sexual orientation and knowledge levels about HIV (see, for example, Kunawararak et al., 1995; Sittitrai et al., 1994; Sriwatjana, 1995). Less consideration has been given to contextual issues, such as the interactions among the sex workers, and their clients, and associated issues of power. What is totally lacking is a challenge to the way in which sex work is socially constructed or a description of how legal issues and policies impinge on sex workers and their practice.

In this paper I partially redress this shortfall by drawing on a series of interviews with gay-identified Thai men, and with male bar workers and their clients in order to chart the traditions, discourses, and institutional contexts contributing to the construction of gender and sexual identity in Thailand. My interest in this topic was prompted by demographic studies of Thai male sex workers highlighting that the majority of the workers do not homosexually identify (Kunawararak et al., 1995; Narvilai, 1994a and 1994b; Nopkesorn et al., 1991; Sittitrai et al., 1992; Sriwatjana, 1995). What was I, a gay-identified Westerner, to make of this? After all, the workers were having sex with men. Should we not focus attention on behaviour rather than on identity? In subsequent sections, I argue against the uncritical application of Western paradigms to the study of Thai sexuality, though this paper is as much about my struggle to avoid falling into the same trap. I begin by presenting a view of gender and sexuality that is "fluid and pragmatic." I then turn to difficulties associated with sexual choice and to levels of acceptance and toleration. Next, I look at examples of how sex work has been socially constructed and discuss how Thai "gay" men define themselves. Finally, I discuss the attachment of Thai male bar workers to this "gay" community. But first, I begin by reviewing the methodology of the research informing these discussions.

BACKGROUND

This paper is based on a larger research study looking at the discursive and sexual practices surrounding male bar work in Bangkok, Thailand. I here draw on a series of in-depth interviews I carried out in Thai over a twelve-month period from April 1994 to March 1995 with male bar workers. I also interviewed men who were regular clients, both Thais and non-Thais (who were either living in or visiting Thailand). All interviews were tape recorded and were typically one-on-one. In addition, I talked with gay-identified Thai men and with *kathoey* (male transvestites and transsexuals). Other sources of data informing the study have been: discussions with managers and waiters in the bars; discussions with others working in HIV/AIDS programs in Thailand; research and government publications; local newspapers; and Thai "gay" magazines.

The male bar workers participating in this study ranged in age from 19 to 28, with the majority between 19 and 22 years of age. Twenty-four bar workers participated in the interviews. In addition, there were 12 clients and five bar staff. The workers were recruited from either inner city bars in the Patpong area of Bangkok or from suburban bars in the Saphan Khwai area of the city. The names of the informants and venues given in this paper have been changed to maintain anonymity. The use of italics in the transcripts indicates either a transliteration of the Thai or words borrowed from English.

Note on Terminology: Many Thai male bar workers are behaviourally bisexual (*ha-sip ha-sip* or "fifty-fifty") and describe their work in terms of economic rather than sexual needs. It appears that many of the clients are also bisexual and that some are married. In this paper, the expression "homosexually active men" will be used to include all male-male sex behaviours. The term "gay" refers to those men who identify themselves as gay, with this originally English term now being widely known and used amongst both homosexual and heterosexual populations in Thailand.

Thai male bar workers, irrespective of their age, are referred to as "boys" or *dek*. The term *dek* denotes someone young, usually younger than the client, and also reflects the low social and cultural status of male sex work. There is, of course, considerable control exercised in this naming, and I will use "boy" only in direct quotation. Otherwise, I will use "worker" or "bar worker" to refer to the commercial male bar workers.[1] The term *farang* is used by Thais to refer to Caucasians and is also used here. When a client takes a worker from the bar, he pays an *"off* fee" (*kha off*) to the bar and then he "tips" the worker after the session. The borrowed English term *off* is part of the vernacular of the bars and is used throughout this paper.

A PRAGMATIC VIEW OF SEXUALITY

A number of demographic studies of male sex workers in Thailand have highlighted that the majority of the workers do not homosexually identify (Kunawararak et al., 1995; Narvilai, 1994a and 1994b; Nopkesorn et al., 1991; Sittitrai et al, 1992; Sriwatjana, 1995). But as I have argued elsewhere (Storer, 1997), gay identification in Thailand is problematic and hampered by a lack of clear terminology. In this section, I will discuss gender and sexuality in Thailand and how they relate to gay-identification among homosexually active Thai men. I include here two other categories, age and class-structure, which interact with gender to construct social practice (Connell, 1995). I note that these categories are not necessarily distinct and that many aspects of trans-generational homosexual relations may be more appropriately considered in terms of the class-structured relations that are apparent in interactions between Thai male bar workers and their clients, where there is invariably a gap in socio-economic standing as well as age. I also note that patron-client relations are pervasive in Thailand and that relationships where men receive "favours" in return for respect or loyalty should not be conflated with prostitution.

In her study of gender and sexuality in Thailand, Rosalind Morris (1994, p. 18) found herself "astounded by the plasticity and heterogeneity of Thai gender and sexual identity." The ease with which *kathoey* and some Thai gay men are apparently tolerated by Thai society challenges preconceived notions of sexuality and reminds us that Western perspectives hold no privilege. There is no "tidy partition of 'nature' and 'culture,' or sex versus gender . . . since each culture posits its own definition of what is natural or social" (Herdt, 1994, p. xiii). Rather, in a particular society, people play out certain sexual roles and assume, are assigned, or are forced into certain sexual identities (Ruse, 1995). Further, these roles may vary over time. The self is not static but is continuously re-defined in one's experiences in interaction with others. There is no necessary relationship between a particular pattern of sexual behaviour and the taking on of a sexual identity: "what is crucial is the meaning that individuals ascribe to their sexual feelings, activity and relationships" (Richardson, 1984, pp. 86-7). Padgug sums it up rather neatly: "To 'commit' a homosexual act is one thing; to *be* a homosexual is something entirely different" (Padgug, 1992, p. 51; emphasis in original).

As issues of identity appear significant in understanding occupational practice among male sex workers (Boles & Elifson, 1994)–male sex workers who gay-identify and who allow themselves sexual feelings during commercial contacts seem more prone to engage in unsafe behaviours than those who do not gay-identify (de Graaf et al., 1994; Storer, 1995)–a closer look at the Thai social constructions of gender and sexual identity, and the discourses and interactional contexts within which these are located, is appropriate here.

ACCEPTANCE OR TOLERATION?

Coming out may be a modern concept but its "practice involves levels of difficulty that has a very long history" including fear of rejection, categorisation, or making the wrong decision (Edwards, 1994, pp. 26-27). While it is not immediately apparent what societal sanctions are at work in Thailand on those men who openly admit to sex with men (Sittitrai et al., 1992, p. 22), I doubt whether the majority of Thai gay men in the 1990s are as confident about proclaiming "I'm gay and I'm a man," as Peter Jackson suggests (Jackson, 1997, p. 185).[2] There is a definite "reluctance and delay in applying stigmatised labels to oneself" (Murray, 1992, p. 31). Anjana Suvarnananda, a member of the lesbian group Anjaree, had this to say about how Thai society views lesbian relations:

> Although Thai people aren't violent or hostile towards homosexuals in a way that some countries' societies are, there is another kind of control mechanism at work here that's just as traumatic for those on the receiving end. . . . [Thai] society doesn't see lesbian relationships as legitimate or meaningful. (Interviewed in Otagnonta, 1995, p. 29)

For Anjana, this denial of social acceptance is one of the most powerful control mechanisms at work in Thai society. It is, in fact, a mechanism of "silencing" as it ensures that there is no discursive space available for debate.

In Thailand, transgender homosexuality is institutionalised in the *kathoey*. The *kathoey* are readily visible in Thai life and run their own businesses, wait on tables in restaurants, work at the post office and so on. It is widely known that one of Bangkok's top models, Ornapha Kritsadee, is a *kathoey*. So is the transsexual singer Jern-jern Boon-song-ngern, whose song *Ni Kheu Achip Khorng Chan* ("This is my profession") has been popular both in drag shows and on Thai radio stations. *Kathoey* are considered, both by themselves and by other Thais, to be a "second type of woman" (*phu-ying praphet thi sorng*), and for a male to engage in sex with a *kathoey* does not imply that he necessarily adopts a homosexual identity (Beyrer et al., 1995; Sittitrai et al., 1992). Same-sex contacts are not necessarily sanctioned negatively if one of the partners assumes a "female" sex-role (De Lind van Wijngaarden, 1995; Murray, 1992), as ultimately it is the role one plays sexually which demarcates one's sexual/gender identity. In this pragmatic and fluid view of sexuality, men are able to enjoy homo-erotic experiences or take on the role of sex workers if these are viewed as something being lived at the moment. But social appearance is well-scripted and one's supposed and presumed sexual behaviour, as can be read from one's appearance, is fixed. As in other parts of the world, anal intercourse remains a "benchmark" of the homosexual (Allyn, 1992, p. 9), and it would be taboo for a man to admit to being anally penetrated as this would directly affect his social representation or "face" (De Lind van Wijngaarden, 1995).

At first glance, the ubiquitous presence of the *kathoey* suggests a challenge to the traditional patriarchal gender system. But while *kathoey* have access to the female domain, the naming of *kathoey* as "a second type of woman" firmly relegates them into an inferior position. Kathoey are symbolically emasculated. This inferior positioning of the *kathoey* reinforces the traditional gender stratification. Morris (1994) describes it thus: what at first seems to be tolerance and the open acceptance of *kathoey* may be merely a preservation of social order through the value dualism of *na* ("face") and *kreng jai* (consideration and "presentation" of appropriate respect).[3] Here Pom, a *kathoey* with whom I talked, describes this complicity of silence:

It seems like Thai society accepts. But I don't think they do. I think they are beginning to now but I still have to be careful. I can't be *over* [i.e., "overly ostentatious"]. It's like there are rules that I have to follow. But really, Thai society is not that accepting. They don't show it but it's in their hearts. And I don't show them how I feel either. (Pom, interviewed 28/11/1995)

Even though *kathoey* have been readily visible in traditional Thai society, the term remains marked and problematised. Nowadays, *kathoey* is often used in a derogatory way similar to the terms "poofters," "queers," "fags" or "bum boys" in Australia, the United States and Great Britain. (Ironically, it is the naming of the *kathoey* as Other which allows Thai men to measure their masculinity; see Jackson, 1997.) Peter Jackson (1995) and De Lind van Wijngaarden (1995) believe that Thai men who like sex with men can avoid such stigmatisation by marrying and establishing a family. But, as in other countries, the perception that homosexual identity negates or violates family roles inhibits disclosure of homosexual identity. However, the decision not to disclose or the avoidance of disclosure raises a further risk–the risk of discovery (Strommen, 1989). This sets up a double prohibition for the male sex worker, the fear that his family will know that he is prostituting himself and doing so with men. I disagree with Allyn's assumption that there is minimal stigmatisation of the Thai male sex worker (Allyn, 1993); any man who identifies himself as a male sex worker servicing men becomes subject to the discourses which stereotype masculinity and effeminacy and which also stigmatise prostitution (Browne and Minichiello, 1996). In addition, each gay bar in Bangkok projects an image which reflects a particular market niche. In some instances, this positioning does not allow for homosexual identification, especially in bars like The Tulip or Big Boy, where clients go to find "real men" (read "muscle men") and where watching the workers lift weights is part of the performance. But in a bar like The Superman, it is acceptable to gay identify.

It is interesting to look at how the culture of a bar defines the boys. For example, the guys at Big Boy or The Tulip all act like 'men,' while in Bar Carousel they act [effeminately] gay. In Superman, you can be either. It's a tolerant environment for those boys who [say they] are gay. (Noel, expatriate Australian, interviewed 8/12/1995)

Thus, while a number of studies of Thai male sex workers highlight that the majority of the workers do not gay identify (Kunawararak et al., 1995; Narvilai 1994a and 1994b; Sittitrai et al., 1994; Sriwatjana, 1995), these findings can be problematised. Questions that ask, for example, "Are you gay?" or "Do you prefer to have sex with men?" invite denial when expressions like "complete man" (*phu-chai tem tua*) or "100 percent man" (*phu-chai neung roi per sen*) retain currency. Identity, as manifested in public appearances and behaviours, is readily separated from private practice (see Morris, 1994) and there is a definite resistance to naming oneself as one's sexuality. My research suggests that Thai male bar workers do not readily talk among themselves about sex with their clients and that maintaining "image" (*phap-phot*) and not "losing face" (*sia na*) are paramount (Storer, 1997). However, this management of impressions (see Goffman, 1969) can inhibit frank discussions with the bar workers about male-male sex and associated risk behaviours. Additionally, it is difficult to target clients when their homosexuality is silenced because of a lack of acceptance or where their contact with male bar workers is a fleeting "night out with the boys" (Storer, 1997).

There is no indigenous Thai noun for a homosexual person other than *kathoey* (Jackson, 1997), and more often than not the language of homosexuality, as heard around the bars and saunas, is English. But while terms like *gay*, *gay king* and *gay queen* have been appropriated and re-invented into the Thai vernacular, they seem to mean different things to different people. Yim, a gay-identified Thai man, resisted the notion that he has to be "active" or "receptive" (i.e., *king* or *queen*). For him, *gay* meant exclusive sexual relations with other men and being able "to do everything" (*pen gay, kor tham dai thuk yang*) (Yim, 28, field notes, 28/11/95). Such resistance defines a space different from that understood by the traditional masculine-feminine opposition which historically structured male-male sex relations in Thailand. It is the cultural presumption that masculinity and homosexuality cannot co-exist (Robinson and Davies, 1991) and the lack of precision in terms to talk about gay identity that enable some Thai men to avoid self-categorisation as homosexual and thereby preserve their masculine self-image.

Despite the poverty of Thai terms for "a homosexual," a complex system of polarised terms describes the sexual roles played out in homoerotic encounters. It is interesting to note how many of the expressions used by my informants amongst male sex workers to describe their same-sex behaviour continue to reinforce the imaginings of the "real man" as dominant and "on top" of the situation. Some of the most common expressions used by my informants are listed below in Table 1.

So far I have come across only one term that challenges the traditional masculine-feminine gender role dichotomy in male-male sexual relations, namely, *kathoey siap* (lit. "a *kathoey* who penetrates [her man]"), although when I asked bar workers about this term, I was often greeted with incredulity, suggesting it is not widely known or used amongst bar workers.

In this section, I have argued that Thai society is tolerant rather than accepting of homosexuality and that gay identification is constrained by a traditional gender role bifurcation. While terms like gay, *gay king* and *gay queen* have been appropriated into the Thai vernacular, they

TABLE 1. Some Paired Thai Expressions for Talking About Male-Male Sex, Ascribed onto the Local Gender System.

phu-chai ("masculine" sexual position)	*phu-ying/kathoey* ("feminine" sexual position)
fai ruk (noun-adjective) ("the invading party")	*fai rap, torn rap* ("the receiving party," "to receive")
siap (verb) ("to penetrate")	*thuk siap* ("to be penetrated")
ao pratu lang (slang) ("to enter the back door")	*khoa ao phom* (literally, "he took me")
phang pratu lang (slang) ("to break down the back door")	*hai pratu lang* ("to give one's back door")
tham or *tham hai* (verb) ("to do" or "to do for")	*hai tham* ("to be willing to be done to")
yet or *yet hai* (verb, vulgar) ("to fuck")	*hai yet* ("to be willing to be fucked")

seem to mean different things to different people. For some, gay has been used as a label for "modern" and "egalitarian" homosexuality through a process of "stigma transformation" (Murray, 1994, p. 297). For others, "the new word has become a euphemism for those men who are homosexually penetrated" in an instance of relexification (Murray, 1994, p. 297). The presumption remains that masculinity and homosexuality cannot co-exist and in the traditional scheme of things, the insertee is an inferiorised kind of man, while the inserter is relatively unstigmatised and generally maintains his masculinity in homosexual encounters. Thus, a homosexually active Thai man may deny being gay, associating it with behaviour expected of a *kathoey*. But not all Thai men buy into these heterosexual presumptions:

> [Male sex workers] can't say that they are men when they sleep with other men and have feelings. At the most, they might be 80% men and 20% gay. They are men . . . They just won't show they are gay. Some have a wife and children, but they work in the bar. If you're 100% man, then you can't sleep with another man. (Sam, interviewed 23/1/1996)

It has not been my intention here to assign a *homosexual* identity to Thai male bar workers, but to challenge representations of gender and sexuality as these relate to male bar work and male-male sex. My position is that a singular focus on identity diverts attention away from discussions of *homosexual behaviours* and encourages a reluctance to talk about same gender sex. Questions about homosexual behaviour invite denial when gender and sexuality are defined through binary oppositions. While there is evidence of an emerging middle class gay lifestyle in some parts of Thailand (see Altman, 1995; Jackson, 1995, 1997), it would be wrong to assume that there is a readily identifiable community of men who have sex with men. This is particularly so for Thai male bar workers, whose support networks are fragmented and whose friendships are usually confined to one or two other men who come from the same village or region (see McCamish and Sittitrai, 1997). It is necessary then to problematise the concept of community when planning HIV/AIDS interventions with male bar workers and to focus attention on both work-related sexual networks and those that extend beyond the bar. In the next section, I will turn my attention to representations of male sex work in research studies and the effects of legal issues and development policies on sex workers and their practice.

CONSTRUCTING THE MALE SEX WORKER

In a study that has been widely publicised in Thailand, Anan Narvilai (1994a) speciously argued that young men from up-country, either out of curiosity or from economic necessity, are lured into prostitution and that, in the process, they become homosexuals (or at least bisexuals). Further, he argued that this trend could lead to an increase in the number of homosexuals and an erosion of Thai society. I make two comments here. First, we need to be wary of being seduced by cause and effect enquiry into homosexual behaviours and the notion that "masculinity is a fragile essence, more easily spoiled than maintained" (Murray, 1992, p. 31). Second, it is possible that for some, male prostitution may be a safe entry to a homosexual experience without being labelled as queer (Shick, 1978). Narvilai's research was apparently prompted by Jackson's early work on homosexuality in Thailand (Jackson, 1989), as he felt that Jackson had applied a very Western perspective in analysing Thai homosexuality (Narvilai, 1994b). Unfortunately, Narvilai did not seem to challenge any of his informants' responses, and his conventional reading of the research data confused sexual behaviour with sexual identity and reinforced stereotypes about homosexual behaviours and desires. Such an ideology of deviance disempowers sex workers (Browne and Minichiello, 1996). It would be more useful to realise the central role played by the bar workers in a complex pleasure economy, and that a diverse workforce extending from the ice vendors and waiters to pimps and accountants depends on this economy to make a living.

It is also important to remember that both male and female prostitution, though highly visible, remain illegal in Thailand. Thus, the bars can provide a safe haven for the workers and their clients outside the law and beyond public gaze. But this protection can be tenuous for the worker:

> In the bar, [the client] told me what he wanted to do. I said 'Okay. If you want to do this, you have to pay me this much, right?' He agreed. But when it was over, he said that I hadn't been any good, that I didn't give it everything (*mai tem jai*). He said, 'I spent my

money at the bar . . . I paid 200 baht [US $7]. Go and get the money from them.' And he walked out of the hotel. [laughing]. You can choose either to work within the law and make 100 per day or you can work outside the law and make sometimes 2,000 per day. Some days, 1,000. Some days, 500. Which one would you choose? (Sam, interviewed 23/1/1996)

The development policies pursued in the Thai government's successive Five Year Plans for the past several decades have unintentionally separated Thai women and men from a rural subsistence lifestyle (Winichakul, 1995) and fostered an economic climate that favours sexual exploitation of the female and, increasingly, of the male body (Lyttleton, 1994). Sulak Sivaraksa (1995), a prominent Thai social critic, believes that the Thai intellect has been colonised by a consumer culture. Charoensin-o-larn (1988) argues that consumer goods have become symbols of "modernization" and the objects of class identification. It is this culture of "wants" and "needs," along with a lack of regular employment in rural areas, that encourages migration to the major cities in the search for work and a "better" life. But work opportunities for migrant youth with little education are limited. The minimum wage in Bangkok is currently 180 baht per day. However, a construction worker may start on less than 100 baht per day, especially if an agent has been involved in recruiting work crews from up-country. A waiter in a restaurant might make as little as 1,800 baht per month with meals thrown in. If we factor in accommodation, daily living costs and transport to and from work, there is little left over, even for those with a "good" job, as Tam explained:

Tam has been working at the Mandrake Bar for about two weeks. During the day, he is a goldsmith and works for a jewellery store. The work is relatively light–he goes into work around nine in the mornings and finishes around 5:00 pm–and he makes 6,000 baht per month: 'But it isn't enough. Without extra money, there's nothing to do.' (field notes, 14/12/1995)

Thus, in many cases, working in a gay bar is not a last resort but a pragmatic economic choice, though it would be naive to suggest that these choices are always made in circumstances of the workers' own choosing (Davies and Simpson, 1990). Most of the men enter the bars because the work provides them with much more money than they could make in any other job and with a modicum of control over their lives. In addition, bar work does not require long hours (Storer, 1995).

RE-DEFINING "GAY"

While the opposition between "male/masculine" (*phu-chai*) and "female/feminine" (*phu-ying*) has local currency, there are signs of resistance. In recent years, there has been a detachment from the "feminine" representation of homosexuality (Jackson, 1997) and constructions of masculinity are slowly changing, notably in Bangkok and other major commercial centres. As in other parts of the world, the gym culture has become a dominant gay image. The Thai gay man now seen cruising the bars or roving the steam rooms of gay saunas is not necessarily sticking to any prescribed sexual role. As Miller so aptly describes: "if this is still *the body that can fuck you, etc.*, it is no longer–quite the contrary–*the body you don't fuck with*" (Miller, 1984, p. 31; emphasis in original).

But it would be wrong to suggest, as Morris has, that Thai gay identity is "an importation from the West" (Morris, 1994, p. 29), a pale imitation of Western clone culture. To do so would be to deny local discourses, traditions and institutional contexts. It would also deny Thai gay men agency within these cultural and situational re-sources.[4] Nor should we view these Thai male bodies as merely valo-rising the male as male. The images have been appropriated and re-presented to challenge the notion that gay means *kathoey*, submissive, weak or wimpish. The play in many Bangkok gay venues is about avoiding stereotypes and rigid categories of exclusion and inclusion (Halperin, 1995, p. 32). Unfortunately, this imaging generates its own commodified techniques of normalisation. There is now a new and right way to be gay in Thailand, which costs a considerable amount of money and many men find themselves unable to afford the lifestyle. Regrettably, the emergence of this masculine-identified gay communi-ty has also further stigmatised the *kathoey* (Jackson, 1995) and, like their "straight" counterparts, Thai gay men now define their identity in opposition to the effeminised *kathoey*.

Pattaya, a popular tourist destination and rest and recreation stop, has grown rapidly from a "sleepy fishing village" into a bustling seaside metropolis. In one area affectionately known as "Boys' Town," commercial gay bars are placed alongside the cafes and pubs which have come to typify gay night life in Thailand. In Boys' Town, gay men who are not engaging in commercial sex brush shoulders with those who are. On Soi 4, a street in Bangkok's Patpong entertainment district, market forces have squeezed out the commercial gay bars to the periphery and replaced them with designer pubs, cafes and discos (although these gay venues are also cruised by free-lance sex workers and, later at night, by bar workers). What I am pointing to here is this–Thai men have been able to define a "gay" sub-culture for themselves in and around spaces created by the male sex workers.

A COMMUNITY OF MEN WHO HAVE SEX WITH MEN

It has not been my intent in this paper to name the Thai homosexual but to offer some explanation for the discursive silence that envelops the subject of male-male sex behaviours. Earlier, I referred to a community of Thai gay men. The notion of "community" is of course ideological and it is still not clear at this point how Thai gay men will define themselves. On the one hand, gay-identification is constrained by a gender-role hegemony that maintains the notion of "real" men versus submissive women, "second type of women" (*kathoey*), or effeminate men. On the other hand, sanctions against male homosexuality tend to be non-interventionist and Thai gays can show their resistance to restrictive social norms by simply ignoring them (Jackson, 1995). For this reason, we would not expect to see a "gay community" as in the West with its tradition of liberation, simply because without oppression, there can be no liberation (Altman, 1972; Plummer, 1992). While there are signs that a Thai "gay" community may be defining itself through a process of resistance to traditional categories, it is important to remember that for many Thai men, their homosexuality is private and outside public purview. For others, same-sex encounters typically comprise only one portion of their sexual wardrobe: homosexuality is what they do, not who they are.

However, there are three reasons why I feel it is important to promote a sense of community among homosexually active men. First, it seems that sexual safety is a social process (Ridge et al., 1994; Weeks, 1995) and that peer support may be critical in promoting the motivation and intention central to behaviour change (McCamish et al., 1993, pp. 190-194). Second, many young Thai men coming to terms with their identity may be excluded (economically and/or socially) from contemporary gay life and there may be a sense of isolation and a corresponding lack of self esteem about who they are. Third, not all Thai male bar workers identify as gay. Many are behaviourally bisexual and their responses to HIV and related health issues may be either (in)formed or limited by their attachment to or isolation from the "gay" scene. HIV-prevention strategies

> *cannot* only be concerned with the specific practices in which HIV transmission occurs . . . a person's sexuality involves a complex of actions, emotions and relationships. Particular practices (such as unprotected anal intercourse) *always* occur in a wider repertoire of sexual and social activities. To change a particular practice requires the reshaping of the wider pattern of sexuality. (Kippax and Crawford, 1993, pp. 256-7; emphasis in original)

At present there is no stable and embracing pattern of mutual interaction among the Thai bar workers (see McCamish, this volume), but one way to begin to develop a sense of community among Thai male bar workers would be to build on affinities in which regional language differences are significant. Another would be to establish a male sexual health clinic which would open from early evening to late at night–a centre where the men could seek advice about health management, referral services and other work-related issues in an informal setting. The challenge will be to promote a community in which "definitions of 'common good' are not all enveloping, yet at the same time bonds of social obligation and affiliation operate to tie the group together" (Tierney, 1993, p. 148). My objective is to seek ways to extend the concept of community to include a culture of need and struggle as well as a culture of sexual practice. But first, it will be necessary to promote a wider institutional acceptance for organising Thai male bar workers in this way.

ACKNOWLEDGMENTS

I would like to thank all the men who gave of their time to inform the research and who agreed to openly discuss their life stories. I would also like to thank Dr. Anthony Pramualratna (Regional HIV/ AIDS Program, UNDP, Bangkok), Greg Carl (Research Associate, Thai Red Cross, Bangkok), and Khun Promboon Panitchthakdi (Country Representative for CARE Thailand) for their comments and advice.

NOTES

1. *Editors' Note*: The term *dek* occurs in the most common colloquial expressions for male sex workers used both in the general population and amongst homosexually active men and male sex workers themselves. The Thai press variously calls male sex workers *dek khai tua* ("kids who sell their bodies") or *phu-chai khai tua* ("men who sell their bodies"). These are variants of the expression *phu-ying khai tua* ("women who sell their bodies") for female sex workers. More formal and bureaucratic terms are *sopheni chai* ("male prostitute") and the euphemistic *phu-chai borikan* ("male service [worker]"), compare *sopheni* ("prostitute") and *phu-ying borikan* for female sex workers. Amongst homosexually active men, male sex workers are commonly called *dek khai nam* ("a kid who sells water"), an abbreviation of the more explicit *dek khai nam-asuji* ("a kid who sells semen"). These expressions are often abbreviated to simply *dek khai* ("a kid who sells . . ."), leaving unstated the service or thing sold. Perhaps the most derogatory expression for a male sex worker, which tends to be used only by the sensationalist press, is *ai tua*, a masculine variant of a similar derogatory expression for female sex workers, *ee tua*.

2. For an example of anti-homosexual attitudes, see the editors' discussion (introduction to this volume) on the threat in late 1996 to identify and ban homosexual teacher trainees from Rajabhat Institute teacher training colleges.

3. Morris describes *kreng jai* as "ubiquitous and obligatory expression of deference" and implying "the presentation of a mask and the veiling of felt emotion through public displays of agreeability." The term *na* means "face" or "front" and also connotes honour and propriety; "*na* is not a *representation* of subjectivity but a *presentation* of public order" (Morris, 1994, p. 36; emphasis in original). Also of relevance here is the work of Komin (1990) on the Thai value system in which she highlights the importance of maintaining "smooth interpersonal relations" (of avoiding conflict). Tan has noted a similar "patronizing" tolerance of the Filipino transvestite, the *bahkla*, who "is tolerated only as long as he remains confined in certain professions" (Tan, 1995, p. 3).

4. One clear example of how Thai gay men are appropriating and reconstituting Western gay culture can be seen at the Babylon in Bangkok. This gay sauna with its marble foyer, gym, restaurant, garden bar, spa area and steam rooms is as much a social venue as it is cruising spot, and unlike the gay saunas I am familiar with in Australia and New Zealand. The Babylon is not the place you stumble into at the end of the night, if you have not scored yet. On the contrary, it is a venue where homosexually active men can cruise, meet up with friends, or have dinner before going off to drink, dance and cruise some more.

REFERENCES

Allyn, E.G. (Ed.). (1992). *The dove coos (Nok Kao Kan): Gay experiences by the men of Thailand*, trans. by N. Benchamat and S. Inpradith. Bangkok: Bua Luang Publishing Co.

Allyn, E. (1993). *The men of Thailand: 1993 guide to gay Thailand*, Fourth Edition. San Francisco CA: Bua Luang Publishing Co.

Altman, D. (1995). The new world of gay Asia. In S. Perera (Ed.). *Asian and Pacific identities: Identities, ethnicities*, (pp. 121-138). Bundoora (Australia): Nationalities, Meridian.

Altman, D. (1972). *Homosexual: Oppression and liberation*. Sydney: Angus and Robertson.

Beyrer, C., Eiumtrakul, S., Celentano, D.D., Nelson, K.E., Ruckhaopunt, S. & Khamboonruang, C. (1995). Same sex behaviour, sexually transmitted diseases and HIV risks among young northern Thai men. *AIDS, 9*, 171-176.

Boles, J. and Elifson, K.W. (1994). Sexual identity and HIV: The male prostitute. *Journal of Sex Research, 31*(1), 39-46.

Browne, J. and Minichiello, V. (1996). The social and work context of commercial sex between men: A research note, *Australian and New Zealand Journal of Sociology, 32*(1), 86-92.

Charoensin-o-larn, C. (1988). *Understanding postwar reformism in Thailand*. Bangkok: Duang Kamol Editions.

Connell, R.W. (1995). *Masculinities*. Sydney: Allen and Unwin.

Davies, P. & Simpson, P. (1990). On male homosexual prostitution and HIV. In P. Aggleton, P. Davies & Graham Hart (Eds.). *AIDS: Individual, cultural and policy dimensions* (pp. 103-119). London: The Falmer Press.

De Graaf, R., Vanwesenbeeck, I., Van Zeesen, G., Straver, C.J. & Visser, J.H. (1994). Male prostitutes and safe sex: Different settings, different risks. *AIDS CARE, 6*(3), 277-288.

De Lind van Wijngaarden, J.W. (1995). *A social geography of male homosexual desire: Locations, individuals and networks in the context of HIV/AIDS in Chiang Mai, northern Thailand*. Chiang Mai: Social Science Research Institute.

Edwards, T. (1994). *Erotics and politics: Gay male sexuality, masculinity and feminism*. London and New York: Routledge.

Goffman, E. (1969). *The presentation of self in everyday life*. London: Penguin Press.

Halperin, D. (1995). *Saint Foucault: Towards a gay hagiography*. Oxford and New York: Oxford University Press.

Herdt, G. (1994). *Guardians of the flutes. Vol. 1: Idioms of masculinity* (Preface to the 1994 edition, pp.xi-xvi). Chicago: Chicago University Press.

Jackson, P. (1989). *Male homosexuality in Thailand: An interpretation of contemporary Thai sources*. New York: Global Academic Publishers.

Jackson, P. (1995). *Dear Uncle Go: Male homosexuality in Thailand*. Bangkok: Bua Luang Books.

Jackson, P. (1997). *Kathoey < > gay < > man: The historical emergence of gay male identity in Thailand*. In L. Manderson and M. Jolly (Eds.). *Sites of desire/economies of pleasure: Sexualities in the Asia and Pacific* (pp. 166-190). Chicago: University Press.

Kippax, S. & Crawford, J. (1993). Flaws in the theory of reasoned action. In D. Terry, C. Gallois & M. McCamish (Eds.). *The theory of reasoned action: Its application to AIDS preventive behaviour* (pp. 253-269). Oxford: Pergamon Press.

Komin, S. (1990). Culture and work-related values in Thai organisations. *International Journal of Psychology*, 25, 681-704.

Kunawararak, P., Beyrer, C., Natpratan, C., Feng, W., Celentano, D.D., de Boer, M., Nelson, K.E. and Khamboonruang, C. (1995). The epidemiology of HIV and syphilis among male commercial sex workers in northern Thailand. *AIDS*, 9, 517-521.

Lyttleton, C. (1996). Messages of distinction: The HIV/AIDS media campaign in Thailand. *Medical Anthropology*, 16, 363-389.

Lyttleton, C. (1994). The good people of Isan: Commercial sex in northeast Thailand. *The Australian Journal of Anthropology (TAJA)*, 5(3), 257-279.

McCamish, M. & Sittitrai, W. (1997). *The context of safety: Life stories of male sex workers in Pattaya*. Bangkok: Thai Red Cross Society, Program on AIDS, Research Report No. 19.

McCamish, M., Timmins, T., Terry, D. & Gallois, C. (1993). A theory-based intervention: The theory of reasoned action in action. In D. Terry, C. Gallois & M. McCamish (Eds.). *The theory of reasoned action: Its application to AIDS preventive behaviour* (pp. 185-205). Oxford: Pergamon Press.

Miller, D. (1984). *Bringing out Roland Barthes*. Berkely: University of California Press.

Morris, R.C. (1994). Three sexes and four sexualities: Redressing the discourse on gender and sexuality in contemporary Thailand. *Positions*, 2(1), 15-43.

Murray, S.O. (1992). The "underdevelopment" of modern/gay homosexuality in MesoAmerica. In K. Plummer (Ed.). *Modern homosexualities: Fragments of lesbian and gay experience* (pp. 29-38). London and New York: Routledge.

Murray, S.O. (1994). Stigma transformation and relexification in the international diffusion of gay. In W.L Leap (Ed.). *Beyond the lavender lexicon: Authenticity, imagination and appropriation in lesbian and gay languages* (pp. 297-315). Amsterdam: Gordon and Breach Publishers.

Narvilai, A. (1994a, December). *Phu-chai Khai Tua* (Men who sell themselves). Presented at the conference, Urban Communities and Their Transformation in Bangkok and the Environs. Sirinthorn Anthropology Center, Silpakorn University, Bangkok.

Narvilai, A. (1994b, July 2). Interview: Young men following in their sisters' footsteps. *Bangkok Post: Outlook*, p. 25.

Nopkesorn, T., Sungkarom, S. & Somlum, R. (1991). *HIV prevalence and sexual behaviours among Thai men aged 21 in northern Thailand*. Bangkok: Thai Red Cross Society, Program on AIDS, Research Report No. 3.

Otagnonta, W. (1995, July 21). Women who love women. *Bangkok Post: Outlook*, p. 31.

Padgug, R. (1992). Sexual matters: On conceptualising sexuality in history. In E. Stein (Ed.). *Forms of desire: Sexual orientation and the social constructionist controversy* (pp. 43-67). New York: Routledge.

Plummer, K. (Ed.). (1992). *Modern homosexualities: Fragments of lesbian and gay experience*. London and New York: Routledge.

Richardson, D. (1983/84). The dilemma of essentiality in homosexual theory. *Journal of Homosexuality, 9*(2-3), 79-90.

Ridge, D.J., Plummer, D.C. & Minichiello, V. (1994). Young gay men and HIV: Running the risk? *AIDS CARE, 6*(4), 371-378.

Robinson, P. and Davies, P. (1991). London's homosexual male prostitutes: Power, peer groups and HIV. In P. Aggleton, G. Hart, G. & P. Davies (Eds.). *AIDS: Responses, interventions and care* (pp. 95-110). London: Palmer Press.

Ruse, M. (1995). Sexual identity: Reality or construction. In H. Harris (Ed.). *Identity: Essays based on Herbert Spencer Lectures given in the University of Oxford* (pp. 65-98). Oxford: Clarendon Press.

Shick, J.F. (1978). *Male prostitution as a deviant career*. Unpublished Manuscript.

Sittitrai, W., Phanuphak, P. & Roddy, R. (1994). *Male bar workers in Bangkok: An intervention*. Bangkok: Thai Red Cross Society Program on AIDS, Research Report No. 10.

Sittitrai, W., Sakondhavat, C. & Brown, T. (1992). *A survey of men having sex with men in a Northeastern Thai Province*. Bangkok: Thai Red Cross Society Program on AIDS, Research Report No. 5.

Sivaraksa, S. (1996, January 22). Interview: Illusions of Wealth. *Newsweek*, p. 52.

Sriwatjana, P. (1995, September). Life styles and health behaviour of male prostitutes in Patpong Area. Paper presented at the Third International Conference on AIDS in Asia and the Pacific and Fifth National AIDS Conference. Chiang Mai, Thailand.

Storer, G. (1995, April). Making choices: HIV/AIDS education and male sex workers. Paper presented at the *Second International Conference on Language in Development*. Bali, Indonesia.

Storer, G. (1997). Bar talk: Thai male sex workers and their customers. In P. Aggleton (Ed.). *Men who sell sex–International perspectives on male sex work and HIV/AIDS*. London: Taylor and Francis.

Strommen, E.F. (1989). "You're a what?" Family member reactions to the disclosure of homosexuality. *Journal of Homosexuality, 18*(1), 37-58.

Tan, M.L. (1995). Tita Aida and emerging communities of gay men: Two case studies from Metro Manila, the Philippines. In G. Sullivan and L.W. Leong (Eds.). *Gays and lesbians in Asia and the Pacific: Social and human services* (pp. 31-48). New York and London: Harrington Park Press.

Tierney, W.G. (1993). Academic freedom and parameters of knowledge. *Harvard Educational Review, 63*(2), 143-160.

Weeks, J. (1995). History, desires and identities. In R.G. Parker and J.H. Gagnon (Eds.). *Conceiving sexuality* (pp. 33-50). New York and London: Routledge.

Winichakul, T. (1995). The changing landscape of the past: New histories in Thailand since 1973. *Journal of South East Asian Studies, 26*(1), 99-120.

The Friends Thou Hast:
Support Systems
for Male Commercial Sex Workers
in Pattaya, Thailand

Malcolm McCamish

SUMMARY. Most studies of male commercial sex workers (CSWs) in Thailand have been framed within a context of HIV risk and have investigated sexual behaviours and HIV knowledge. However, Mann et al. (1992) have identified health and social services and a supportive social environment as equally essential partners in an HIV-preventive triumvirate. This paper is based on extended observation and a series of in-depth interviews with forty-three male CSWs who are both organised (bar workers) and freelance as well as a number of clients (*farang* and Thai) and bar management. This paper examines the social environment in which male CSWs operate. It considers workplace conditions and support, the personal relationships workers have with parents, friends, clients, other bar workers and management, and how these are influenced by workers' cultural norms. A number of recommendations designed to reduce HIV-infection rates are made. *[Article copies available for a fee from The Haworth Document Delivery Service: 1-800-342-9678. E-mail address: getinfo@haworthpressinc.com]*

Address correspondence to: Malcolm McCamish, Chemistry Department, The University of Queensland, Brisbane Qld, 4072, Australia.

[Haworth co-indexing entry note]: "The Friends Thou Hast: Support Systems for Male Commercial Sex Workers in Pattaya, Thailand." McCamish, Malcolm. Co-published simultaneously in *Journal of Gay & Lesbian Social Services* (The Haworth Press, Inc.) Vol. 9, No. 2/3, 1999, pp. 161-191; and: *Lady Boys, Tom Boys, Rent Boys: Male and Female Homosexualities in Contemporary Thailand* (ed: Peter A. Jackson, and Gerard Sullivan) The Haworth Press, Inc., 1999, pp. 161-191; and: *Lady Boys, Tom Boys, Rent Boys: Male and Female Homosexualities in Contemporary Thailand* (ed: Peter A. Jackson, and Gerard Sullivan) Harrington Park Press, an imprint of The Haworth Press, Inc., 1999, pp. 161-191. Single or multiple copies of this article are available for a fee from The Haworth Document Delivery Service [1-800-342-9678, 9:00 a.m. - 5:00 p.m. (EST). E-mail address: getinfo@haworthpressinc.com].

BACKGROUND

The first reported AIDS-related death in Thailand, that of a bisexual Thai male who had travelled to the USA, was reported in 1984 (Kanai & Kurata, 1995). Of the country's first seventeen reported cases of AIDS, 15 were identified as homosexually active men. This was followed by observed infections among injecting drug users (Nelson, 1994; Weniger et al., 1991) which led to a belief that Thailand would follow a pattern of infection similar to that of North America, northern Europe and Australia. This assumption, however, was soon disabused by surveillance reports of high levels of HIV infection among female commercial sex workers (CSWs) (Weniger et al., 1991). More recent studies of molecular epidemiology (Weniger, Takebe, Ou & Yamazaki, 1994) suggest that two independent epidemics were initiated at about the same time: a sexually driven epidemic associated with HIV sub-strain E, a recombinant form which had its origins in Africa, and a hypodermic epidemic associated with the American and northern European HIV sub-strain B.

This rapid spread of infection was not matched by an equivalent explosion among male CSWs, whose infection levels remained not dissimilar to those of sexually active heterosexual males of similar age. However, while this latter group has now been identified as the third wave of the Thai epidemic (Brown, Sittitrai, Vanichseni & Thisyakorn, 1994; Weniger et al., 1991), with educational campaigns developed to target them, no equivalent response has been developed for homosexually active men.

A number of explanations have been advanced for the fact that "since 1991, men who have sex with men have become almost invisible in the eyes of the public health establishment" (Sittitrai & Brown, 1994, p. S149). These include low infection rates and a reluctance to address the behaviour (Sittitrai, Brown & Sakondhavat, 1993a; Sittitrai, Brown & Virulak, 1991) leading to a "lack of information," which Sittitrai and Brown (1994, p. S150) argue, "should not be construed as a lack of a problem."

Information on prevalence levels of HIV infection among homosexually active males in Thailand is restricted to surveillance data of male CSWs (Weniger et al., 1991) or is gleaned from surveillance of military recruits. Earlier studies of military recruits in Northern Thailand (Nopkesorn et al., 1993a; Nopkesorn et al., 1993b) showed no correlation between male-male sex and HIV infection. However, data from a more recent study by Beyrer et al. (1995) of male CSWs in Chiang Mai showed an HIV-prevalence of 17.7 percent and a study of military conscripts from six northern provinces by Celentano et al. (1996) identified having sex with other males (though not necessarily male CSWs) as a risk factor for HIV infection.

Lifestyle characteristics of the male CSW can place him at considerable risk of HIV infection. Many are behaviourally bisexual, and considerable evidence exists that condom use in their commercial homosexual transactions is greater than during recreational heterosex[1] (Sittitrai, Phanuphak & Roddy, 1993b), whether paid for or *gratis*. As male CSWs occasionally have considerable disposable income, this heterosexual companionship is often associated with the consumption of alcohol (Fordham, 1995), a combination identified with enhanced risk. Thus even though a male CSW may be scrupulously safe in his own profession, income and intoxication can result in exposure to greater risk of infection than that threatening his lower income peers. The case load of HIV-infected men supposedly heterosexually exposed may well include a number who have been infected through commercial sex with other men. Though male homosexual activity is proscribed by neither the law nor religion in Thailand, and though the level of stigmatisation attached to homosexual activity in Thailand is much less than in many western countries, the Thai desire to avoid even mild social disapproval of unconventional behaviour may nevertheless inhibit the reporting of same sex behaviour (Jackson, 1989).

Male CSWs can be highly itinerant, drifting in and out of the bar scene, free-lancing on the streets or returning home to rural villages when work is scarce or farm labour is required. Tanasugarn (1989) reported that workers in Bangkok bars tended to shift bars every three months and that the average time of current bar work was six months. Similarly, Sittitrai, Phanuphak and Roddy (1993b) found that fifty percent of the workers in five Bangkok gay bars had worked there for less than two months and only about one half had worked in the same bar for more than two months. In his study in this volume, De Lind van Wijngaarden reports similar work mobility amongst male sex workers in Chiang Mai. This high level of mobility could result in the failure of periodic surveillance to reach many male CSWs. Moreover, even if work-related HIV infection had occurred, for some it could go undetected for they would not have yet seroconverted.

In summary, there is considerable justification for regarding male CSWs as being at heightened risk. Early attempts to address the problem amongst this group faltered when the epidemiology of HIV spread revealed greater epidemics among the injecting drug population of Bangkok and female CSWs, especially in the north. Recent data show that HIV prevalence among northern male CSWs is significantly greater than levels among military recruits from the same region (Beyrer et al., 1995), and that the difference is "too high not to have [infection levels] be part of their occupational risks" (Beyrer, 1997). These data demand that efforts to address this problem be renewed.

In their book *AIDS in the World*, Mann, Taratola and Netter (1992, p. 325) stated that

> An analysis of prevention programs worldwide has identified three elements as essential to the success of HIV prevention: information and education, health and social services, and a supportive social environment. . . . Yet if any of the three elements are [sic] missing, it can be stated unequivocally that prevention is not being given a fair chance to succeed.

Others have previously reported on general levels of AIDS knowledge and awareness among the general population (e.g., Sweat et al., 1995) and for male CSWs (Sittitrai et al., 1993b). This study arose out of discussions starting in 1990 with officers of the Thai Red Cross Society Program on AIDS and our joint desire to investigate the level or lack of the other two components of Mann's requirements, namely, health and social services and a supportive social environment. In this paper, I report on part of an ongoing study of male CSWs in Pattaya and examine the level of support from some of the men's institutional and personal relationships–parents, bar, clients, friends–to consider access to health services, and levels of financial security. I conclude by making some recommendations which might, hopefully, contribute to HIV prevention in the population of male CSWs.

A NOTE ON TERMINOLOGY AND LANGUAGE

Though Thai male CSWs are referred to and refer to each other as "boy" (*dek*), a term which reflects younger age, lower social status and an inherent imbalance of power and control, I shall use other descriptors, reserving "boy" for direct quotation. *Farang* is the Thai term for a Caucasian person, while "foreigner" here denotes a non-Thai Asian person. I distinguish a *customer*, for example, from a *client* who engages the services of a worker. In local terminology, a worker is taken *off* from the bar, or goes *off* with a client after a bar fee or *off* fee is paid. It is easier to describe sexual behaviour than sexual identity, and terms such as *gay* have been reserved for those who so self identify, with "homosexually active men" being used to describe men who engage in male-male sexual activity. Descriptions of Pattaya refer to 1993-94 when the detailed interviews were held.

THE MALE COMMERCIAL SEX SCENE IN PATTAYA

Pattaya is located on the Gulf of Siam, about 140 kilometres south east of Bangkok. Initially a fishing village, it was transformed by US soldiers on "rest and recreation" (R and R) leave during the Vietnam war. For a considerable time the pace of development in Pattaya, one of the closest beach resorts to the capital, outstripped the supporting infrastructure, resulting in a beach too dirty to traverse and water too polluted to swim in. More recently, serious attempts to grapple with problems of water supply, drainage and sewage treatment have been made.

While these modifications may help convert Pattaya into a family resort, they were irrelevant to its reputation of being associated with beer halls and street sex catering predominantly to heterosexuals. Pattaya has also been described as "one of the world's major gay tourist destinations" (Allyn, 1992, p. 231). Though it is relatively easy for homosexually active men to find Thai sexual partners almost anywhere in Pattaya, recruitment of participants in this study occurred in three localities: the South Pattaya bars, the "gay" section of Jomtien Beach, and the South Pattaya waterfront.

The Gay Bars. The history of the commercial gay scene in Thailand has been described by Jackson (1995) and the more recent bar scene in Pattaya by McCamish and Sittitrai (1997). Bars are either Thai style[2] or go-go bars.

When the field work for this study was conducted, there were about two dozen gay bars. Most crowded into one side-street of South Pattaya which, with its congestion of seven go-go bars, two beer bars with *off* facilities, three gay coffee shops, two gay restaurants and two gay hotels (and one tourist hotel with a large gay clientele), caroused under the banner of "Boy's Town." This, in the words of one of the proprietors, "may well be the greatest concentration of gay establishments in the world." Within two minutes walk another half a dozen go-go bars can be found. With few exceptions, the bar staff and dancers who participated in this research were recruited from this area.

Jomtien Beach. Jomtien Beach stretches to the south east of Pattaya, much of it divided into concessions providing shelter from the sun, deck chairs, and a variety of food and drink. The gay concessions are only a ten minute bus ride followed by a five minute walk from South Pattaya. Workers, most of whom are otherwise unemployed, parade the beach and eye contact is easy to establish. Occasionally, once-off Thai visitors appear on the beach, such as a student needing money to pay for a trip home, or a soldier without money who is about to embark on a military expedition. Another feature of the gay beach is the number of young men offering Thai massage, until recently a service provided almost exclusively by older men and women who plied a less diverse trade but who now have been almost totally supplanted by more youthful surrogates. Some of these masseurs blatantly tout for sex, while others use "massage" as a discreet euphemism. A small number do not provide sexual services at all.

The Waterfront of South Pattaya. In the evenings from about eight until late, freelance sex workers congregate, walking or sitting on the South Pattaya beach front. They may wait until approached or signal their availability to passing pedestrians. They are generally otherwise unemployed. In the past, freelance men would sit silently on the line of motor cycles parked outside the bars of Boys Town in direct and visible competition with the workers employed by the bars. This pattern of behaviour has since changed, the common wisdom being that bar owners have forced them away to reduce competition.

METHODOLOGY

This work forms part of a larger study of Thai male sex workers in Pattaya and their clients. It draws on direct observation and extensive field notes made intermittently over more than six years, and specifically on a series of interviews carried out in December 1993-January 1994. Sex workers interviewed during this period were recruited from the three sites described above–the bars, the beach and the water-front.[3]

The methodology has been detailed elsewhere (McCamish & Sitti-trai, 1997). Most interviews were carried out in a hotel room, which provided privacy, absence of distractions and an environment with which participants were conceptually familiar and comfortable. At the beginning the purpose of the interview was explained. In all inter-views, the interviewer, after having specifically sought permission from the worker, took detailed notes. Some interviews were taped with permission. Before the interview started it was explained that what was documented would not be shown to anyone or discussed in a way that would identify the worker. Nicknames were always used and have been further altered in this paper.

Interviews generally lasted between one hour and ninety minutes. They were carried out in English or "Thaiglish" (a functional mixture of English vocabulary and Thai syntax) by the author, or in Thai by a Thai research assistant provided by the Thai Red Cross Program on AIDS. Interviews were relatively unstructured. A schedule of question prompts ensured that all important issues were covered, but their sequence depended on the way participants responded. Extreme care was taken so as not to appear to direct the answers in any way. After the interview had been completed, participants who had revealed un-safe practices were advised about them and what should be done to avoid risk. Condoms and sachets of water-based lubricant were also distributed. Finally, participants were paid a small sum.

Beach workers were recruited during the day. They were asked if they would participate in an interview, though at that time its purpose was not explained. They were told they would be paid for participating and asked to arrive at the hotel at a predetermined time, late afternoon or early evening. Waterfront workers were recruited between 8:00 pm and 1:00 am using a similar procedure, and interviewed forthwith. Recruitment in the bars was generally carried out late at night for interviews scheduled for the next afternoon. Only one worker who was asked refused to participate. All who agreed arrived on time for the interview.[4]

Other workers, bar owners/managers, and Thai and *farang* clients have also contributed to this study. Bar owners/managers were repre-sentative of the bars from which workers were recruited. Clients pro-vided a convenient sample of people met in the bars, on the beach or through other social contacts, or who were contacted to corroborate statements. "Conversations" were not recorded, but documented as soon as possible afterwards.

During recruitment, no attempt was made to explore sexual identity. The only criteria for inclusion in the sample group were that the participant was currently or recently had been a commercial sex worker and that he was at least eighteen years old.

Workers ranged in age from 18 to 29, though the majority were between 19-22 years of age. Workers as young as 24 identified the fugacity of their career opportunities. More than 50 percent of the interviewees came from Isan, the Northeastern region, which is the largest, most populous and poorest of the major geopolitical divisions of Thailand. A number of interviewees estimated that 60-70 percent of the bar workers in Pattaya came from Isan. Sittitrai et al. (1993b) found in their study of bar workers in Bangkok that most of the workers came from this region.

Typically, both parents were still alive, though a number were separated or divorced. When parents were separated, the men talked more about their mothers, suggesting the greater strength of these ties. Parents were generally poor rice or general farmers with small farms (2-10 *rai* in area)[5] considered insufficient to support a family (Ekachai, 1990, p. 20). Some owned no land and therefore had to work as labourers. A few participants came from wealthy families, including ones with large land holdings (400 *rai*) which were rented out for income.

Four workers reported that they had been married, and two of these were parents. All four indicated that the relationship had ended. The remainder were single. Almost twenty percent self-identified as gay, with only one of this sub-group expressing an interest in sex change surgery.

LIMITATIONS OF THE STUDY

As well as the obvious disclaimers surrounding convenience sampling, certain features of the Pattaya bars may make generalisation outside Pattaya unwarranted. All bar workers came from go-go bars owned by *farang* who, as a group, may make fewer or different demands than Thai owners. Certainly where differences of opinion existed, workers regarded *farang* owners more favourably than Thai managers.

The male sex industry in Pattaya also depends heavily on overseas tourism. The holiday mood provides a fantasy environment which can maximise the opportunities for *sanuk* ("fun," "a good time") and a party, for it is often the case that a client purchases companionship as much as sexual services, and neither client nor worker has a job which requires early rising next morning. The long-time *off* is commonplace, embracing the worker too in a holiday atmosphere.

The dependence on international tourism means that the economics of the industry is highly sensitive to fluctuations in the gay population from high and low seasons. It also has an influence on the migratory habits of the workers. In Bangkok workers change bars frequently to maximise variety for the clients (Sittitrai et al., 1993b), but in Pattaya it is the *farang* who come and go. Consequently, it is not uncommon to find workers at the same bar for a number of years.

WORKPLACE CONDITIONS AND SUPPORT

Comparisons of Bar and Freelance Conditions

All workers agreed there were advantages associated with working at bars. Prostitution in Thailand is illegal, and bars provide protection from unwanted harassment by authorities. Also, by their recruitment choices, some bars can provide a relatively friendly environment for the workers. Though the larger bars cater to a wide spectrum of client tastes, smaller bars sometimes exercise specific recruitment policies, targeting, for example, the workers' geographical origins or body size. This means a worker should be able to find compatible workmates by carefully selecting the bar, and quickly discovering whether or not he fits into that environment. As Tee, a worker, and Alan, a bar owner explained:

> I went to [name] bar because I'm small and [name] takes small boys whereas [other name] takes bigger boys. (Tee: ex-dancer, doorman, age 24)

> Often the [other] boys decide, and after about five days a new boy will know if he's welcome or not. (Alan: bar owner)

Bar owners took pains to point out that, by holding copies of work-ers' identity cards, they provided considerable security for clients. If a problem such as theft from a client's room were to occur, the bar would be able to identify the worker and provide his home address to police. Though less publicised, the bars can also provide security for the workers. It is not unknown for bar owners/managers to expel clients[6] who treat the workers harshly or who try to force them to participate in unwelcome sexual acts. This is appreciated as most workers reported favourably on the bar owners and environment.

Such security and privacy are not available to the freelance worker. They, especially beach workers, are less able to avoid public displays of affection, which tourist handbooks identify as a Thai taboo. Many resist the overt advances of clients, urging, "Wait till we get to the room. Not on the beach. I'm shy." The word *ai* ("shy" or "modest") was used by some bar workers to explain why they preferred bar to beach work, and by local gay men who did not engage in sex work to explain why they avoided the beach in the company of *farang,* as this implied they were CSWs.

I'm shy. I don't go to Jomtien beach. (Sun: bar manager)

As well as "modest," *ai* implies shame and embarrassment and expresses "apprehension of criticism" (Mulder, 1992, p. 109). Sun and others who expressed similar reservations about working on the beach were subtly identifying some of their internal conflict over sex work, wanting to contain it within the environs of the bars.

But to preserve modesty is also to sacrifice freedom. Independence has been identified as an important Thai national characteristic[7] and freelance workers contrasted the regimentation of bar workers with their own lifestyle, in which it was "up to themselves" (*laew tae rao*) when they started work, how long they worked and whether they would work at all on a particular day. Another identified attraction of freelance work was that it could be combined with other work, like being a masseur. Freelance workers also identified, as disadvantages of bar work, the atmosphere thick with smoke, and the air condition-ing which, designed to cater for fully dressed customers, could be uncomfortably cold for the scantily dressed workers.

These choices should be interpreted carefully. They were often prefaced by comments that revealed previous bar work terminated because of an unidentified "problem." Bar workers identified the positive social aspects of their work and occasionally spoke pejoratively about freelance men:

> I don't like the boys on the beach who [have to] walk, walk, walk all the time [looking for *farang*]. If a client wants me, they come to my bar. (Not: dancer in a bar, age 21)

The reverse was never encountered. It would seem therefore that Coleman's (1989) observation that "bar hustlers have a higher status than street hustlers [in the USA]" is equally true in Pattaya.

FINANCIAL RELATIONSHIPS

Different bars have different policies regarding the payment of workers (see above). The go-go bars of South Pattaya generally paid their dancers a retainer of about one thousand baht per month. Workers got a percentage of the *off* fee, generally fifty baht, and ten baht for every drink which a customer bought for them, though dancers were sometimes instructed to order orange juice or beer as "I forfeit this tip if I order whisky."

Some bars would advance wages to meet room rental and other financial emergencies. But bars that paid wages also imposed a system of fines. Breaches of smoking and cruising regulations, being late, or not attracting a sufficient number of clients in a month had graded penalties. Absenteeism, even if due to sickness, was penalised with the equivalent of the *off* fee (to prevent freelancing). At times a monthly wage was completely forfeited, and workers were known to have paid their own *off* fee to satisfy a house minimum and preserve their job. These financial policies were the source of a number of complaints from workers, especially if they felt they had been unfairly treated.

Other schemes to extract money from bar workers were also identified. One Thai manager forced dancers to pay him in order to take their entitled day off, and a *farang* bar owner reported that he had dismissed his Thai manager for demanding a percentage of the money workers earned from clients. Some waiters and the *mamasan* in charge of the dancers exerted a quiet coercion on workers by recommending them or conversely discrediting a worker to potential clients-"Number [xx] is a good/bad boy"-whether or not the advice was sought. This control was increased if the bar provided *offs* ordered by telephone, or with clients negotiating with the *mamasan* rather than directly with the worker.

Despite these practices, workers acknowledged that bar work payed better than freelance.

> I worked at the [name] bar for one-and-a-half years and I have been six months on the beach. The money was better at the bar especially at high season, but I left because of a problem. I cannot go back. (Tia: beach worker, age 21)

> I used to work at [name] bar. It was difficult. Part of me liked it and part did not. Now I work the waterfront but I think bar was better for money [clients pay more]. I prefer the waterfront to the bar because I am free and nobody controls me. (Nut: waterfront worker, age 22)

The observations of Tia and Nut were supported by a number of *farang* clients who stated that they paid beach workers less than bar workers, even though with the former they could avoid the *off* fee. Bar workers generally seemed to have more and better clothes than freelance men, even allowing for the different and more casual environment of the beach.

HEALTH AND HIV RELATIONSHIPS

Bar managers in Pattaya were conscious of the HIV/AIDS epidemic and the risks of other sexually transmitted diseases. The most conscientious provided weekly medical checks for *Neisseria gonorrhoea*, comprising throat, urethral and rectal swabs which are stained and examined by microscopy. Though workers invariably referred to the clinician as "doctor," the swabs were taken by a nursing sister and examined on site by a technician. These visits were purely for clinical testing. No general or specific advice was given on safe sex. At some bars the weekly service was free; in others the staff were expected to contribute towards the costs.

A dancer with a positive stain for *N. gonorrhoea* was given antibiotic tablets and forbidden to work for a number of days. Some bars covered the costs of medication but others expected staff to pay. The policy of some bars was to dismiss a dancer if he had more than a certain number of positive stains for gonorrhoea, though another owner dismissed gonorrheal infection, particularly of the throat, as "an occupational hazard."[8]

Blood tests for syphilis and HIV were less well organised and infrequent, if they occurred at all. One bar owner said he sent his workers to a medical practitioner, another bar organised monthly blood checks which management paid for, but most bar workers claimed that they had to organise and pay for any blood test themselves.

Some bars provided general warnings about HIV, instructing their staff to "always use condoms," which they claimed to provide free of charge, though, according to some *farang* clients, these were not always in evidence. No bar in Pattaya was reported to provide free water-based lubricant. Bar workers were exposed to occasional educational visits by FACT (the Fraternity for AIDS Cessation in Thailand) and its affiliated Sen See Khao (White Line) dance troupe, a non-government organisation (NGO) which used to present its safe sex show to workers in the area about every six months. Prudence Borthwick notes the work of FACT amongst homosexually active men in Chiang Mai in northern Thailand in her paper in this volume.

Though conscientious regarding health checks, no bar cultivated any overt safe sex ambience for customers. Workers, consequently, might have wondered if management were less concerned about the health of their workers than the profitability of their business, and clients could be forgiven for concluding that the bars were unconcerned about the protection of their staff. All workers had heard about AIDS and identified the media, specifically TV, as their source of information, which is consistent with results from other studies on sources of HIV information (Lyttleton, 1994; Sittitrai et al., 1993b). All workers failed to distinguish HIV from AIDS, using the latter term exclusively. It would be surprising if a number also did not confuse the gonorrhoea checks for HIV tests.

Health checks were not obligatory for freelance workers. All knew about AIDS and knew condoms provided protection, but for some the cost of condoms was a barrier to their use. Most freelance workers claimed occasional checks for STDs, though some, like Tik, were fatalistic regarding their risk of infection and death and neither took precautions nor appeared to care at all.

Condoms are unnecessary, as I may die tomorrow. . . . If a *farang* does not want to use a condom, it is not important. I know about AIDS, but . . . [he shrugs]. (Tik: beach worker)

WORKERS' RELATIONSHIPS WITH PARENTS

Most participants said their parents did not know they sold sex. They generally explained the money they sent home by claiming to work in a hotel or a restaurant, despite the amounts sent home being patently incompatible with the earning power of these putative jobs. This parental "blind-eye" must be interpreted in the context of Thai patterns of non-involvement in the affairs of others, especially where closer scrutiny could lead to conflict. It is better not to ask than to force an unsettling confrontation which could cause the worker to be stigmatised or to lose face.

Allyn's (1992, p. 120) statement that there is minimal stigmatisation of male sex workers is inconsistent with the findings of Sittitrai et al. (1993b) and of this study. Most workers indicated that fear of being shamed prevented them from revealing their occupation to their parents, as Chai explained,

My family knows I am a sex worker–so too do many people from the village. The village people understand that what I do is for my parents, who are very poor, but I am shy [*ai*], which is why I don't go home often. (Chai: waterfront worker, age 25)

Like Chai, most workers belong to the poorer rural classes where children by 15-16 years of age must shoulder a full adult work load (Smith et al., 1968) and where their inescapable and lifelong obligation to parents is a fundamental cultural characteristic (Mulder, 1992, p. 64).[9] In return for the initial care provided by parents, especially the mother, the child, as soon as (s)he is economically independent, must start to repay that obligation. A young man in the prime of life would neither expect nor seek support. Thus Bee, a waterfront worker, described an earlier time in Pattaya when he had no money and had been without food for four days:

Maybe I could speak to my family, but I don't like my mother to give me money, because I am a man, and I can work, and so I think I won't go to my house [to ask for help]. (Bee: waterfront worker, age 21)

None of the men mentioned that they could seek help from their parents when asked whom they could turn to in time of need. Powerful cultural forces determine that at this time of life the flow of obligations is unidirectional.[10]

WORKERS' RELATIONSHIPS WITH CLIENTS

Cohen (in Leheny, 1995, p. 368) has argued that female "prostitution represents a rather unstable livelihood bringing moments of temporary affluence but frequent concerns about safety and financial security." While this is also generally true for male workers, sex work for some men can provide a long-term, sometimes permanent, escape from life as an unskilled farm labourer. This is because the gay sex industry is more than a process of mutual exploitation in which the *farang's* greater wealth is exchanged for the youth of the worker. Though one *farang* informant joked about his long-term Thai acquaintance in the following way, "When I arrive at the airport, Moo greets my wallet, and then welcomes me," he has nevertheless repeated this ritual for almost a decade, suggesting a considerable degree of commitment and emotional involvement.

As in the case of Moo and his *farang* friend, some stories of financial support extending beyond a short vacation were confirmed. One participant who stated that he "stayed with a German for eight months who gave me about 100,000 baht," produced telegraphic receipts showing that he had sent most of the money home to his family. Another informant, who lived with his *farang* lover (also interviewed) who had business interests in Pattaya and regularly spent about half the year in Thailand, stated:

I do not go to the beach much by myself as it does not look good, and I do love [name]. We have been together now for two years. He has given me about 100,000 baht. (Sorn: ex-barworker, age 22)

Such long-term relationships were generally sought by older *farang* who continue to visit or who have retired to live in Pattaya, having left countries where homosexual behaviour is (or at least when they were younger) proscribed by law, or where it still at least carries significant stigma. One retired *farang* who was interviewed reported visiting his friend and family in Isan twice a year and contributing significantly to their support. Another had formally adopted a younger Thai lover, buying property in his name where they continued to live, even though the intimacy had ended. First reported with Thai female CSWs, this phenomenon of "open-ended prostitution," defined by Cohen (see Ford & Koetsawang, 1991, p. 410) as a "peculiar mixture of pecuniary interest and emotional attachment [which] in extreme cases may become purely emotional," can also be observed in the relations between some male CSWs and clients.

The majority of workers, however, sought a more conventional future. Nevertheless, while acknowledging "I work for money," many workers were happy to stay with a client for a week or two–the length of their holiday.

> I can care for and be happy with a good client for a long time–though primarily it means I can send money home. (Joi: bar worker, age 25)

The opposite view was expressed by Lek, who was worried about his future, because "at twenty-four, I'm too old, I'm no longer handsome," a declaration which was rejected by a "straw poll" of gay farang taken at the beach a few days after he made the comment. He had formerly worked as a dancer but more recently had gone free lance, occasionally working the beach or the streets outside the bars. Because of previous bad experiences, he only went "short time."

> I don't want to stay a long time with a farang in case he doesn't like me. The first day is good and the second is OK but then they get bored. (Lek: ex bar dancer, beach worker, age 24)

Nearly all the workers had stories to tell of good and bad clients. Assessments were most frequently based on the sexual demands of and economic rewards from clients. All workers interviewed said they would masturbate (*chak wao*)[11] and perform oral sex (*samok*)[12] on clients. All said they would engage in penetrative anal sex with a client, though some would not take the insertive role and the majority stating that they did not like to be fucked. The men interviewed expressed little concern about being involved in more esoteric sexual practices, providing they were the performers or active party. The men only infrequently referred to clients who wanted to be fist fucked, beaten or who liked to be tied up, handcuffed, or otherwise restrained during sex. Some of the men told of occasions when they were asked to urinate or defecate on clients. The workers thought these behaviours were amusing and their descriptions were often accompanied by uproarious laughter. Inaccurately, but almost universally, such clients were called *sadit* (from the English term "sadist").

Sadly, at times, brutality from clients was also revealed. A few workers said that they had been beaten because they refused to be fucked, or refused to be fucked without a condom.

> Some customers do not want to use condoms–especially Germans. That is *ok* by me. I am worried that I will lose customers if I insist on [using] condoms. (Nut: waterfront worker, age 22)

> Germans are no good. They treat boys badly. They want too much sex, all the time, but they pay well. Germans like to fuck but don't want to use condoms. If I insist, they get angry and hit me. When they want to fuck without a condom, I refuse. They usually accept but pay less money. (Yar: dancer at a bar, age 28)

While clients from most western countries were complimented or condemned randomly, Germans seemed to be singled out for their negative attitudes towards using condoms. It has been reported by Kleiber and Wilke (1993) that the percentage of German sex tourists who use condoms is "alarmingly low," and that sex tourism accounts for perhaps ten percent of all Germans who are HIV-infected. However, many workers spoke especially highly of the Japanese, specifically in terms of their generosity and their simple sexual needs (compared to many western clients). This view was confirmed by one bar owner, "The Japanese are big tippers, three to five thousand baht, and they generally only want to be fucked." It was not uncommon to see a group of Japanese tourists in a bar partying with a number of workers or stuffing 500 baht banknotes down the briefs of a fancied worker while he danced on stage. I once witnessed a bar worker trying (successfully) to break a previously negotiated engagement with an American *farang* because of a subsequent higher offer from a Japanese so, he said, he could "make big, big money."

Almost all men interviewed expressed a preference for *farang* or foreign clients. Reasons, when given, formed a consistent pattern. Workers feared that Thai clients could make more trouble, they "know too much," talk among themselves, and it is "less easy to hide things from the Thai [client]." Thai clients reportedly paid less, or were sometimes drunk and did not want to pay at all. Workers would be less likely to complain to a Thai client and would find it much harder to challenge a refusal to use condoms by a Thai, who would inevitably assume a socially superior position as client. They therefore felt more comfortable with foreigners who, more ignorant of or less concerned with the subtle hierarchies of the Thai social system, would be less likely to cause workers to lose face.

However, some self-identified gay workers expressed the desire to establish long-term relationships with another Thai. They saw these desired relationships purely in terms of emotional involvement, whereas workers who expressed interest in a long-term relationship with a *farang* sought economic benefits as well.

SELF-RELIANCE: SAVINGS AND THE FUTURE

One stereotype of the Thai, widespread even in Thailand, is the belief that they tend to live for today, with little planning or concern for the future. William J. Klausner, in his book *Reflections on Thai Culture* (1987, p. 86), has written:

> Research studies have defined Thai national character in terms of self reliance, independence, pragmatism, status consciousness, enjoyment of living (*sanuk*), present oriented and the like.

Such a lifestyle assumes that a worker will spend tomorrow what he is paid tonight, and so be poorly equipped to face an accident or crisis. While sometimes true, such stereotyping is over-simplistic and may have different consequences. Conspicuous generosity–the gentle and good heart–confirms status, however temporary, on the spender, and contributes to establishing and maintaining a complex web of obligations which will ensure, as much as possible, that the giver will not go hungry should he too fall on hard times.

But money must not only support the worker and maintain his social networks and provide assistance to parents, it must also provide savings for the future. It is expected that when a man marries and settles down he will be able to support his wife and family, as "No lady will want a man with no money!"

Those interviewed formed two distinct groups when discussing their future. Lon typified those who supported parents and saved, having plans for the future and some idea of how much it would cost. Lon was proud of his independence and his ability to help himself "if there were a problem, or if [I] got sick."

> I send money through the post to my parents, and now I have saved 10,000 baht. My room is near work so I can walk to work but I am looking for a new room as this one costs 1,300 baht. When I have enough money [identified as 100,000 baht], I want to go back home and work the farm. Then I will marry and have children. (Lon: dancer in bar, age 22)

The absence of savings cannot of itself be used as a measure of the absence of future planning. Daeng was representative of a small group of informants who shared goals similar to Lon, although temporarily lacking savings at the time of this study.

> I have no savings. I share a room with three friends from [home town] and they would have to take care of me if I became sick, as I have no money. When I have enough money, about 80,000 baht, I can go back to the farm. I would like to get married when I am 23-24. (Daeng: motor cycle taxi driver, age 20)

Daeng used to be a bar worker. Because few customers came to his bar, he stopped work eighteen days prior to his interview–he was precise about dates–returned home and borrowed his father's motor bike which he then operated as a taxi. "I have greater freedom. I make about 200 baht a day, and now I can tell my parents what I do."

Contrasted with Lon and Daeng were the workers described by Dee, a Thai bar manager:

> Some boys save, but when they are young they don't think of the future, and even if they do save, they are not always in control. (Dee: bar manager, age 27)

Characteristically, such workers were either fatalistic about their future (e.g., Tik, above) or, at best, passively unconcerned.

> When I have money, I can give some to my parents, but now I
> have no money. I would like to go back home and open a shop
> but that will cost me 40-50,000 baht, so it will take me a long
> time to save, as when I have money, I like to spend it [laughing].
> (Tia: beach worker, age 24)

Tia worked the beach sporadically. Unlike most workers, his
clothes were dirty and remained unchanged and unwashed for several
days. Though "I know about AIDS and must protect myself," he only
occasionally uses condoms with male clients or female friends. His
responses to questions about his future were characteristic of those
reported by Boles and Elifson (1994) in their study of male sex workers in Atlanta, Georgia. Pollack's hypothesis (1992) that attitudes of
fatalism contribute to continuing levels of unsafe sex in gay men, a
correlation which has been observed in homosexually active men in
Australia (Bartos et al., 1993) and Singapore prostitutes (Wong et al.,
1993), is no less germane to Pattaya.

FRIENDSHIPS AND LIVING ARRANGEMENTS

Perhaps the first and greatest difference a *farang* notices in Thailand is the seeming pervasiveness and intimacy of social relationships.
Everybody knows everybody else, identifying them as friend (*pheuan*)
or in some relationship term Westerners reserve for blood kin. Sharing
is a way of life. On the beach or in the street it is common to see one
person buy food, and several share the meal. Yet the Thai distinguish
between such "eating friends" (*pheuan kin*) and "friends to the
death" (*pheuan tai*). As one informant more dramatically expressed it:

> There are two types of Thai: those who will kill you and those
> who will kill for you. (Noi: beach worker, age 26, field notes,
> 1991)

Consequently it would be dangerous to interpret this apparently
smooth cultural interaction as being more than superficial or being
capable of translation into support.

The willingness to share can rapidly disappear and a fierce independence exert itself, especially when problems are faced. Then the Thai
become unusually taciturn and inwards looking. A solicitous question

of "What's the matter?" is likely to be met with "Not your problem," just as the desire to share a concern with a Thai friend will be ignored with "Not my problem!" When a Thai has a problem, he is most likely to excuse himself from company to be by himself: "I need to think."

This separation of sharing the good and isolating the bad operates at a number of levels. A Thai expects to take care of himself and to be self-reliant (see Note 7).

Most importantly, he must preserve face, which, by sharing a problem, may be sacrificed. The price of maintaining face is sometimes loneliness and isolation–magnified more in the less familiar environment of the bar and the beach where the support of kin, however fragile, is absent. This self reliance (and isolation) is reflected when the workers talk about their friends and their choice of accommodation. Rooms in Pattaya are expensive by non-metropolitan Thai standards, with monthly rates generally in the range of 1,200-1,500 baht. There would be obvious financial benefits of sharing a room–and the rent–yet many workers preferred to live alone.

When precise reasons were given, they generally reflected an absence of social compatibility or betrayed a fear of theft.

> I have four or five good friends but at [the bar] when I work I don't have friends. That is why I don't share a room, because I don't like to. Some boys drink and smoke too much–me I drink only a little. (Chao: bar worker, age 25)

> I live alone and don't share a room as a roommate may take my money. (Joi: bar worker, age 25)

Like others who had considerable savings and possessions, Joi did not trust his eating friends with more than a meal. One bar worker related how he took his motor bike into his room at night so that it would be safe. The description of his security system of locks and chains made it sound more like New York than Pattaya.

Many workers said that they did not have special or close friends whom they trust. Those who identified close friends identified them as coming from the same village (like Daeng, above) or else the friendship had developed over a long period of time.

> I share a room with a friend whom I have known for 2-3 years.
> (Ton: waterfront worker, age 21)

There was never expressed any feeling of community or indication of solidarity based on the common bond of their work. The friend to the death who will stand by and be supportive even in difficult circumstances is rare. Jackson (1995, p. 52) maintains that a Thai is lucky to have one *pheuan tai*, while Forster's (1976) study of friendship in rural Thailand claims that a Thai would have fewer than three. Thus, for most, the bosom friend is a fiction.

Thai social relationships are based on status differences between individuals rather than between classes, and so there is no culture of forming groups for collective support based on shared interests (see Smith et al., 1968, p. 113). Such issues of non-equality have been blamed for the failure of Thai soccer teams, of cooperative farms (Klausner, 1987, p. 360) and the low membership of trade unions (Mulder, 1992, p. 107; Kulick & Wilson, 1992, p. 142). In a number of countries, effective anti-HIV interventions based on community development models have been able to tap pre-existing social or community organisation. These structures do not yet exist among male commercial sex workers in Pattaya.

IMPROVING HEALTH AND SOCIAL SERVICES FOR PATTAYA MALE SEX WORKERS

The above stories clearly identify the vulnerability of the Thai male sex worker in terms of Mann's (1992) three *sine quibus non* of effective HIV-preventive measures, namely information and education, health and social services, and a supportive social environment. The men are separated from any supportive environment that the home and village might provide. Because of the shame associated with their work, they feel unable to discuss it with kinsfolk. They operate in a culture which militates against the formation of intimate supportive friendships which can be relied upon positively in circumstances of crisis. The worker exists, despite the appearance of well being, in an isolated and often threatening world. Notwithstanding this, a number of immediate simple and inexpensive responses at an institutional and at a personal level are possible.

INFORMATION AND EDUCATION SERVICES

In his study in north east Thailand, Lyttleton (1994) has reported that "when asked what causes AIDS" the majority of respondents identified sex and injecting drug use, but "only 15 [out of 435 villagers questioned] said AIDS is caused by a virus." No participant in the current study distinguished between AIDS and HIV infection. This failure to differentiate between act and virus may confuse conceptualisations of condom use. For some, sex *per se* may be identified as the risk without any realisation that condoms allow sex but deny entry of the virus into the body. The lack of understanding of how and why condoms provide protection may also explain the lack of skills in condom use. While the desire to keep messages simple in general campaigns is laudable, it may be advantageous to provide more detailed information to CSWs.

Greater detail might also counter the over-simplistic messages of "always use condoms with clients," advice sometimes given at the weekly checkup but never extended to sex outside work with commercial or social female partners. It may be that media warnings directed towards unprotected heterosexual intercourse had been subsumed by these more specific work-related messages, for while a number of workers claimed they always used condoms for penetrative sex with clients, none admitted to always using them with female partners.

SUPPORTIVE SOCIAL ENVIRONMENT

Bars made no attempt to supplement the infrequent educational visits from outside organisations. Safe sex policies could be easily reinforced among bar staff and customers by simple messages on drink coasters or on account slips. Such messages would also assist workers to inform potential clients of bar policy that condoms must be used.

Bars could exploit Thai cultural norms and social networks that already exist among workers from the same area. Within Thai families, older siblings have responsibility for and authority over younger ones (Smith et al., 1968, p. 122), and juniors are not expected to contradict their seniors (Mole, 1973, p. 52). Bars could foster *phinorng* ("older brother-younger brother") relationships so that a newly recruited bar worker could be paired with an older, more experienced mentor, preferably from the same region of the country. This would provide a new recruit with useful instruction, support and access to a source of practical survival tactics until he settled into what is, at least initially, an uncomfortable experience.

Bars also provide a setting in which interventions could reach free lance workers as well as the recreational sexual partners of workers. Despite the byzantine sexual networks of sex workers and clients and the bewildering taxonomy and geographies of sites where male-male sexual recruitment occurs, it has been shown that a successful bar-based intervention can reach far beyond the physical confines of its place of delivery (McCamish et al., 1997).

HEALTH SERVICES

A number of limitations of the weekly medical checks for gonorr-hoea could be addressed. One bar owner stated that a number of workers, when suspended from work because of infection, would go and freelance. He argued that, where feasible, medication should be administered via injection and the worker kept in the bar as long as possible to allow the injection to take some effect. Proper medical advice should be sought to determine the clinical validity of such actions, and to assess whether it should be implemented. Another owner claimed that some clinics/clinicians falsely identified infections (especially of the throat) so that they could profit from the increased sale of antibiotics.

A need also exists for more specialised HIV testing, counselling and support services. The size of the total sex industry in Pattaya could justify an extension of Bangkok's anonymous HIV clinic operated by the Program on AIDS of the Thai Red Cross, or a similar agency. The clinic could possibly be self-supporting, funded by the fees already paid by bars to have their staff tested and, as its services to the bars could be regimented, it could operate for an appropriate number of days per month. The use of rapid, saliva-based agglutination testing means that the service could dispense with expensive laboratory pro-cedures. This would guarantee quality service at no added cost.

COMMUNITY DEVELOPMENT

In his evaluation of health education concerning HIV/AIDS, Aggleton (1989, p. 226) stated that community development health models "reject the idea that the individual is responsible for his/her own health and suggest that people should act collectively to identify and satisfy their health needs." Also, peer support has been shown to be fundamental in a number of successful HIV-preventive interventions (McCamish et al., 1993, pp. 190-194). Unfortunately, among Thai sex workers little evidence of community exists and would have to be created *ab initio*. Community development programs would be better based on occupation rather than sexual identity.

As a "gay" community program is likely to be unattractive to the majority of workers who do not identify as gay, there is also need for gay community development. Though Thailand has played host to an International Asian Gay and Lesbian Conference (Allyn, 1992, p. 94), there is little evidence of any organised Thai gay community. As one gay Thai doctor stated:

> Because of the absence of criminal sanctions in the past against homosexuality, there has been no community formed–for example to agitate for law reform–which could be mobilised to address the challenge of AIDS. (Dr. T., fieldnotes, 1992)

This, however, may be changing, for experiments in community development have begun. The FACT group, formed in 1989 specifically to respond to the AIDS epidemic in Thailand but with a gay identity, later expanded its activities to include monthly social meetings which were initially held at the home of the founder. These moved when a community centre, FACT House, was developed, but this has subsequently closed. In Chiang Mai, partly with Australian Government funds, the community program Chai Chuay Chai (Men Helping Men) was established in the mid-1990s for men who have sex with men. Though FACT no longer seems to operate and Chai Chuay Chai is defunct, future organisers should learn from those experiences. Prudence Borthwick provides a report on the activities of Chai Chuay Chai in her paper in this volume.

The attempt of Chai Chuay Chai to meet the needs of both the gay-identified and the male CSW communities (Greg Carl, personal communication, 1996) caused considerable problems. The attraction of an inclusive program is that continuity is more likely to be provided by local gay men rather than itinerant sex workers. The price is that if the aims of the group are perceived to be too closely allied with a gay agenda, then the group becomes less attractive to the majority of sex workers who identify as heterosexual and who may feel alienated and disenfranchised.

For a community development model to be implemented, a community of male sex workers would first need to be generated, based on occupation. A number of sex-worker collectives, including Thailand's EMPOWER for female sex workers, might provide useful insights and models. Given that one aim of any community development scheme is that it become self-supporting, difficulties which would need to be addressed include the itinerant nature of male sex workers, both between bars and from bar-to-home when labour is needed on the farm. One of the benefits from a community model is that it would extend beyond the bars to other sexual localities.

Another non-government organisational (NGO) model which might provide insights is the Wednesday Friends' Club, an initiative of the Chulalongkorn Hospital and the Thai Red Cross Society, which provides support for people infected with HIV. But even these NGOs can have identity problems. It took a long time for people in Australia who were not gay-identified but who were HIV-positive to feel comfortable with the support services provided by AIDS Councils and similar organisations which were perceived to be "gay." The reverse concern has been expressed by a gay Thai man with HIV, when informed of the services and facilities of the Wednesday Friends' Club. He was not interested because he perceived it would be "family" oriented.

CONCLUSION

Currently, no Thai national program is focussed on male commercial sex workers, though considerable evidence exists that they are at heightened risk of HIV infection. I have attempted to contextualise a number of these vulnerabilities in terms of the working environment, the relationships workers have with family, friends and clients, and the traditional Thai cultural frameworks in which the workers operate. I believe that such an understanding can facilitate the development of targeted anti-HIV interventions which are effective, so that the successes now being experienced with other vulnerable and targeted communities can also be reproduced with these men.

ACKNOWLEDGMENTS

The study reported in this paper grew out of a number of discussions starting in 1990 with officers of the Thai Red Cross Society Program on AIDS, specifically Dr. Werasit Sittitrai whose encouragement, especially in the early stages of this project, I gratefully acknowledge. The Program on AIDS also made funds available which were used to pay workers for their interviews. I would particularly like to record my gratitude to Manoon Chomkhamsing who assisted in the recruitment of workers, acted as translator when necessary and with good humour rejected the advances of a number of *farang* who misinterpreted his role.

Most importantly I register my indebtedness to the men whose life stories are chronicled here. Without exception they spoke openly and with good humour of their experiences and of the events which shaped their lives. It is also my sad responsibility to record that since the interviews took place, at least one of the men has died and at least two others are known to be suffering from AIDS-related illnesses. There could be others. It is to all the participants but especially to these men that this paper is humbly dedicated.

NOTES

1. In January 1990 I witnessed, with permission and for the first time, one of the weekly check-ups for gonorrhoea at one of the male go-go bars in Pattaya. The nurse taking the swabs maintained that most of the gay clients acted responsibly, "the homos are not the problem, it is the heteros," and indicated one of the workers who had recently been cured of gonorrhoea transmitted, she maintained, from a female US tourist (McCamish, fieldnotes 1990).

2. In Thai style bars workers generally sit at one end of the bar in street clothes. They tend to be approached indirectly through the mediation of a person in charge, whether the manager, *kaptan* (i.e. "captain") or *mamasan*. The *kaptan* will ask a client, "What type of boy are you looking for?" and make a recommendation, thereby exercising considerable control (Storer, 1996). Workers may or may not be paid a retainer wage by the management. They may be paid if they dance or participate in a show, but if this performance results in an *off* they may forfeit this pay. Sittitrai et al. (1993b) report in their study of male sex workers in Bangkok bars that the majority

did not receive any money for drinks bought for them by clients, nor any basic salary. Salary policies vary with bar owners and bar style. One Pattaya worker who had worked in a Bangkok bar where workers sat in street clothes stated that he received neither a wage nor a share of the *off* fee. He was paid 60 baht if he danced, but only if he did not attract a client. If he did attract a client, he forfeited the 60 baht! Storer (1996) reports a similar payment structure in Bangkok bars. In go-go bars workers take turns dancing on stage in bikini briefs. When not dancing they dress, generally in an identifying uniform. Dancers are paid a monthly retainer. Introductions between a customer and a dancer can be direct without going through another staff member. My observations are that *farang* may seek the advice of bar staff but prefer to establish contact directly, whereas Thai customers almost invariably negotiate through the *kaptan*.

3. Recruitment figures for interviews were: bars 18, beach 13, waterfront 5. Bar workers, irrespective of where they were recruited, were so categorised. Seven ex-workers who now have other employment but who may "occasionally go with *farang*" were also interviewed.

4. The arrival of participants in the hotel lobby "on the hour" caused some amusement for the staff, who marvelled at the appetite and stamina of the interviewer, until the more mundane purpose of the visits was explained to them.

5. The Thai measure of land area, the *rai*, is equal to 1600 square metres or 0.16 hectare or 0.396 acre.

6. The manager of one bar, now closed, instructed workers to get dressed and leave immediately if a client refused to use condoms for penetrative sex. The bar guaranteed to pay the worker a minimum reasonable tip so he would not be tempted by financial need to take unnecessary health risks.

7. Suntaree Komin (1991) in her national study of the Thai value system found that of the 23 values studied, those associated with ego, independence, pride, dignity and self esteem were most highly rated (p. 133), while those associated with ambition and hard work ranked as least important (pp. 197-198).

8. According to one venereologist interviewed, while genital and rectal tests for gonorrhoea are accurate, the myriad bacterial flora of the throat render the results from standard methylene blue gram staining more suspect.

9. While it was never acknowledged, it is possible that the desire of parents for material possessions and hence dependence on the income-earning capacity of their unskilled offspring may influence the decision to become a CSW. The expressed need by a number of interviewees to remit to parents more than could be earned through other work available to them is consistent with this hypothesis. Thus, though the methods are less overt than the sale of female children in prostitution, the outcomes are not dissimilar.

10. This sense of obligation does not mean that parents will not help, merely that they cannot be asked. This feeling was tapped by one former bar owner in his anti-HIV message: "If you got AIDS you would get sick and in order to look after you, your parents would have to sell their land [buffalo, gold, or whatever] that you helped them buy."

11. *Chak wao* literally means "to pull on a kite [string]" or "to fly a kite," and this idiomatic description of the motion of repeatedly tugging on a kite string being the most common colloquial Thai metaphor for male masturbation.

12. *Samok*, from the English "to smoke [a cigarette]," is a common Thai idiom for oral sex.

REFERENCES

Aggleton, P. (1989). Evaluating health education about AIDS. In P. Aggleton, G. Hart & P. Davies (Eds.). *AIDS: Social representations, social practices* (pp. 220-236). Philadelphia, PA: Falmer Press.

Allyn, E. (1992). *The men of Thailand: 1993 guide to gay Thailand*. Fourth Edition. San Francisco, CA: Bua Luang Publishing Co.

Bartos, M., McLeod, J., & Nott, P. (1993). *Meaning of sex between men*. Canberra: Department of Health Housing and Community Services.

Beyrer, C., Eiumtrakul, S., Celentano, D.D., Nelson, K.E., Ruckphaopunt, S., & Khamboonruang, S. (1995). Same-sex behaviour, sexually transmitted diseases and HIV risks among young northern Thai men. *AIDS, 9*(2), 171-176.

Boles, J & Elifson, K.W. (1994). Sexual identity and HIV: The male prostitute. *Journal of Sex Research, 31*(1), 39-46.

Brown, T., Sittitrai, W., Vanichseni, S., & Thisyakorn, U. (1994). The recent epidemiology of HIV and AIDS in Thailand. *AIDS, 8*(suppl. 2), S131-S141.

Celentano, D.D., Nelson, K.E., Suprasert, S. et al. (1996). Risk factors for HIV-1 seroconversion among young men in northern Thailand. *Journal of American Medical Association, 275*(2), 122-127.

Coleman, E. (1989). The development of male prostitution activity among gay and bisexual adolescents. *Journal of Homosexuality, 17*(2), 131-149.

Ekachai, S. (1990). *Behind the smile: Voices of Thailand*. Bangkok: Thai Development Support Committee.

Ford, N., & Koetsawang, S. (1991). The socio-cultural context of the transmission of HIV in Thailand. *Social Science and Medicine, 33*(4), 405-414.

Fordham, G. (1995). Whisky, women and song: Men alcohol and AIDS in Northern Thailand. *The Australian Journal of Anthropology (TAJA), 6*(3), 154-177.

Forster, B.L. (1976). Friendship in rural Thailand. *Ethnology, 15*(30), 251-267.

Jackson, P.A. (1989). *Male homosexuality in Thailand: An interpretation of contemporary Thai sources*. Elmhurst NY: Global Academic Publishers.

Jackson, P.A. (1995). *Dear Uncle Go: Male homosexuality in Thailand*. Bangkok: Bua Luang Books.

Kanai, K., & Kurata, T. (1995). Review: Collected materials and records of HIV/ AIDS prevalence and the contemporary social changes in Thailand. *Japanese Journal of Medical Science and Biology, 48*(1), 1-48.

Klausner, W.J. (1987). *Reflections on Thai culture*. Third Edition. Bangkok: Amarin Printing Co.

Kleiber, D., & Wilke, M. (1993, June 6-11). *Sexual behaviour of German (sex) tourists*. Paper presented at IX International Conference on AIDS, Berlin. (Abstract No. WS-D10-02)

Komin, S. (1991). *Psychology of the Thai people: Values and behaviour patterns.* Bangkok: Magenta Co.

Kulick, E., & Wilson, D. (1992). *Thailand's turn: Profile of a new dragon.* New York NY: St Martin's Press.

Leheny, D. (1995). A political economy of Asian sex tourism. *Annals of Tourism Research, 22*(2), 367-384.

Lyttleton, C. (1994). Knowledge and meaning; The AIDS education campaign in rural Northeast Thailand. *Social Science and Medicine, 38*(1), 135-146.

Mann, J., Taratola, D.J.M., & Netter, T.W. (Eds.). (1992). *AIDS in the world.* Cambridge MA: Harvard University Press.

McCamish, M. (1990). Gay sex and AIDS in Thailand. *National AIDS Bulletin, 4*(3), 25-26.

McCamish, M., Timmins, P., Terry, D., & Gallois, C. (1993). A theory based intervention: The theory of reasoned action in action. In D. Terry, C. Gallois & M. McCamish (Eds.). *The theory of reasoned action: Its application to AIDS preventive behaviour* (pp. 185-205). Oxford: Pergamon Press.

McCamish, M., & Sittitrai, W. (1997). *The context of safety: Life stories and lifestyles of male sex workers in Pattaya.* Bangkok: Thai Red Cross Society Program on AIDS, Research Report No 19.

Mole, R.L. (1973). *Thai values and behaviour patterns.* Rutland, VT: Charles E. Tuttle Co.

Mulder, N. (1992). *Inside Thai society: An interpretation of everyday life.* Bangkok: Duang Kamol.

Nelson, K.E. (1994). The epidemiology of HIV infection among injecting drug users and other risk populations in Thailand. *AIDS, 8*(10), 1499-1500.

Nopkesorn, T., Sweat, M.D., Kaensing, S., & Teppa, T. (1993). *Sexual behaviours for HIV-infection in young men in Payao.* Bangkok: Thai Red Cross Society Program on AIDS, Research Report No 6.

Nopkesorn, T., Mastro, T.D., Sangkharomya, S., Sweat, M., Singharaj, P., Limpakarnjanarat, K., Gayle, H.D., & Weniger, B.G. (1993). HIV-1 infection in young men in Northern Thailand. *AIDS, 7*, 1233-1239.

Pollack, M. (1992). AIDS: A problem for sociological research. *Current Sociology, 40*(3), 85-102.

Sittitrai, W., & Brown, T. (1994). Risk factors for HIV infection in Thailand. *AIDS 8*(suppl 2), S143-S153.

Sittitrai, W., Brown, T., & Virulrak, S. (1991). Patterns of bisexuality in Thailand. In R.A.P. Tielman, M. Carballo, & A.C. Hendriks (Eds.). *Bisexuality and HIV/AIDS* (pp. 97-117). Buffalo NY: Prometheus Books.

Sittitrai, W., Brown, T., & Sakondhavat, C. (1993a). Levels of risk behaviour and AIDS knowledge in Thai men having sex with men. *AIDS Care, 5*(3), 261-271.

Sittitrai, W., Phanupak, P., & Roddy, R. (1993b). *Male bar workers in Bangkok: An intervention trial.* Bangkok: Thai Red Cross Society Program on AIDS, Research Report No 10.

Smith, H.H., Bernier, D.W., Bunge, F.M., Rintz, F.C., Shinn, R-S., & Teleki, S. (1968). *Area Handbook for Thailand.* Washington DC: U.S. Government Printing Office.

Storer, G. (1996, October). *Bar talk: Thai male sex workers and their customers.* Chiang Mai: Paper presented at VI International Conference on Thai Studies.

Sweat, M.D., Nopkesorn, T., Mastro, T.D., Sangkharomya, S., MacQueen, K., Pokapanichwong, W., Sawaengdee, Y., & Weniger, B.G. (1995). AIDS awareness among a cohort of young Thai men: Exposure to information, level of knowledge, and perception of risk. *AIDS Care, 7*(5), 573-591.

Tanasugarn, C. (1989, January 24-27). *Condom education among gay bar men in Bangkok.* Bangkok: Paper presented at 2nd International Congress on AIDS in Asia.

Weniger, B.G., Takebe, Y., Ou, C-Y., & Yamazaki, S. (1994). The molecular epidemiology of HIV in Asia, *AIDS, 8*(suppl 2), S13-S28.

Weniger, B.G., Limpakarnjanarat, K., Ungchusat, K., Thanprasertsuk, S., Choopanya, K, Vanichseni, S., Uneklabh, T., Thongcharoen, P., & Wasi, C. (1991). The epidemiology of HIV infection and AIDS in Thailand. *AIDS, 5*(suppl. 2), S71-S85.

Wong, M.L., Archibald, C., Roy, K.W., Chan, C., Goh, C.L., & Tan, T.C. (1993). *A qualitative investigation of condom use negotiation among prostitutes in Singapore.* Berlin: IX International Conference on AIDS. (Abstract No. WS-D10-1)

Between Money, Morality
and Masculinity:
Bar-Based Male Sex Work in Chiang Mai

Jan W. De Lind van Wijngaarden

SUMMARY. This paper focuses on the supply-side of Chiang Mai's gay bars, that is, the male sex workers called *dek bar* or "bar boys"[1] in Thai. I formulate some explanations why these young men–more than half of whom do not consider themselves to be "homosexual"–take on a job as a male sex worker. In this analysis I focus on certain notions in traditional Thai society, trends in contemporary urban Thai society, the economics of work in a gay bar, as well as the sexual behaviour of male sex workers and the concepts they use to describe their work. *[Article copies available for a fee from The Haworth Document Delivery Service: 1-800-342-9678. E-mail address: getinfo@haworthpressinc.com]*

INTRODUCTION

Chiang Mai is Thailand's second largest city after Bangkok and in early 1996 around ten gay bars[2] (*bar gay* or *bar go-go* in Thai) were located in the city area. It is only ten years since the first gay bar, called the Siamese Cat, was established in this northern Thai city and

---

Address correspondence to: Jan Willem De Lind van Wijngaarden, Niewe Achtergracht t.o. 65, 1018 WX Amsterdam, The Netherlands.

[Haworth co-indexing entry note]: "Between Money, Morality and Masculinity: Bar-Based Male Sex Work in Chiang Mai." De Lind van Wijngaarden, Jan W. Co-published simultaneously in *Journal of Gay & Lesbian Social Services* (The Haworth Press, Inc.) Vol. 9, No. 2/3, 1999, pp. 193-218; and: *Lady Boys, Tom Boys, Rent Boys: Male and Female Homosexualities in Contemporary Thailand* (ed: Peter A. Jackson, and Gerard Sullivan) The Haworth Press, Inc., 1999, pp. 193-218; and: *Lady Boys, Tom Boys, Rent Boys: Male and Female Homosexualities in Contemporary Thailand* (ed: Peter A. Jackson, and Gerard Sullivan) Harrington Park Press, an imprint of The Haworth Press, Inc., 1999, pp. 193-218. Single or multiple copies of this article are available for a fee from The Haworth Document Delivery Service [1-800-342-9678, 9:00 a.m. - 5:00 p.m. (EST). E-mail address: getinfo@haworthpressinc.com].

over the past decade Chiang Mai has come to host the fourth largest concentration of gay bars in Thailand, after Bangkok, Pattaya and Phuket. Gay night-life is scattered throughout the city, rather than being localised in certain areas as is the case in Bangkok. However, this night-life is focussed around male prostitution, with only a few "non-prostitution" gay localities existing in the city, and even in these places one can often see male hustlers hanging around.

The Chiang Mai gay bar scene has been growing over the past ten years due both to an increased demand and to a "green light" implicitly given to poor young men to engage in this occupation by an increasingly money-dominated Thai society. The increased demand has come from both an expansion of gay tourism from western and from Asian countries (especially Japan, Singapore, Hong Kong, Taiwan), as well as from the growing wealth of the Thai middle class, with more Thai men being able to afford to visit male prostitutes more frequently. The fact that there is a steady supply of "fresh" (*sot*) men or "new faces" (*na mai*) is here explained in terms of the operation of traditional Thai concepts (such as social hierarchy) and also as the result of contemporary trends in Thai society, in particular, the commodification of many aspects of social life.

The data presented in this paper were collected during anthropological fieldwork carried out in Chiang Mai in 1994. I conducted in-depth interviews with 52 homosexually active men, of whom 20 at some stage had been bar-based male sex workers. The interviews took place outside working hours. This information was supplemented and quantified through questionnaires collected by volunteers from the Chai Chuay Chai ("men helping men") Project, a now defunct HIV/AIDS intervention program for homosexually active men in Chiang Mai which I worked with following my period of fieldwork research. Prudence Borthwick's paper in this volume provides more information on the activities and philosophy of the Chai Chuay Chai Project. The volunteers distributed HIV/AIDS information in the gay bars and completed a questionnaire on the basis of responses provided by the male sex workers during interviews conducted on a one-to-one basis. Before presenting these results, I will begin with a brief description of Chiang Mai's gay bars and the way they function.

GAY BARS: PLACES FOR TRADING MONEY AND DESIRE

Usually gay bars in Chiang Mai have a counter with stools, chairs, or sofas where drinks are served by a number of "hosts" who can be "bought out" or "taken off" (called *off* in Thai, from the English "to take off [the premises]") by paying the management a fee of between 120 and 200 baht.[3] On top of this so-called "off fee" (*kha off*), a client has to negotiate a price with the sex worker that he chooses to take out. When no negotiation takes place, both parties assume that the price is the going rate, which in 1996 was 500 baht for a "short-time" or 700-1000 baht for "all-night."

Though many of these venues call themselves a "bar" and maintain the air of a "normal" bar where one would go to chat, drink and relax, in fact most clients go to such venues with the specific intention of picking up a male sex worker and enjoying sexual pleasure with him in exchange for money. To encourage clients to take a sex worker "off," so-called *ten go-go* ("go-go-dancing") shows are performed in most venues. Young men dressed in fancy underwear, and sometimes completely naked, (try to) dance sensually and make movements suggestive of sexual acts.

Clients are usually approached by one or more sex workers, who can be invited to sit at their table. If clients are not approached, they can call one or more of the young men to their table, or they can call for the manager or a waiter and ask him to send the man of their choice to their table. Depending on the tone of the conversation, and the assessment by the client of the sex worker, or *vice versa*, compliments are exchanged and some physical contact may take place, such as stroking the leg or touching the crotch. The bars try to create a stimulating, erotic atmosphere for the client with music and dimmed red or purple neon lights, and young men that are (or seem to be) "willing to please." The bar management aims to achieve a maximum number of sex workers who are "taken off" each night. The number of men working in each venue varies from between four to almost 30, with numbers depending on the season, the time of the day, the working conditions imposed by the venue's management, and the perceived popularity of the bar with clients. The function of a venue as a place to buy sex is strengthened by the high prices of drinks, with a glass of beer costing between 65 to more than 100 baht, significantly more expensive than the price of a bottle of beer from a liquor store. For most clients, drinking all night and "only watching" is just too expensive, so most relax with their selected man at another location (see De Lind van Wijngaarden 1995a, 1995c, 1996, forthcoming).

MASCULINITY, "IDENTITY" AND SAME-SEX RELATIONS

In traditional Thai society, sexual relationships and sexual encounters between two males are interpreted through prevailing perceptions about gender roles and power relationships between the two sexes. According to the dominant gender ideology in traditional Thai society, a sexual encounter or relationship between two men is possible only if one assumes a feminine gender role and the other takes a masculine gender role. Gender role is important, although as discussed further below it can never be seen in isolation from social hierarchy. Hence, at least in terms of their public self-representation, homosexually active men tend to stick to one type of sexual practice, either receptive or insertive anal intercourse, in accord with the notions of female or male gender identity that are respectively associated with these sexual practices. These men tend to perceive themselves as either feminine (in the case of a man who is anally receptive) or as masculine (if the man is anally insertive). In fact, in terms of traditional values it does not really matter whether a man's sex partner is another male (which would stigmatise him as a "homosexual" in the West). Instead, it is the sexual act that a man performs with his sex partner that counts. That is, in terms of sexual behaviour, it does not matter much with *whom* one has sex, but rather *what position one takes in penetrative sex.* This means that if a male sex worker wants to be seen as a "real man" in his social environment, he can do so by limiting his sexual script with clients to "masculine" sex acts, at least in his public accounts of his interactions with clients. Therefore, working in a gay bar does not necessarily mean that a Thai man abandons his masculine status, and for many sex workers this occupation has nothing to do with "being gay." This situation partly explains the "fluidity" and contradictions that were found when male sex workers were asked to describe themselves with one of the terms that are commonly used to describe male sex/gender behaviours and identities in Chiang Mai (see Table 1).

TABLE 1. Preferred Self-Description Terms

Question: "How do you describe yourself?"

	n.	%
Phu-chai ("man")	69	52.7
Gay	22	16.8
Gay king	8	6.1
Gay queen	7	5.3
Seua bai	15	11.5
Kathoey	1	0.8
Don't know	5	3.8
Other	4	3.1
Total	131	100.0

Note: When an interviewee chose more than one label to describe himself, he was then asked to select the label that he felt best described himself.

Brief Glossary (terms are described in more detail below):

phu-chai–A normatively masculine male, often also colloquially called a "real man" (*phu-chai tem tua*).
gay king–prefers insertive role in sex with men.
gay queen–prefers receptive role in sex with men.
gay–sexually versatile, no preferred sexual role in relations with men.
seua bai–bisexual.
kathoey–transgender.

Even in western societies the use of the expression "sexual identity" is often problematic. This is even more the case in Thailand. Male sex workers often had quite some difficulty choosing for themselves just one of the "gender identity labels" provided in the questionnaire, and which are the most common descriptive terms used within the community of homosexually active men in Chiang Mai. Some men chose more than one label to describe themselves. In fact, the above "identities" tended to be understood more in terms of the preferred sexual habits and behaviour of the person involved, and to a lesser extent their appearance (i.e., style of dressing, hair-do, etc.) In responses the basic dimorphic system of two genders prevailed, with *kathoey* being included within the female gender. This means that the importance of "being gay" or adhering to a "gay identity" as opposed to a "male" or "female" gender identity was not an issue for the men in this sample. It was more important for them to find and combine the right gender presentations in order to fulfil different roles in different social contexts, such as "night-time" (working) and "day-time" (non-working) identity (see Watney, 1993). This explains, for example, why self-identified "real men" (*phu-chai*), who constituted 52.7 percent of the sample group, could take up this profession with little apparent psychological stress. The label "gay" was used by 28.2 percent of respondents, including the terms *gay queen* (usually denoting being receptive in anal intercourse, feminine-identified or looking somewhat feminine) and *gay king* (insertive role in sex, masculine-looking).

However, many different meanings were attributed to the expression *gay king*. There appeared to be almost as many definitions of the *gay king* as men in this sample (see De Lind van Wijngaarden, 1995a, forthcoming). Some respondents equated a *gay king* with a *phu-chai* or gender normative male. Another group said *gay kings* were "gays who want to keep up a masculine appearance." Some of these respondents laughingly referred to *gay kings* as *ee aep*, which literally means "a female being who surreptitiously has sex (with *phu-chai*)," and denotes closetted homosexual men who pretend to be straight. *Ee aep* present themselves as *phu-chai*, but in fact they are not "really" masculine because behind closed doors they engage in receptive anal sex, and for this reason do not genuinely deserve the *king* predicate. Some self-identified *kings* who admitted that this indeed happens, said that they engage in receptive sex only for money and do not experience any sexual pleasure. But some respondents who called these men *ee aep* did not believe that somebody would sell his masculinity for only 500 baht if he did not enjoy "being taken."

The term *seua bai* means literally a double-edged knife that can cut with both sides of the blade, and has a similar sense to the English idiom "to swing both ways." *Seau bai* was also the name of well-known Thai gangster in the 1960s and furthermore is an interesting conflation of the Thai word for "tiger" (*seua*) and the first syllable of the borrowed term *bai*, from the English word "*bi*sexual" (Jackson,

1995: 61). It is used to denote a person who can have sex with every gender and in all positions. *Seua bai* do not identify as, or choose between being a *gay king*, *phu-chai* or *gay queen*. They seem to view themselves as sexual beings who can have sex with other sexual beings, regardless of the sex of their sex partners. Some people express clear pride that they are able to have sex in all positions, roles, and with all kinds of partners. That they *can* have sex with every type of person was often explained by several factors, such as that they needed money, they were drunk, they enjoyed it, and so on. However, which sex partners they themselves really *desire* remained unclear from the interviews.

Interestingly, the number of male sex workers using the label *kathoey* to describe themselves was very small. *Kathoeys* tend to find sex partners or clients in the "regular" (ostensibly heterosexual) entertainment sector, often acting as a kind of "wild" or "free" woman and looking for sex partners who are *phu-chai*. Rich and older (that is, less beautiful and sexually less successful) *kathoeys* were prominent among the clients of Chiang Mai's gay bars and favoured especially the men who are *phu-chai*.

In summary, the meanings of the "identity"–concepts mentioned by male sex workers were very fluid and often contradictory. However, in general, these concepts were defined by a presumed gender role (masculine or feminine) as this related to sexual practices and to a man's physical appearance (e.g., as "butch" or "sweet") in certain social settings. Usually these labels were not used to denote the Western conception of an alternative "gay life-style" on the part of the male sex workers, nor to express a desire to "deviate" and be different from the dominant gender ideology. (The latter may be the case in other parts of the Chiang Mai "homosexual" subculture or in other regions of the country.) In addition, it cannot be stressed too much that *public* performance and *private* praxis are two different things. For example, a man who is a *phu-chai* in public presentation may be anally penetrated behind closed doors with several motives, ranging from sexual desire to financial gain. Indeed, human sexual desire is too complex and varied to be captured within any sexual ideology.

SOCIAL HIERARCHY

Social hierarchy is an important factor facilitating sexual contacts between persons of the same sex within the Thai system. When there is a difference in power position, be it economic (employer/employee), religious (monk/novice), social (teacher/pupil) or age-related (senior-junior), then favours may be sought by the "higher" person in the relationship. In certain circumstances these favours may include sex. In most cases it is implied that the "higher" person will take the "dominant" role of anally penetrating the lower/junior person. In such situations the lower/younger person will, in many cases, view his "feminine" sexual behaviour as a result of his dependent and weak position, rather than as the result of a "feminine identity" (see De Lind van Wijngaarden 1995b, forthcoming). The cultural expectations associated with the pervasive character of social hierarchy in Thai social life mean that young male sex workers may not necessarily experience a threat to their masculine gender identity from engaging in sex work. However, this cannot be generalised to all cases, as there are many young men who cannot tolerate sex work and leave the occupation soon after beginning work in a bar. Such men probably have not been reached in this survey and may have left because of a perceived conflict between sex work and their masculine gender identity.

It should be added that the cultural expectation that the senior person will play the inserter role in anal sex is not always met. The sexual "service" demanded of a junior man by a senior man may be to be anally penetrated. This is often the case when the latter adheres to a feminine self-concept, the *kathoey* manager of a Chiang Mai restaurant who often had affairs with young waiters being a case in point.

SOCIETAL TRENDS IN CONTEMPORARY CHIANG MAI

Certain trends in contemporary urban society help us understand the growth in the number of men working in the gay bars in recent years. An important trend is the obvious growth in the importance of money and conspicuous consumption in Thai society. It seems that more and more people tend to sympathise with men who try to make money this way. There seems to be relatively little societal disapproval of the profession of the male sex worker, and the existence of "men who sell their bodies" (*phu-chai khai tua*) is relatively, although not completely, ignored in the media, which instead tends to focus on female and child prostitution.

Most male sex workers made more money than they ever could in any other occupation given their generally low level of education.

Only 17.6 percent of the men reported that they were going to school in the daytime.[4] Only six years of primary school education or less was completed by 26.6 percent of the men. Half of the sample (54.3 percent) had completed three years of secondary schooling (called *mor 3* level in Thai), with 15.5 percent having completed the full six years of secondary schooling. Only 1.6 percent had undertaken any education higher than secondary school. The average number of years of completed education was 8.6, or somewhere between the second and the third year of secondary school education.

The male sex workers are "good friends" in their social circle of youth friends. For example, they often have money to buy drinks for their friends, and often dress according to the latest fashion. Because of this, they are popular friends and often very much sought after by local young women. They maintain an air of being rich and of being able to enjoy a consumerist lifestyle. Most of their male friends know what they do to earn a living and many of the male sex workers have introduced several of their friends to the scene. Only a small minority of the male sex workers had *not* been introduced to the scene by more experienced workers. This suggests that people within the young men's social environment of peers do not discourage or openly disapprove of the work they do. On the contrary, the strong growth of a consumerist mentality promoted through both the media and education provides a positive influence on the men's decision to work in a gay bar.

SOCIAL CONTROL

Many men had rural backgrounds and in the urban environment of Chiang Mai they experienced a marked decrease in social control exerted by the people around them compared to the situation when they lived in their home villages. This may facilitate their decision to begin working in a gay bar. However, even in a case where a certain degree of social control continues to be exercised in the young men's environment by older family members or others, working in a gay bar (or for that matter, in any sex-work profession) may still be possible. As often seems to be the case with many phenomena considered abnormal (*phit-pokati*) in Thai society, neighbours, family, parents and others tend to abide to what Brummelhuis (1984) has called a "conspiracy of silence," through which painful questions and painful answers are avoided and harmonious relations are maintained. The same phenomenon operates in many social settings where a friend or family member is gay or *kathoey*. When one asks most people whether working in a bar is good or bad, whether prostitution is good or bad, or whether being a *kathoey* is good or bad, the answer will almost always be that these things are considered to be "bad." However, to prevent social disharmony around the self or the person concerned, such issues are almost always ignored in the proximity of a person who is known (or privately suspected) to fall into a publicly disapproved category. This suggests that the decision to engage in prostitution would, in a Thai setting, have fewer life-long consequences than, for instance, in a European setting. Brummelhuis (1993, p. 14) states it this way:

> The integration of prostitution into Thai society provides also certain benefits. There seem to be greater opportunities to use prostitution as a temporary occupation and to return to normal life without great psychological or social difficulty; the period as a sex worker is often used to gain access to resources and the work itself is not an impediment to a social career.

SELF-REPORTED MOTIVES FOR WORKING IN A GAY BAR

It is often assumed by both Thai and foreign observers that money is the only motive for men to enter the bar scene. Indeed, two-thirds of the men interviewed mentioned money as a factor. However, significantly, there were also a number of other important motives, as shown in Table 2.

The importance of the money-making motive increased significantly in comparison to the other motives when compared to data the author collected in a previous study (De Lind van Wijngaarden 1996), suggesting a rapid change in values with the phenomenal expansion of the Thai (and local Chiang Mai) economy in the first half of the 1990s. Still, more than half of the men also reported that they entered the bar scene because the work is "light" or "easy," with relatively short working times and a high degree of autonomy to decide whether to work or take a night off.

THE ECONOMICS OF INNOCENCE VERSUS EXPERIENCE

As seen in Table 2, 66.4 percent of the men mentioned money as one out of three possible reasons for starting a career in a gay bar. In this section I formulate some hypotheses for describing the economic dynamics of work in a Chiang Mai gay bar. In the tourist high season (November to April), the average number of clients that men reported serving was 3.4 per week, dropping to 2.2 clients per week in the low season (May to October).[5] By multiplying the average number of clients in the high season by 4.5 (the average number of weeks in one month), and then multiplying this result by the average reported profit per client (604 baht), I found that the workers surveyed had an average monthly income of 9,928 baht for this period. In the low season the average monthly income dropped to 5,825 baht, with the annual average monthly income being 8,105 baht. Considering their young age and low levels of education, this is considerably more than most of the men could make in any other profession outside the criminal circuit.

Many regular bar patrons expressed the view that bar workers could make more money when they were young and "new" (*na mai*, i.e., "a new face"), and that later on their income would decrease. But do young men indeed make more money than older bar workers? Table 3 breaks down average monthly income by age.

From Table 3 it is clear that younger bar workers do not make more money than their older colleagues. An explanation for this counter-intuitive result could be that older men have more experience and have

TABLE 2. Self-Reported Motives for Working in a Gay Bar (N = 131)

Reason Given	No. of Mentions	%
Good money	87	66.4
Easy work	67	51.1
"Free" work, i.e., no fixed working time, etc.	47	35.9
To get experience	44	33.6
No opportunities for other job	30	22.9
Other	14	10.7

Note: Interviewees could mention up to three reasons for starting bar work.

mastered the art of bargaining a higher price for their services. If this is the case, then "experience" should be the distinguishing variable influencing income, not age. To test this hypothesis I divided the sample group into three income sub-groups: low (under 5,000 baht per month), medium (between 5,001 and 10,000 baht per month) and high (over 10,000 baht per month). If we then look at the variable "duration of work," it seems that this is a plausible explanation. I then compared these three income subgroups against the average duration of bar work reported by the members of these groups. The results are shown in Table 4.

It appears that length of experience in bar work does indeed influ-

TABLE 3. Self-Reported Average High-Season versus Low-Season Monthly Income Related to Age (in Thai Baht, "B")

Age	Low Season	N	High Season	N	Annual Average	N
Under 18	4,206 B	13	8,363 B	6	6,713 B	6
18, 19	5,594 B	36	8,297 B	24	6,877 B	23
20, 21, 22	5,908 B	31	9,450 B	27	7,944 B	26
23 and older	6,854 B	26	12,723 B	22	9,961 B	22
Average	5,825 B	106	9,928 B	77	8,105 B	77

Note: The number of workers surveyed (N) is higher in the first column because more data were collected from more workers in the low season, when they have more spare time to be interviewed. The annual averages in the third column are only calculated from data provided by workers who were interviewed in both the high and low seasons.

TABLE 4. Standardised Monthly Income-Group Related to Average Duration of Bar Work in Weeks

Income Group	Average Duration of Work in Weeks
Low (N = 26)	13.9
Medium (N = 32)	35.5
High (N = 19)	41.4
Average	18.8

ence a worker's earning capacity, with the highest income group on average having about 10 months work experience and the lowest income group only three months. Furthermore, if we look at another measure of bar work experience, namely, the answer to the survey question "Have you ever worked in another bar before starting work here?" the same trend becomes clear, as shown in Table 5.

Men who reported having worked previously in another bar can be assumed to have more experience than those who had only ever worked in their current bar. Moving to work in another bar might be taken to be a measure of "self-confidence." Some clients who I interviewed suggested that men who move bars are attracted by the idea of being a *na mai* ("new face") in their new bar, increasing their value in the eyes of the steady clients of that bar. However, this does not appear to be a major factor in influencing movement between bars. The gay bar-scene is quite small in Chiang Mai, and few clients restrict themselves to frequenting only one bar. This means that it is not so easy to "fake" being a *na mai*. More common reasons that workers cited for moving to another bar were problems with the management in the old bar and the belief that the new bar attracted more clients than the old one.

The average duration of work in workers' present bar was 18.8 weeks, or a bit more than four months. However, including the men with a history of having worked in at least one other bar (46.5 percent of the total), the average duration of sex work increased to 44.5 weeks or approximately 10 months. 20.5 percent of the men interviewed were in the first week of their career in their current bar, although many of these had worked somewhere else before. Sixty-three or 49.6 percent of the men were in the first three months of their career as sex workers, of whom 9 (14.3 percent of 63) had switched bars in this three month period.

Taking a closer look, it appears that the asset of being a "new face" does make sense for the men, and they can indeed make more money in their first week in a bar than in subsequent weeks. But then their

TABLE 5. Average Monthly Income in Thai Baht Related to Working Experience

Have you worked in another bar before?	Average income	N
NO	7,554 B	34
YES	8,498 B	41

earnings decrease in the following three weeks, with even less being earned per week in the second and third months. However, as a worker slowly masters the skills of sex work, his income increases again in the fourth and subsequent months of sex work, as is shown in Table 6.

Looking at workers' average monthly income, one can say that over-all the longer men worked in bars, the more able they became at making money. In the long term, age seems less important than experience, but a *dek mai* (lit. "a new kid") is nevertheless still perceived as fresh and "unspoiled" (*borisut*) and can ask more for his services during his first few weeks at a bar. After this initial period his income drops, but then he learns to "bargain" better with clients and acquires "captivating skills" such as "sweet talking" (*pak wan*) clients to increase his in-come. Workers' average profit per client also reflected the commercial value of experience, with average profit dropping marginally after the first week and then increasing progressively from 571 baht per client for "new faces" to 772 baht per client for men who have more than a year's experience. The average number of clients per week in the low season also reflects the impact of experience, with experienced workers having a higher average number of clients per week. The average number of clients per week rises steadily, finally decreasing slightly amongst the most experienced group. One reason for this slight decline appears to be that with a higher average profit per client, these men may become more selective about who they take as a client and may refuse to go *off* with some clients that they do not particularly like.

TABLE 6. Income Related to Length of Working Experience

Duration of Work	First Week	1-4 Weeks	1-3 Months	4-12 Months	Over 1 Year
Average Monthly Income in Baht	9,200 (n = 8)	7,600 (n = 10)	6,800 (n = 29)	9,600 (n = 17)	9,800 (n = 11)
Average Profit per Client in Baht	571 (n = 34)	565 (n = 21)	580 (n = 36)	630 (n = 18)	772 (n = 11)
Average No. Clients per Week in Low Season	1.8 (n = 26)	1.9 (n = 20)	2.15 (n = 33)	2.2 (n = 18)	2.0 (n = 11)

Some men increase their income-earning capacity by building up a network of clients (usually non-resident foreigners) who support them with regular payments from overseas. Thirayut was an example of such an extremely successful male sex worker:

By the age of 19, Thirayut had 23 *farang* men sending him money, mostly on a monthly basis. He had to write almost 50 letters a month to keep the contacts going, and he had to manage his time very well in order not to let two of his sponsors meet each other in Thailand. For example, if one of his sponsors was to arrive on say the 3rd of July, and another on the 5th of July, then he would say to the July 5th man that he had to study till the 10th, after which the July 3rd man would have left. None of the 23 overseas men knew that other people were also sending money to Thirayut. At one point, there was 400,000 baht in his bank account, which he used to build a new concrete house for his parents. During this period he didn't go to Ngok Bar [his place of work] often, only 3 or 4 times a month. (Thirayut, 24 years old, from a rural district of Chiang Mai Province) (De Lind van Wijngaarden 1995a)

Knowledge of such success stories might enhance the appeal of working in a gay bar, especially for men who are gay or *kathoey* and do not want to start a family with children who can support them when they are old. Some leave the bar for good to live with a lover in a Western country.

However impressive the careers of some male sex workers may seem, it should not be forgotten that only a small minority of the sex workers are so successful. The results in this study are biased towards the positive, with those men who hated the job and left after perhaps only a few days not having been reached. Indeed, the average duration of work was low, 18.8 weeks, suggesting that many men could not stand remaining in this occupation for too long a period of time. Earnings may have been lower than they expected, which may be a reason for many "unsuccessful" men to leave sex work. Violence and humiliation inflicted upon the sex workers by some clients no doubt also lead some men to quit. One must also mention the young men who become HIV-infected and experience seroconversion illness in the first months of their career due to a lack of knowledge about safe sex activities (De Lind van Wijngaarden 1995a, 1996; Kunawararak et al. 1995). Fear of contracting AIDS is another reason for quitting sex work, and I now turn to consider the sexual behaviour and sex partners of the male sex workers.

SEXUAL BEHAVIOUR AND SEX PARTNERS OF CHIANG MAI MALE SEX WORKERS

As can be seen from Tables 7a and 7b, about half of the interviewed men were single, with almost one third having a regular female partner (girlfriend or wife), one sixth having a regular male partner and a small number having regular partners of both sexes.

TABLE 7a. Current Relational Status of Workers

Current Status	No.	%
Currently single	67	52.0
Currently with steady female partner	38	29.5
Currently with steady male partner (incl. *kathoey*)	21	16.25
Currently has regular male and female partners	3	2.25
Total	129	100.0

TABLE 7b. Marital Status of Workers

Question: "What is your current relational/marital status?"

Marital Status	N.	%
Never Married: Single	62	48.0
Steady girlfriend, but not (yet) married	34	26.4
Steady male partner (incl. *kathoey*)	14	10.9
Both male and female steady partners	3	2.3
Currently married	3	2.3
Divorced and currently single	5	3.9
New girlfriend after having divorced	1	0.8
Male partner (incl. *kathoey*) after having divorced	7	5.4
Total	129	100.0

TABLE 8. Lifetime Experience of Different Types of Sexual Partners

Question: "Have you ever had the following type of sex partner, either inside or outside of your work?" (more than one response possible, N = 131)

Type of Sexual Partner	% YES
Client	96.1
Steady Girlfriend	51.1
Steady Boyfriend (including *kathoey*)	29.8
Thai female casual partner	56.5
Thai male casual partner	34.4
Female sex worker	28.2
Male sex worker	6.1
Farang female casual partner	0
Farang male casual partner	2.3
Kathoey casual partner	3.1

About half of the men were in what they considered to be a "steady" relationship, with either a woman, man or *kathoey*. In previous research I found that almost 60 percent of male sex workers' relationships lasted less than one year (De Lind van Wijngaarden 1995c). Of the men in the current sample, 9.9 percent had one or more children. Only 8.4 percent of the men lived with their parents, with 19.8 percent residing at the bar where they worked, and the rest living alone or with friends of their regular partner. Three bars in Chiang Mai provided their workers with free lodging, in part to ensure that they worked regularly.

From Table 8 it is apparent that as a group the male sex workers should not be clearly or categorically distinguished from the general "heterosexual" youth population. After clients (96.1 percent of respondents reported having had at least one client, with some "new faces" not yet having had a client), the second and third most common types of sex partners were casual female partners (56.5 percent) and steady female partners (51.1 percent).

The range and variety of individual workers' sex partners seem to be related to the men's self-reported gender concept, as shown in Table 9, which traces lifetime experience of different types of sexual partners against gender self-concept.

TABLE 9. Type of Sexual Partner Related to Gender Self-Concept (see Table 1)

Question: "Have you ever had the following type of sex partner?" (N = 130, % answering "Yes")

Worker's Reported Self-Concept	Regular female partner	Regular male partner	Casual female partner	Casual male partner	Male client	Female sex worker	Other male sex worker
Phu-chai (n = 69)	65.2	13.0	73.9	10.1	95.7	37.7	0
Gay (n = 22)	36.4	50.0	22.7	68.2	95.5	13.6	9.1
Gay king (n = 8)	62.5	37.5	50.0	50.0	100	25.0	25.0
Gay queen (n = 7)	14.3	71.4	0	85.7	100	0	28.6
Seua bai (n = 15)	20.0	40.0	60.0	66.7	100	20.0	6.7
Don't know (n = 5)	60.0	60.0	20.0	40.0	80.0	20.0	0
Other (n = 4)	50.0	25.0	100.0	0	50.0	50.0	0

Note: The one self-identified kathoey in the sample group of 131 respondents did not reply to this question.

The self-identified *seua bai*, *gay king* and gay respondents reported sexual experiences with all identified categories of partners. It should be noted that unfortunately the category of *kathoey* is included in the columns "steady boyfriend" and "casual male partner," which probably offers an explanation for the significant scores of *phu-chai* for these partner types.

SEXUAL BEHAVIOUR WITH CLIENTS

In the following tables, I explore the question of what bar workers are prepared to do sexually with their clients.

From Table 10, it can be seen that less than 20 percent of the men were unconditionally prepared to engage in receptive anal or oral intercourse. More than 50 percent replied that under no circumstances were they prepared to engage in receptive anal intercourse. However,

TABLE 10. Preparedness to Engage in Different Sexual Acts with Clients, in Percentages (N = 131, Kissing: N = 130)

Question: "If a client takes you out tonight, are you available for the following sex acts?"

DEGREE OF PREPAREDNESS	Unreservedly Prepared	Depends on the Person and/or the Fee	Absolutely Not/ Under No Circumstances
ACTIVITY			
Kissing	42	45	13
Hugging	50	50	–
Receptive Oral Sex	10	52	38
Insertive Oral Sex	18	70	12
Receptive Anal Sex	14	48	38
Insertive Anal Sex	78	19	3

over 75 percent were prepared to be the insertive partner in oral or anal intercourse. It is interesting that kissing was more often unconditionally rejected (by 13 percent or respondents) than insertive anal intercourse (3 percent) or being fellated (12 percent). This may be for the same reason that Sophie Day (1990) found in her study of female sex workers in London, namely, that kissing was reserved for persons with whom one is romantically involved and was not "done" with clients. In the following tables I take a closer look at the role of "self-concept" in influencing the sexual behaviours that workers were prepared to engage in with their clients.

It is clear in Table 11 that self-identified *gay queens* were the group who were most prepared to be the receptive partner in anal intercourse. This is not surprising given that the desire or preparedness to engage in receptive anal sex is a key defining characteristic of the Thai *gay queen*. Also in accord with expectations is the finding that only a very few self-identified *phu-chai* admitted that they were prepared to engage in receptive anal sex with clients. One unexpected reason given by one self-identified *phu-chai* when asked to explain his preparedness to be the receptive partner in anal intercourse with clients was that he could not maintain an erection with male sex partners due

TABLE 11. Preparedness to Engage in Receptive Anal Sex with Clients, Related to Self-Concept

DEGREE OF PREPAREDNESS	Unreservedly Prepared	Under Some Circumstances	Under No Circumstances/ Absolutely Not
SELF-CONCEPT			
Phu-chai	0	13	87
Seua Bai	25	55	20
King	13	64	23
Gay	32	56	12
Queen	84	16	0

to lack of erotic interest, and had consequently decided that the only clients he could satisfy were those who wanted to play the insertive role.

Again, not unexpectedly, self-identified *gay queens* were the most distinctive group in Table 12, with less than 30 percent being prepared to play the inserter role in anal intercourse, while significant majorities of all other groups were prepared to engage in this sexual activity with clients. Interestingly, the self-identified *seua bai* group, that is, the "sexual omnivores," were even more ready to engage in insertive anal sex with clients than the group of self-identified *phu-chai*.

Also in Table 13, the self-reported *gay queens* were the group who were most prepared to "use their mouth" (*chai pak*) with a client. In general, none of the informants reported being unprepared for a client to perform oral sex on them.

In Table 14 we see an interesting and different pattern from the responses to the previous sets of questions, with the sexually omnivorous *seua bai* group being the most prepared to kiss a client, followed by the *gay kings*, then the *gay queens* and gays, with the self-identified *phu-chai* group being the least prepared to kiss a client. These results suggest that there are in fact significant differences between *seua bai* and *gay kings*, on the one hand, and *phu-chai*, on the other hand, despite all three groups enacting a masculine public persona and having somewhat similar responses to questions about preparedness to engage in varieties of anal and oral sex. If we can take kissing as a more "romantic" erotic behaviour, involving the men's erotic attraction and emotional responses to other males much more than the immediately physical genital contact of anal and oral sex, then the results in Table 14 suggest that *seua bai* and *gay kings* have a greater emotional involvement in same-sex eroticism than do self-identified *phu-chai*. Homoerotic desire and emotional interest perhaps also explain why, as seen in Table 12, *seua bai* are more prepared than self-identified *phu-chai* to be the insertive partner in anal sex, despite the fact that engaging in insertive sex can be considered a defining

TABLE 12. Preparedness to Engage in Insertive Anal Intercourse with Clients, Related to Self-Concept

DEGREE OF PREPAREDNESS	Unreservedly Prepared	Under Some Circumstances	Under No Circumstances/ Absolutely Not
SELF-CONCEPT			
Phu-chai	78	22	0
Seua Bai	94	6	0
King	86	14	0
Gay	82	18	0
Queen	28	29	43

TABLE 13. Preparedness to Perform Oral Sex on Clients, Related to Self-Concept

DEGREE OF PREPAREDNESS	Unreservedly Prepared	Under Some Circumstances	Under No Circumstances/ Absolutely Not
SELF-CONCEPT			
Phu-chai	4	39	57
Seua Bai	12	75	13
King	36	64	0
Gay	8	68	24
Queen	42	58	0

TABLE 14. Preparedness to Kiss Clients, Related to Self-Concept

DEGREE OF PREPAREDNESS	Unreservedly Prepared	Under Some Circumstances	Under No Circumstances/ Absolutely Not
SELF-CONCEPT			
Phu-chai	38	60	2
Seua Bai	64	31	5
King	49	39	12
Gay	41	37	22
Queen	43	32	25

feature of heteronormative masculinity. Perhaps *seua bai* enjoy homo-erotic activity, of all forms, more than *phu-chai*.

In summary, there appear to be significant differences in individual worker's preparedness to engage in different homoerotic acts if we look at their self-concept. This indicates major differentiations within the cohort of male sex workers, who are by no means a uniform group. For most respondents the above "self-concept labels" were mere descriptors of preferred sexual behaviour and did not necessarily relate to core gender identity. Nevertheless, work experience also appears to have influenced the men's sexual behaviour with clients. For example, men who had worked for a longer period of time seemed more prepared to kiss their clients, and were also more prepared to be the insertive partner in anal intercourse. Interestingly, workers also became less prepared to be the receptive partner in anal intercourse over time. This appears to confirm a common but until now mostly anecdotal belief amongst HIV/AIDS program workers that the men who are newest to the scene, the "new faces," are at greatest risk of HIV infection. As an example of how more experienced men are able to avoid certain sexual acts that they do not like or do not dare to do with clients, one young worker, Rin, told me of some techniques that he used in order to protect himself when with an insistent client:

First, when a client is dirty or has a very big penis, but still wants to fuck me, I say to him that I have never been fucked before, but that I will try. I let the man press a bit, start moaning loudly and then run into the toilet. There I draw some blood from my arm or finger and put the blood on my anus. Then I go back to the client and say, 'I'm bleeding!' Usually clients, especially *farangs*, feel very sorry then. They don't try to continue fucking me, and usually I get a big tip to ease the pain. Second, whenever you are fucking a client and you are not sexually aroused, moan as if coming and then quickly run into the toilet to flush an empty condom. Third, if you don't want to perform oral sex on a client, for whatever reason, you say that you never do that kind of thing. If the client insists, you take his penis in your mouth and bite a bit, so that it hurts. Usually the client will refrain from insisting after that. (Rin, 19 years old, student, from a district 30 kilometres from Chiang Mai, working in a bar)

From reports such as Rin's, we can see that more experienced male sex workers who have learnt the "tricks of the trade" can engage in sex work with little risk of HIV infection.

CONCLUDING REMARKS

An important explanation for why a career in the bars is an option for Thai men who regard themselves as *phu-chai* is the way that Thai culture deals with masculinity or "masculine honour." This is determined more by sexual behaviour than the gender of a man's sex partner. As long as a man (says that he) limits himself to the "dominant" role in anal and oral intercourse with clients and also maintains an active sex life with women, he does not perceive having sex with male clients as unmasculine. This is because he does not perceive these sex partners as real *phu-chai*. In western societies, having sex with somebody of the same gender (regardless of the sex acts performed with that person) is a direct threat to the masculine status, which for many "straight" men blocks the option of a career in the gay prostitution scene.

Another notion explaining the steady supply of men to gay bars is the Thai system of social hierarchy, in which a less powerful person is supposed to submit to the wishes of a superior. This means that even if male sex workers are anally penetrated by clients, they may not perceive this as resulting from an ascribed female gender identity, but rather as resulting from their (temporary or permanent) lower position in the "power rankings" with regard to their clients.

A further factor facilitating a man's career in prostitution is the "conspiracy of silence," which can be considered to be an unwritten rule stating that it is better to avoid publicly confronting people who demonstrate "bad" behaviour or work in "bad" professions. This enables men to work in bars without being openly disapproved and without being ostracised within their social environments. However, the influence of this "conspiracy of silence" is partly dependent on the class and ethnicity of the family the man comes from, as well as the degree of anonymity that his working place can achieve in an urban setting. Nevertheless, due to this "conspiracy of silence" a temporary career in sex work has no necessary life-long stigmatising consequences.

It is clear from this study that western concepts such as "homosexual," "gay" or "heterosexual" are inappropriate in some Thai settings, especially in describing the group of male sex workers in Chiang Mai. This is illustrated by the way male sex workers used my "What-do-you-call-yourself?" labels. Rather than denoting "sexual identity" as we understand this concept in the West, the men tended to use these labels merely to reflect (presumed) sexual behaviour, habits and appearance. Using a concept such as "gay identity" assumes an identification of the self with a life-style based on a different sexuality, often acquired after a struggle with the self and in solidarity with other "different" individuals. Among Chiang Mai male sex workers this is not necessarily the case. Traditional notions and modern trends (urbanisation, commodification, globalisation, consumerism) create a complex and continually changing context for sexual personae, who, depending on class, social status, sex, and habitat (city or countryside) are in the midst of a process of defining and redefining sexualities and gender concepts, using both "traditional" and "modern" notions. In order to study these developments, it is crucial for scholars in Thai studies to redefine and re-invent the tools and concepts that they use to describe sexual behaviour, sexual otologies, sexual ideologies, and for that matter, Thai sexual culture as a whole.

NOTES

1. "Boy" here translates the Thai word *dek* (literally "child"). The use of *dek* refers to the male sex worker's youth and social inferiority with respect to customers and does not mean that they are children. Only 12.3 percent of the young men or *dek bar* interviewed in this study were under 18 years old.

2. As elaborated below, a "gay bar" in the context of this paper and within the prevalent discourse of the Thai gay entertainment sector means a venue where male sex workers can be picked up.

3. At the time of this study in 1996 $1US equalled roughly 25 baht. However, since the floating of the Thai currency in July 1997, the exchange rate has dropped to around $1US to about 36-37 baht.

4. A popular way of increasing the educational level amongst older people who may have had to leave school to work when younger is the so-called Kor Sor Nor School, an abbreviation of *kan-seuksa nork rong-rian* ("study outside school"). This is a type of government school which requires only half a day of contact hours per week with a teacher.

5. The high season corresponds with the dryer months of the year, the low season with wetter months, when fewer customers tend to go out at night and when more farm labour is required for planting the annual rice crop. For Chiang Mai gay bars the low season is therefore a time of reduced demand and also of reduced supply, as some young men return to home villages to work in the fields.

BIBLIOGRAPHY

Balzer, E. & Ratchanee Srionsri. (1996, October 14-17). The lifestyle of the *Wairun Caj Taek* (teenagers with broken hearts). Paper presented at the 6th International Conference on Thai Studies, Chiang Mai.

Brummelhuis, Han ten. (1993, July 5-10). Do we need a Thai theory of prostitution? Paper prepared for the 5th International Conference on Thai Studies, London.

Brummelhuis, Han ten. (1984). Abundance and avoidance: An interpretation of Thai individualism. In Han ten Brummelhuis & Jeremy Kemp (Eds.), *Strategies and structures in Thai society* (pp. 39-54). Amsterdam Publikatieserie Vakgroep Zuid- en Zuidoost Azie no 31: Anthropologisch-Sociologisch Centrum Universiteit van Amsterdam.

Day, Sophie. (1990). Prostitute women and the ideology of work in London. In Douglas A. Feldman (Ed.), *Culture and AIDS*. New York: Praeger.

De Lind van Wijngaarden, J.W.de. (1995a). *A social geography of male homosexual desire: Individuals, locations and networks in the context of HIV/AIDS in Chiang Mai, northern Thailand*, Chiang Mai: Social Research Institute.

De Lind van Wijngaarden, J.W.de. (1995b). *The dilemma of tackling male homosexual HIV-transmission in Thai Buddhist temples*. unpublished.

De Lind van Wijngaarden, J.W.de. (1995c, November). *Condom use and sexual networks of men having sex with men at public places and in the boy brothels in Chiang Mai, northern Thailand*. Chiang Mai: Second Chai Chuay Chai Data-analysing Report for NAPAC (Thai-Australian Northern AIDS Prevention and Care Program), unpublished.

De Lind van Wijngaarden, J.W.de. (1996). *Between money and masculinity: Bar boys in Chiang Mai. Third data analysing report for NAPAC*. unpublished.

De Lind van Wijngaarden, J.W.de. (in press). The variety of same-sex experience in Chiang Mai, northern Thailand. In Peter Jackson & Nerida Cook (Eds.). *Gender and sexuality in contemporary Thailand*. Chiang Mai: Silkworm Books.

Jackson, Peter A. (1989). *Male homosexuality in Thailand: An interpretation of contemporary Thai sources.* New York: Global Academic Publishers.

Jackson, Peter A. (1995). *Dear Uncle Go: Male homosexuality in Thailand.* Bangkok: Bua Luang Books.

Kunawararak, P., Beyrer, C., Natpratan, C., Feng, W., Celentano, D.D., de Boer, M., Nelson, K.E. and Khamboonruang, C. (1995). The epidemiology of HIV and syphilis among male commercial sex workers in northern Thailand. *AIDS, 9,* 517-521.

Watney, S. (1993). Emergent sexual identities and HIV/AIDS. In P. Aggleton (Ed.). *AIDS: Facing the second decade.* London: The Falmer Press.

About the Contributors

Prudence Borthwick has worked in the field of community AIDS education in Australia since 1985, developing resources on AIDS for disadvantaged groups ranging from remote communities to young suburban gays and lesbians. Prue lived in Bangkok as a child, where she was educated in Thai. She returned to Thailand in 1993 to take up a position with the Northern AIDS Prevention and Care Programme (NAPAC) in Chiang Mai. In 1993 she published *Mothers and Others: An Exploration of Lesbian Parenting in Australia*. Prudence has recently worked as a consultant on Communities and AIDS in Australia and Southeast Asia and is currently International Projects Officer for the Bamrasnaradura Hospital HIV/AIDS Ambulatory Care Project, a bilateral Australia-Thailand project coordinated from the Albion Street HIV/AIDS Clinic in Sydney.

Han ten Brummelhuis, PhD, is Lecturer in Anthropology at the University of Amsterdam. Most of his research relates to Thailand. He recently reconstructed an epsiode of the history of irrigation from the Thai national archives and he has also worked on AIDS-related themes and on Thai migration to Europe, including a chapter on Thai migrants in the Netherlands in *Sexual Cultures and Migration in the Era of AIDS,* edited by Gilbert Herdt (1997). With Gilbert Herdt, Dr. Brummelhuis edited *Culture and Sexual Risk: Anthropological Perspectives on AIDS* (1995).

Malcolm McCamish, PhD, is Senior Lecturer at the University of Queensland in Brisbane, Australia. He is a foundation member, long time board member and currently Secretary of the Queensland AIDS Council. He has published numerous papers dealing with HIV prevention and is co-editor of *The Theory of Reasoned Action: Its Application to AIDS Prevention Behaviour* (1993).

Stephen O. Murray, PhD, lives in San Francisco, California, and is the author of numerous books including *Angkor Life* (1996), *Islamic Homosexualities* (1997), *Oceanic Homosexualities* (1992), and *Taiwanese Culture/Taiwanese Society* (1994). He is currently working on a theoretical synthesis of historical and ethnographic material on homosexualities around the world (*Homosexualities* 1998).

Megan Sinnott is a graduate student in Anthropology at the University of Wisconsin, Madison, and is currently undertaking dissertation fieldwork research on lesbian identities and communities in Thailand.

Graeme Storer is currently completing a doctorate in Applied Linguistics in the School of English, Language and Media Studies at Macquarie University in Sydney, Australia. His research interests include the application of critical discourse analysis to social science research and, in particular, to studies of homosexually active men in Thailand. He works as a freelance consultant to non-government organisations in Asia, providing management and human resource development training and workshop facilitation.

Jan W. De Lind van Wijngaarden conducted research on homosexually active men in Chiang Mai, northern Thailand, in the early 1990s while an MA scholar in the Amsterdam School for Social Science Research, University of Amsterdam, The Netherlands. After completing his Masters dissertation, Jan Willem worked with the Chai Chuay Chai, which undertook HIV/AIDS education activities among homosexual men in Chiang Mai city. He currently works in Bangkok, Thailand.

Index

Notes: Page-numbering differentials for the Foreword section in the co-published versions of this book are denoted as follows: square brackets indicate the *Journal of Gay & Lesbian Social Services;* parentheses indicate the Harrington Park Press imprint version.

Page numbers followed by "n" indicate information found in the specified end-of-chapter Note number.

Personal names are indexed only when cited in full.

Thai personal names are alphabetized according to the orthographic guidelines explained on pp. 23-24 of this book (i.e., first name first).

All Thai-language words, including English words adopted into Thai, are collected under the subject entry titled: Thai-language terms and phrases, translated. (Note that selective terms are also indexed as subject entries.)

NEW BOOKS FROM HAWORTH GAY & LESBIAN STUDIES

NAVIGATING DIFFERENCES

Friendships Between Gay and Straight Men
Jammie Price, PhD
Explores the gender and sexual identities of gay and straight men who become friends and how those identities influence their behavior with one another.
$24.95 hard. ISBN: 0-7890-0619-7.
Text price (5+ copies): $17.95. 1998. 172 pp. with Index.
Features numerous interviews, surveys, interview checklists, and 4 appendixes.

IN THE PINK

The Making of Successful Gay- and Lesbian-Owned Businesses
Sue Levin, MBA
Offers insights from over 650 gay and lesbian entrepreneurs into why and how they started their businesses and how they currently manage them.
$24.95 hard. ISBN: 0-7890-0579-4.
$17.95 soft. ISBN: 1-56023-941-7.
1999. Available now. 171 pp. with Index..
Features case studies, numerous interviews, tables, a list of organizations, Web site/Internet addresses, survey methodology, and recommended books.

LILA'S HOUSE

A Study of Male Prostitution in Latin America
Jacobo Schifter, PhD
You will learn about the culture of juvenile prostitution and learn from the immediate intervention program that was implemented.
$29.95 hard. ISBN: 0-7890-0299-X.
Text price (5+ copies): $24.95. 1998. 133 pp. with Index.
Full of interviews with actual prostitutes.

DRY BONES BREATHE

Gay Men Creating Post-AIDS Identities and Cultures
Eric Rofes
"Useful to gay men and other sexually active people struggling to reconcile pleasure with safety."
—*The Nation*
$49.95 hard. ISBN: 0-7890-0470-4.
$24.95 soft. ISBN: 1-56023-934-4.
1998. 352 pp. with Index.
Features interviews, personal revelations, and article and book reviews.

LOOKING QUEER
Body Image and Identity in Lesbian, Bisexual, Gay, and Transgender Communities
Edited by Dawn Atkins, MA
Looks at body image issues among lesbian, bisexual, gay, and transgender people.
$69.95 hard. ISBN: 0-7890-0463-1.
$32.95 soft. ISBN: 1-56023-931-X. 1998. 467 pp. with Index.
Features interviews, book reviews, and personal accounts.

LOVE AND ANGER

Essays on AIDS, Activism, and Politics
Peter F. Cohen
One of the first books to take an interdisciplinary approach to AIDS activism and politics by looking at the literary response to the disease, class issues, and the AIDS activist group ACT UP.
$39.95 hard. ISBN: 0-7890-0455-0.
$16.95 soft. ISBN: 1-56023-930-1. 1998. 194 pp. with Index.
Features interviews, recommended readings, a bibliography, and analyses of plays and books.

QUEER KIDS
The Challenges and Promise for Lesbian, Gay, and Bisexual Youth
Robert E. Owens, PhD
"Examines the unique challenges faced by today's homosexual young adults.
—*Outlines:* A newsletter for Ithaca's Lesbian, Gay, and Bisexual Community.
$49.95 hard. ISBN: 0-7890-0439-9.
$24.95 soft. ISBN: 1-56023-929-8.
1998. Available now. 355 pp. with Index.
Features recommended readings, tables, reviews, lists of organizations, and Web site/Internet addresses.

ACTS OF DISCLOSURE
The Coming-Out Process of Contemporary Gay Men
Marc E. Vargo, MS
"A singularly fair and even-handed evaluation of the pluses and minuses of coming out."
—*Michael's Thing*
$39.95 hard. ISBN: 0-7890-0236-1.
$17.95 soft. ISBN: 1-56023-912-3. 1998. 164 pp. with Index.
Features a list of coming-out resources, appendixes, and a bibliography.

THE EMPRESS IS A MAN

Stories from the Life of José Sarria
Michael R. Gorman, MA
"The first comprehensive biography of one of the most colorful and important figures of queer history since the second world war."
—*The Harvard Gay & Lesbian Review*
$39.95 hard. ISBN: 0-7890-0259-0.
$19.95 soft. ISBN: 1-56023-917-4. 1998. 278 pp. with Index.
Features photographs and interviews.

Textbooks are available for classroom adoption consideration on a 60-day examination basis. You will receive an invoice payable within 60 days along with the book. **If you decide to adopt the book, your invoice will be cancelled.** Please write to us on your institutional letterhead, indicating the textbook you would like to examine as well as the following information: course title, current text, enrollment, and decision date.

AVAILABLE FROM YOUR LOCAL BOOKSTORE

If unavailable at your local bookstore, contact: Harrington Park Press,
10 Alice Street, Binghamton, New York 13904–1580 USA
Phone: 1–800–Haworth (outside US/Canada + 607–722–5857)
Fax: 1–800–895–0582(outside US/Canada + 607–771–0012)
E-Mail: getinfo@haworthpressinc.com • Web: http://www.haworthpressinc.com